DR. JACK

on Winning Basketball

DR. JACK RAMSAY AND
NEAL VAHLE

Blue River Press
Indianapolis, IN

TABLE OF CONTENTS

Portland Memories: Dr. Jack Ramsey coaching the Portland players during a timeout (upper left corner). Dr. J. driving to the hoop against Bob Gross (upper right corner). Maurice Lucas channels George McGinnis toward the baseline where Bill Walton waits (bottom). (All photos by Roger Jensen)

PROLOGUE: HOW BASKETBALL SAVED MY LIFE

Cancer is the ugliest, scariest, most dreaded word in the English language. My credentials for saying so? Head-to-head, firsthand close encounters with different versions of the fiendish devil. And …

Whoa, there. This is supposed to be a book about basketball, not cancer. You're right. Absolutely right. But bear with me for a minute. I want to make the case that my long life in basketball helped me cope successfully with … that other thing. But to do so, I must first explain my urgent need to draw on all those rich memories of the game I love.

Dr. Jack Ramsay at the 1993 Portland ceremony retiring number 77 in his honor.

Now, where was I? Oh, yes …

I went through my entire athletic life as a basketball player with only minimal physical setbacks, the worst being a couple of brain concussions, one in a college game in 1948, the other in 1954 while playing in the Eastern League, from which I recovered without permanent damage.

And all the stress and general wear and tear on body and soul from 37 years of coaching at the high school, college, and professional levels? Hard to measure, of course, but I don't regret a single minute that I spent on the sidelines of the game to which I've devoted my entire adult life.

Then, in 1999, a routine medical exam turned up an opponent I hadn't reckoned with—prostate cancer. Fortunately, it was caught early on, and after radiation therapy and a procedure that shot radioactive iodine pellets into the prostate gland, my doctors assured me that they'd gotten it all. Arranging my treatments around my work schedule, I didn't miss a single game that season as a TV color commentator with the Miami Heat.

I didn't tell anyone about my condition, not even my family. Why worry them? I was convinced I could overcome the Big C on my own. I tried to live as I usually did, getting in my daily run and swim workouts at the beach and staying on top of my duties at home caring for my wife and on the job doing television commentary for ESPN and the Miami Heat. I felt a little more fatigue than normal during workouts on radiation treatment days, but other than that I felt fine. My most recent scans in the fall of 2010 revealed no tumors anywhere.

But in October 2004 I went up against the toughest opponent I had yet to face anywhere at any time in my life—melanoma cancer. It started tamely enough, with three small spots under the skin on the instep of my left foot. I'd been running barefoot a lot on the beach near our summer home in Ocean City, New Jersey, and I figured I must have picked up a few thorns. No big deal. But the spots didn't go away, so I had them examined back in Florida that fall by my dermatologist, Dr. Jerry Lugo, who ordered up biopsies "just to be on the safe side." Two days later Dr. Lugo called with the results: melanoma.

I had recently lost a close friend to melanoma, so I asked, "This is like a death sentence, isn't it, Doc?" He responded quickly, completing an exchange that I remember as if it had taken place yesterday: "No, no, Jack. Some people live with this three years."

Three years?

He recommended that I see Dr. David Ritter, a Naples oncology surgeon, who promptly ordered up a PET scan procedure that revealed that the melanoma had quickly metastasized from my foot to my calf. Not a good sign.

I had outpatient surgery three days later to remove the melanoma from my foot and my calf. When I awoke from the anesthesia, Dr. Ritter told me that he had removed most of the sole of my left foot and a part of my calf to get to the melanoma and that he had taken seven lymph nodes from my groin and five from around my spine for closer examination. I left the hospital on crutches and was driven home by a friend. I felt okay—not great, but okay. At least they'd caught it soon enough to get the damned things out of my leg.

A few days later, it was more bad news: they found a melanoma in one of the lymph nodes taken from my left groin. I passed that information on to Dr. Bruce Nakfoor, my prostate physician (and good friend), who told me, "You've got to go to Anderson."

That would be the M. D. Anderson Cancer Center in Houston, where Bruce had a connection with a Dr. Merrick Ross. Bruce called Dr. Ross, explained the details of my condition, and then put me on the phone.

"I know who you are, Dr. Jack," Dr. Ross said after I introduced myself. "I listen to you all the time on NBA games. We've got to get you better." He then explained a procedure called isolated limb perfusion, in which high-dosage chemotherapy would be pumped into a vein in my left leg and circulated there to kill any existing cancer cells. Also, all the lymph nodes in my left leg would be removed for testing.

Hey, fine, okay, let's get it done. Sooner the better, right?

The following week, after I was prepped for surgery, Dr. Ross came into my room. A little pregame pep talk? Sure. Why not? I was feeling confident. But after reviewing the procedure, Dr. Ross said, "Dr. Jack, I must tell you there's a 2 percent chance that you'll lose your leg."

What?

"Look, Dr. Ross," I said, "if you have to take off my leg, don't wake me up." I was dead serious. Soon after, the anesthesia kicked in, and the next thing I knew I was coming out of a sweet, dreamy fog in the recovery room. As soon as I could move my arm, I reached down where my left leg was supposed to be.

It was still there.

This time, I was in the hospital for nine days. I'd had six incisions on the left side of my body in a three-week period, including one from my stomach to mid-thigh that left some severed muscles and nerves. Something as simple as turning over hurt like hell. Dr. Ross visited me at least once every day. When I asked him if he had a family, he answered, "Sure, Dr. Jack. You're my family."

I kidded him, "I bet you tell that to all your patients."

But you know what? I bet he does, and I know he means it. He has that level of commitment to people he's trying to help.

Later in the week, he told me that the results of my procedure were positive but that he would need to see me in a month to check on my recovery. I left Anderson on November 9, 2004, and returned home to Naples, feeling pretty good about things.

A little over two months later, on January 20, 2005, I did my first NBA broadcast for ESPN Radio at Orlando, tipping off a once-a-week NBA game schedule for the rest of the season. I felt great—mentally. But not yet physically: the incisions in my groin and foot became infected and wouldn't heal completely. My left foot was too swollen to wear a shoe, so I wore a soft moccasin. Walking was painful.

But what bothered me the most was that I couldn't get into my usual workout routine that had become a daily part of my life. I couldn't run because of the soreness in my left foot, nor swim because of the open wounds. Even my "room workout" consisting of full-body stretches, running in place, crunches, and push-ups was put on hold.

It took a year and a half before I could resume full physical activity. Years before, I had set a goal of doing a push-up for each year of my life on my birthday, and I'd been able to reach "the number" through my seventies. But I turned 82 on February 21, 2007, and I didn't make it. I got stuck on 78. I'm hopeful that in 2011 I'll be back on track, but it will take 86 pumps of the body.

Then, in March 2006, during a regular checkup, Dr. Ritter recommended another PET scan to make sure that the melanoma hadn't spread. Another routine test? Fine, sure—let's get it over with before the playoffs.

More bad news.

Make that *really bad news*, as in melanoma tumors in both of my lungs.

In April I returned to M. D. Anderson, where I was admitted to an experimental drug program designed to shrink and eventually eliminate the tumors in my lungs. (Surgery wasn't an option; there were too many of them.) This required weekly trips to Houston for two hours of chemotherapy. I scheduled the treatments to avoid, in so far as it was possible, conflicts with my NBA broadcasts on ESPN.

At first, the results were encouraging. The tumors in both lungs grew smaller or disappeared altogether. But in late November, an MRI of my brain showed a tumor there, and a CAT scan of my lungs turned up evidence of new tumors there.

Damn!

Next stop: Massachusetts General Hospital in Boston to see Dr. Jay Loeffler, who had developed a procedure in which high-dose radiation beams are aimed directly at tumors in the brain to destroy them.

At Mass General in January 2007, Dr. Loeffler's team attached a ring-shaped metal frame to my head with four pins. Then I went to the radiation center, where they strapped me to the treatment table and secured the head frame so that I couldn't move. I held that position for about an hour while proton beams were fired directly at the tumor from different angles.

After a brief recovery period following the procedure, Dr. Loeffler gave me the news: "That tumor is gone and won't come back. You may get others, but that one is gone forever."

I liked the sound of that, but two months later I was back in Boston to go through the same procedure for a new tumor that had turned up in my brain. The procedure seemed to go a bit easier this time, or maybe it was just the confidence I felt from the previous experience. But I have to say that those trips to Boston without doing a Celtics radio broadcast got tiresome.

Meanwhile, I was given a new drug, Temodar, which is used primarily to prevent recurrence of tumors in the brain. Then a most unusual effect took place. Not only did Temodar prevent tumors from returning to my brain, but the ones in my lungs began to disappear! I was told the chances of that happening were something like 1 in 20,000. My most recent scans—in the summer of 2010—revealed no tumors anywhere.

"I don't use the word *miracle* very often," Dr. Nakfoor told me later, "but this might just be one."

This seems like a good point to say that I also prayed a lot during this ordeal. As a practicing Catholic, I pray more fervently (and more frequently) at a time of crisis. Suddenly, my need was great—very great. I found myself at Mass focusing my prayers directly at the figure of Jesus Christ suspended on the cross at the front of the church. I began to think of him as the "Big Man."

There is a prayer said aloud by the congregation in a Catholic service just before Holy Communion that goes, "Lord, I am not worthy to receive you, but only say the word and I shall be healed." Every time I went to my knees for that prayer, I silently added, "Come on, Jesus, heal me! You can do it, Big Man! Heal me!"

I have to believe the Big Man heard me.

I approached cancer as if I were preparing for a game against a tough opponent. I "scouted" it, learning as much about melanoma as I could. I took on a medical staff of "coaches" who were experts at dealing with this particular version of the disease. I followed the game plan they laid out but made adjustments when the "game" took different directions.

I used stats—readings from scans and blood analyses—to confirm that my body was handling chemo treatments without damage to my overall system.

This was pretty much the same approach I used to get my Portland Trail Blazers ready to go up against the Philadelphia 76ers in the 1977 NBA Finals … only with different stakes on the line.

To win, you have to *prepare* yourself to win. You have to be ready. You can't expect a W to just happen. That's the credo I always expected of my players. And that's what I demanded of myself when I was battling cancer.

Knowing I was going to have to use crutches *after* my surgeries, I practiced with them weeks *before* I had the surgeries. After the surgeries at Anderson, I did leg lifts while in bed. I started using my crutches (old friends by now) to walk around the perimeter of the eighth floor as soon as they would let me—first once around, then twice, then three times as I built up stamina.

I did isometric exercises in bed to regain my upper-body strength. I never stopped pushing myself and never *ever* eased up on my conditioning program, even on those days when I'd have to stop every few steps to catch my breath.

Another key basketball skill is imagery. The best players "see" situations before they happen so they can be prepared to take best advantage of them when they transpire.

I used imagery to "see" myself in pleasant surroundings while I was getting MRI and CAT scan treatments. I used imagery to see myself reaching my goals. As I got my strength back, I used imagery to see myself walking on my own, then jogging, swimming, and then playing golf again. I used imagery to stay so focused on my job that I could fall asleep inside a closely enclosed MRI machine, with all its banging and buzzing, where you have to remain absolutely still, regardless of any discomfort you might be experiencing.

The best players I have seen and known have confidence in their teammates. They know that basketball's not a one-man game. That confidence brings out the best in everybody, because it's contagious.

I had complete confidence in my medical team. They were not only superbly skilled, but they cared for me—and every other patient they treated—as if we were the most important people in their lives. That gave me confidence that I could win my battle with cancer.

I never thought of losing. Not once. I never let a single doubt or fear creep into my subconscious. When challenges arose, my question was always, "What can I do *now*?" When my doctors revised a game plan, I went at it full bore.

But understand this: my commitment to living in the *now* means I'll never ever say that I've beaten cancer. To do so would be living in the "tomorrow," if you will, and melanoma is far too erratic an opponent to go around making predictions. But I can tell you for sure that I'll never give in to it. Life is too precious to give it up without giving everything you've got—*now*.

Not exactly what you expected to be reading about in a book from an old basketball junkie, huh? Don't worry, this book is *not* about cancer, a word you won't encounter from this point forward. This book is about *basketball*. It's about the attitudes and methods and values and people I have encountered in over 70 years of playing, coaching, and broadcasting basketball and how that unbelievably rich life experience guides me in my biggest off-court challenge.

I received truly extraordinary medical care from a great team of ferociously dedicated men and women. I will never be able to thank them enough.

But I believe in my heart that without being able to draw on my life in basketball for strength, I would be dead right now.

Okay?

Let's get it on. One, two, three…WIN!

INTRODUCTION

One of the benefits of my long association with the NBA, both as a coach and ESPN broadcaster, is that I have gotten to know personally the game's finest players and coaches. I count many of them as my good friends. In preparing this book I decided to draw upon their valuable knowledge and wisdom. I have listed the names of those that I have consulted. Their insights have helped me to gain a better understanding of what it takes to win, not only in basketball, but in life as well. The approach of these players and coaches to the game of basketball has inspired me during my years in the game. I am sure their words will inspire you as well.

Our experience has taught us that athletic skills, which include strength and coordination, make up only part of what it takes to be a winner. These skills are indeed necessary, but those qualities are not what separate the best players from lesser ones, the winners from the losers. Winners break the game down in their minds and sharpen their focus in game situations. We describe in detail the mental makeup of winning players and coaches, focusing on their savvy, know-how and smarts, their ability to focus on the present moment, and their use of intuition and imagery. We let you know how winners handle their fear, control their anger, and develop self-confidence. Finally, we tell you how winners develop the mental toughness and the competitive mind-set than enables them to lead their teams to victory.

Ramsay with wife Jean and daughter Carolyn riding down Broadway in the Portland parade following the team's defeat of Philadelphia for the NBA championship in June 1977. (Roger Jensen Photo)

Ramsay with outstanding Saint Joseph's player Bob McNeill at a 1980s university function.

1

PLAY SMART

Chris Paul, the splendid point guard for the New Orleans Hornets, has a unique penetrating technique. Lightning quick, and with excellent control of his dribble, he gets into the paint consistently, often using screen-and-roll plays with his big men, David West and Emeka Okafor. Once in the paint, instead of driving to the basket like other penetrators, Chris glides laterally, luring the opposing big man to him to try to block the anticipated shot. If the big defender goes for the block, Chris lobs a pass to his teammate left open by the shot blocker for an easy dunk. If the big defender stays on the floor, Chris floats the ball into the basket.

This tactic takes great skill and poise, and Chris Paul is the only player in the NBA who does it consistently. I've watched with admiration as he's performed this ploy successfully against Tim Duncan, Shaquille O'Neal, Marcus Camby, Dwight Howard, and other great skilled NBA shot-blockers.

For a taped ESPN Radio segment called "Meet the All-Stars" at the 2009 All-Star Game played in Phoenix, I asked Chris to talk about this unusual bit of legerdemain in the basket area. He stared at me for a full five seconds and then said with a smile, "Doc, you're going to give away my best secret."

But he did talk about it, about how he and his big men work on their timing and execution at practice and how he learned to stare down opposing big men for a split second while deciding whether to pass or shoot. We're talking a nanosecond of thought process at work here that only Chris Paul has mastered.

But for your information, Chris, what you do is no secret to other NBA teams. Scouting reports detail every maneuver of your game. Videos are run forward and back as you do your thing. Opposing teams know exactly what's coming. They just can't stop it.

It's smart, thinking basketball.

Smart basketball teams play with poise. Smart teams never appear ruffled by anything that happens. They're fiercely competitive to be sure, but they play with controlled aggression. They extract the utmost from the individual skills of each player and then blend those skills into their team game. Smart teams don't beat themselves; they consistently win the close ones.

The fact is, I've never seen a championship team in *any* sport that didn't play smart. And while smart teams may not always win championships, they are always competitive. It's no surprise that those teams are comprised of players who *think* the game—who make productive plays under pressure and seldom, if ever, make game-costing errors. They consistently outthink their opponents. They master the game's finer points, the little details that almost always determine the difference between a W and an L.

"Play smart," says Jerry West. "Your brain is as much a weapon as your legs and your arms."[1]

The ability to make the correct split-second decision and execute a critical play consistently is a key attribute of a great player. Regarding the mental game within basketball, Phil Jackson says, "It's not how hard you play, it's how smart you play." I agree with Phil, with the caveat that if you don't play hard it may be too late to play smart. Smart players *always* play hard. It's not that great players stop to mull over a decision as to what to do next. They *anticipate* what needs to be done, which enables them to do the right thing.

The Boston Celtics have won more NBA championships than any other franchise—17 and counting. The teams of the 1950s and 1960s were led by Bill Russell, Bob Cousy, Tom Heinsohn, Bill Sharman, John Havlicek, Sam Jones, and K. C. Jones and were coached by Arnold "Red" Auerbach. After Red retired in 1967 to become the Celtics GM, he named Bill Russell as player-coach, the first African American coach in the NBA. Combined, those Celtics teams won 11 championships in 13 years. (Hardcore Celtics fans are still bitter about those other two seasons.)

The next Boston championship outfit (1974, 1976) was coached by Heinsohn and included Havlicek, Dave Cowens, Jo Jo White, Paul Silas, and Don Nelson. In the 1980s there were the great teams of Larry Bird, Robert Parish, and Kevin McHale, coached by Bill Fitch and then K. C. Jones. The most recent championship team (2008) was coached by Glenn (Doc) Rivers and was led by Kevin Garnett, Paul Pierce, and Ray Allen.

Great players? Certainly. Outstanding coaches? Of course. But each of those teams was characterized by an extremely high level of *team* play, meaning each was supported by strong contributions from role players. The star players in each group made certain that those role players had an opportunity to contribute. That's smart basketball. That's *championship* basketball.

I found competing against the Russell-coached teams especially intriguing. Because Russell stayed in the game until the outcome was decided, he was seldom on the bench. The other players (Havlicek, Sam Jones, Satch Sanders, Larry Siegfried, Bailey Howell, Wayne Embry, Don Nelson) substituted themselves into and out of the game without any indication from Russ, and during their orderly timeouts, it seemed that anyone could speak while the others listened. Coach Russell either nodded in agreement or offered a final declaration, and the game went on. That method worked well. Those smart, veteran players were totally involved in the game and committed to winning. The system allowed Russell to concentrate on what he did best—shut down the opposing team's offense. The Celts won the NBA championship twice (1968 and 1969) in the four years that Russell was player-coach.

One of those former Celts, Paul Silas, played 15 seasons with six NBA teams and became a great offensive rebounder by using his smarts. Undersized at 6'7" for the power forward position and without great leaping ability, Paul worked constantly on how to out-position his opponent. "I never gave an opponent my whole body to block out," he once told me. "The best he got was my hip. Then I could spin off him and use my foot quickness to get inside." Another trick he used was to go out of bounds, over the end line, and then come back onto the playing floor and block out the defensive rebounder, giving himself an offensive put-back opportunity. Positioning was everything for Paul.

That was smart basketball.

Not everybody gives the attention to detail that Silas did. Some never learn how to do it. Everybody in the NBA can jump. Many rebounders want to show how high they can jump to get a rebound. They like the glamour of going high to get a rebound, then letting everybody see that they have the ball by holding it aloft with one hand. Those players haven't developed their basketball smarts. They count on their natural gifts. That's a mental mistake, a lack of understanding about what it takes to succeed. You see it a lot.

Old-timers like Mikan, Russell, Chamberlain, and, in more recent years, Shaquille O'Neal, had the size and strength to dominate rebounding without having to bother with blocking opponents out. They were around the basket on offense and defense anyway, so they just went up and got the ball.

In today's game, Tim Duncan and Kevin Garnett, both with career marks of over 11 rebounds per game, are prototypes of grade-A rebounders executing basic skills. First, they use good footwork to gain inside position. Then, their thrust to the ball comes off both feet and goes straight to their target, both arms fully extended. The ball, once acquired, is strongly clamped with two hands and kept above the shoulders.

Smart basketball.

How many times have you seen a shot-blocker swat the ball into the second row? Exciting, right? In my view, that's just plain dumb basketball. I never saw Bill Russell block a shot that went out of bounds—not once, and I saw him block a lot of shots. Russell touched the ball just enough to change the shot and tip it to one of his teammates. Over and over, I watch college big men block a lot of shots out of bounds. All that does is give their opponents another chance to score. It demonstrates a lack of understanding about how to play the game.

Walton considered Russell to be one of the smartest players ever, a player who combined intelligence with great physical skills. Bill once said to me, "To Russell, basketball was first and foremost a mental game. He studied everything. He knew the best way to start the fast break, get a rebound, block a short, set a screen, or make an outlet pass."

Red Auerbach had a great knack for getting the maximum performance from his players. Red had just six plays for his Celtic teams to run in their half-court offense once Russell arrived on the scene in 1956. He knew that the Celts were going to get most of their scoring from fast breaks triggered by Russell's shot-blocking and rebounding. The six plays were simple, effective ways to get his best shooters open looks.

Smart coaching.

Pat Riley recognized that players needed to be able to think on their feet while on the court: "The difference between ordinary and extraordinary players," he often said, "is that the great ones are always thinking one to three plays ahead." Riley could have had Chris Paul in mind.

Phil Jackson believes that players who are really savvy about the game have paid their dues to the "basketball gods." By that he means that they played by the game's "irrefutable principles." Among them: "Hit the open man. Help each other out on defense. Box your man out. Play inside the system. Don't break off plays. Don't force the action if you're being doubled."

Jackson adopted the Bulls' half-court triangle offense from its origi-
nator, assistant coach Tex Winter. It's an offense in which player positions
are interchangeable and requires definite player requirements for each
pass, cut, and screen. I watched Tex direct the offense during practices,
while Phil stood by. Then Phil took over the defensive drill work. Phil
always gave Winter credit for the offense but was smart enough to expand
the triangle to accommodate the special skills of Michael Jordan and Kobe
Bryant. His teams in Chicago and Los Angeles have won 11 championships.

Case closed.

Both Riley and Jackson had excellent personnel over their coaching
careers, and both maximized their teams' potentials by insisting on smart
team play. Their approaches were different. Jackson often let his teams
"play through" tough game situations without a timeout, so that they could
learn how to deal with adversity on their own. Riley, by contrast, was
quick to call a timeout and demand of his players, "Get your […] heads
in the game!"

Kareem Abdul-Jabbar, who together with Oscar Robertson led the
Milwaukee Bucks to an NBA championship in 1971, told of the smarts
the Big O brought to the game, particularly during the last years of his
career:

> Oscar had this incredible court vision and a complete un-
> derstanding of the dynamics of the game. Not only did he
> see guys open on the periphery for a jumper, he knew when
> each of us would fight through a pick or come open behind
> a screen, and the ball would arrive and be there like you
> were taking it off a table.[2]

Larry Costello coached the Bucks at the time, but Robertson was
the team leader. Oscar set the tempo, ran the offense, and was a steady-
ing influence on defense. In the 1971 playoffs, he averaged 18.3 points,
8.9 assists, and 5 rebounds.

20 • DR. JACK on Winning Basketball

Robertson was 32 at that time and had lost a half step in speed. (Oscar once surprised me by saying that he was "never a great runner.") But he still maintained enough quickness to orchestrate brilliantly the Bucks' game at both ends of the floor. Oscar knew that his window of opportunity to win a championship was closing, and he was *not* going to let it slip by. It was Robertson's only NBA championship. He retired two years later.

Clyde Drexler came into the NBA in 1983 after an outstanding college career at Houston. I coached Clyde during his rookie season at Portland. He joined a good team with two outstanding players, 2-guard Jim Paxson and small forward Calvin Natt, already in place at his positions.

Drexler had never come off the bench at either the high school or college level, and he certainly didn't expect that to happen in the pros. But it did. In that first season, Clyde averaged about 18 minutes of playing time and just under 8 points a game coming off the bench. I can tell you that he was not a happy camper. But he worked hard at his game over the summer, and the following season he broke into the starting lineup and averaged 17 points, 6 rebounds, and over 5 assists per game. It was the beginning of a great career that culminated in an NBA championship with the Houston Rockets in 1995 and his election into the Naismith Basketball Hall of Fame in 2004.

I interviewed Clyde the Glide on ESPN after the Rockets won that championship and told him that all the drill work I had forced on him during the years I coached him at Portland was for moments like this, when you revel in winning a championship.

"I know that now, Coach," Clyde responded. "I know that now."

As he got older in a young man's game, Drexler learned to use his smarts even more to stay up with the competition. Jim Paxson, who played with Clyde for five seasons in Portland, told David Halberstram that Drexler "kept figuring out what he needed to do to be better. He wasn't as physically dominating, but he was a more efficient player later in his career."

Reggie Miller, the best player I ever saw move without the ball to get open shots, was both tireless and smart. He always seemed to be wide open for his shots. Reggie says that basketball is like a chess game:

You've got to be able to read the pieces—reading where the screens are, reading where you can slip screens. Do you want a 17-footer as opposed to a 19-footer, which is a three-pointer now? What does the team need? You missed your last five shots, why don't you try to take this one all the way to the hole so you can get your rhythm back? That's what's going through my mind out there.[3]

Nowhere in the game does "play smart" apply more than at the point guard position. NBA history is studded with great players at that spot, from Slater Martin (Minneapolis) and Bob Cousy (Boston) in the 1950s, to Nate Archibald (Kansas City) and Walt Frazier (New York) in the 1970s, to John Stockton (Utah), Kevin Johnson (Phoenix), Isiah Thomas (Detroit), and Magic Johnson (L.A. Lakers) in the 1980s and 1990s, to Tim Hardaway (Miami) and Avery Johnson (San Antonio) in the 1990s, to today's game with Jason Kidd (Dallas), Tony Parker (San Antonio), Chauncey Billups (Denver), Deron Williams (Utah), Rajon Rondo (Boston), Steve Nash (Phoenix), and Chris Paul (New Orleans).

The latest phenoms are Derek Rose (Chicago), Russell Westbrook (Oklahoma City), and John Wall (Washington).

The common denominator? Basketball smarts.

The point guard runs the show. He's the designated "coach on the floor," the guy charged with carrying out the head coach's game plan. He orchestrates the fast break, he sets up the half-court offense, and he makes sure that his teammates get the ball where and when they like it. Oh, yes, as if the job description wasn't already large enough: the point guard is also the first line of defense.

Two of the most interesting point guards that I observed closely over the years were Muggsy Bogues and Steve Nash.

Muggsy was the smallest player (5'3") ever to play in the NBA. He went to Dunbar High School in Baltimore and played on teams that were undefeated in 1982 and 1983, winning 60 consecutive games and state championships those two seasons. He then played four solid years at Wake Forest and was Washington's first pick (#12) in the 1987 NBA Draft.

Many astute followers of the NBA thought that Bogues would never make it because of his size. My assistant coach at Indiana, Dick Harter, bet me a dollar that Muggsy would not be on any team's roster at the beginning of the 1987 season. I won the bet: Bogues played not only that season but 13 more in the league for Charlotte, Golden State, and Toronto.

I enjoyed coaching against Muggsy. He was always upbeat and in full control of his game. He was deceptively quick and difficult to double team. He never lost his dribble until he delivered a productive pass or got the shot he wanted. He scored enough to keep the defense honest. His teammates loved him.

Bogues took strong exception to the stereotyping of athletes as intellectually inferior. He explained that his success as his team's floor general was based on his ability to think clearly and make split-second decisions:

> *I hate it when people call athletes "dumb jocks." Hey, we're always thinking out there. It's a thinking game. If you go out there light-headed you'll easily get lost. If I'm coming down the middle and looking at a play, a play that's already in my mind, I have to carry it through so it develops that way in reality. It has to develop in your mind before it ever happens on the court. You have to think. Could a dumb jock do that?*[4]

Steve Nash was born in Johannesburg, South Africa. His father was a soccer coach, and Steve didn't play basketball much until the family moved to British Columbia, Canada. He learned the game well enough there to be recruited by the University of Santa Clara in California. He went on to become a first-round pick (#15 overall) of the Phoenix Suns in the 1996 NBA Draft.

Steve Nash takes a breather against Detroit.

Nash is a cerebral player with great ball control and footwork, the latter helped no doubt by his soccer background. He's also an ambidextrous passer with eyes in the back of his head; he scores when needed. Nash was named the NBA's Most Valuable Player in 2005 and 2006 while playing with Phoenix. In a 2008 ESPN Radio interview, Nash said how soccer helped his basketball game: "The games are similar. For me, it's advancing the ball and finding open teammates. Only in basketball, you can use your hands. At first, it felt like it was cheating."

Nash, who turned 36 in February 2010, keeps himself in excellent physical condition through a combination of total-body stretching and weight work. He still plays soccer in the summers, and he seems not to have lost a step on the hardwood.

The teams with the most savvy and know-how *learn* how to win. "We believed that if we were within four or five points with a minute to go," says Bill Russell, "we could win." All the Celts had to do, he says, was get the ball to Sam Jones. "We knew we had to create the opportunity for him to take those shots. Nothing happens by accident. It had to do with knowing our team—and ourselves—so well that we nearly always had the right guys in the right place at the right time."[5]

Magic Johnson was constantly working on how to make his teammates more successful. Lakers coach Pat Riley explains that "Magic was an avid student of all the styles of basketball. Instead of crushing his teammates under his own greatness, he studied their styles and figured out how he, as the man controlling the movement of the ball, could help them get the most of the abilities they had. He dealt in their strengths."[6]

In the fall of 1991, I was giving a coaching clinic in Paris at the same time that the Lakers were preparing to play in a preseason tournament against FIBA teams. (*FIBA* is the French acronym for *Féderacion Internacional de Basketball*.) I attended a Lakers practice there when then Lakers coach Mike Dunleavy put Magic in charge of running the team through its offensive sets. (Magic was not feeling well and was not to play in the game that night.) I watched him take the team through its various set plays. Magic knew every player's position—when to cut, where to screen, when to shoot. If the team didn't execute perfectly, Magic told them to "run it again," which the players did until Magic was satisfied. (A physical examination given to Johnson when the Lakers returned to Los Angeles revealed his infection with the HIV virus.)

Larry Bird was a half-step slower than a walk, and the Statue of Liberty could jump higher. Normally, that's a double whammy in basketball, but Bird made up for those basic deficiencies with extra effort and mental toughness. In the first game I coached against Bird, the Blazers back-doored him for field goals on our first two possessions. No team that I coached ever back-doored him again in his 13-year career with the Boston Celtics. And, as for his lack of speed and hops … well, I never saw him caught from behind in the open court, by even the quickest guards, and the man averaged 10 rebounds a game for his career.

"Larry could outthink his opponents," says Michael Jordan, who knows a few things about basketball smarts. "And he had a great heart."

Red Auerbach obviously sensed that dimension of Larry Bird when he took Bird in the first round of the 1978 NBA Draft. But Red admitted that he had no idea how great the Hick from French Lick would become: "Anyone tells you they knew Bird would be as good as he turned out—including me—is a liar. Did I know he had one of the greatest work ethics ever? No. Did I know he had a genius IQ for the game? No. Smart, yes, genius, no."[7]

Another perfect example of smart basketball making the difference between winning and losing came in the first round of the 1977 NBA playoffs between Portland and the Chicago Bulls. Bill Walton was matched up against the powerful Artis Gilmore. The three-game series was tied after two games, and Gilmore was hurting us big-time inside. Artis was bigger (7' 2") and stronger (265 pounds) than Bill (6' 11" and 235 pounds), and I reasoned that we couldn't let him receive the ball as freely as we had been in Game 2, when Gilmore scored 27 points.

Problem was, throughout his college career at UCLA and up to that point in the pros, Walton had always played behind his matchup and had good success blocking shots. I met with Bill to see if he thought he could front Artis, that is, play between him and the ball. Bill thought about it for a minute. "I don't know if I can, Coach," he told me. "But if you think it's the best way to defend him, I'll certainly try."

There's often a huge gap between theory and reality. Walton had to decide just how he was going to get front position on Gilmore. That required a game plan of its own. When Game 3 began, Walton met Gilmore before he reached his usual low-post position and, using quick feet, established front position on him and then fought for his life to keep between Artis and the Bulls passers. A combination of tremendous physical effort and smart planning made the tactic work. Bill kept Gilmore under better control (16 points on 5-for-9 shooting from the field), and we advanced to the next round.

Walton believes that smart basketball players play the game in their minds before stepping onto the court. He says that players shouldn't expect to go into a game, score, and play good defense without intense mental preparation: "Smart players have already mapped out their strategy and played the game a million times over in their heads. Bad and undisciplined ballplayers arrive at the arena and haven't given the game a second thought."[8]

At away games in my first season coaching the Blazers, I noticed that Bill always spent some of his pregame warm-up time dribbling the ball on different sections of the floor, examining the backboards, testing the bounce of the ball off the rims, checking the position of the 24-second clocks (not always above the backboards, as they are today), where the scoreboards were located, what stats were kept on them—all data that he felt he needed to know before the game began. Walton didn't want to have to search for information during a game, and he didn't want to be surprised by a dead spot on the floor or discover after the game had started that the basket rims were springier than he was accustomed to.

Smart stuff.

Bill Russell, to me the smartest center in the history of the game, says Willis Reed was the most intelligent big man he faced. Russ had the habit of visiting with his matchups off the court, learning about them and what they thought about the game. He sat down with Reed on one occasion for a little dinner and some shoptalk:

> *I asked him how he played every center in the league. As we swapped yarns, Willis confirmed my hunch that he knew what he was talking about. He didn't play his opponents the same way I did, because he was a great big ox who loved to remind people how strong he was, but he was shrewd in his analysis.* [9]

Teams known for playing tough defense rely on brainpower to be effective. Walt Frazier, whose Knicks were among the top defensive teams of his era (1967–77), describes how he used his smarts to defeat the player he was defending:

> *A key element in playing good defense is savvy. A lot of defense I played was illusion. I would try to beguile my opponents. I gave them plenty of room to hang themselves. My reasoning was that if I was all over my opponents on defense, they would be more alert. I would play off them, so it looked like they could do a lot of things.* [10]

Then, when Walt's opponents began to take him for granted, he swooped in: "They'd start to feel comfortable that they could do anything, and they'd become careless or lazy. That's when I made them pay." [11]

Frazier did that with amazing quickness and smart anticipation. He never seemed to be exerting himself but instead had whatever speed the situation required. Frazier had some great matchups with Randy Smith, my 2-guard at Buffalo. Randy had incredible speed, but he was never able to capitalize on it against Frazier like he did against other guards in the league. Frazier played off Randy just enough to prevent him from blowing by, yet he was always somehow close enough to challenge Randy's dribble or shot.

Smart.

Kareem boosted his ability to concentrate during a game by blocking out distractions in the locker room during the hours before the game. Magic Johnson says that simply by observing Abdul-Jabbar's pregame prep, he was able to improve his own ability to focus on the court:

Kareem would sit there in his underwear and read. He had incredible ability to shut out all the extraneous noise and just concentrate. Nobody could enter his zone. If you talked to him, there was nobody home. If you called his name, he wouldn't answer. He was off in his own world, getting ready to play basketball.[12]

Magic said that Abdul-Jabbar discouraged him from talking with the press before a game. The big man saw it as a potentially harmful distraction. One time he noticed that Magic was giving an interview right up until 6:45 p.m., which was 45 minutes before game time and when members of the press had to leave the locker room. "You shouldn't be doing that," Jabbar told Johnson. "You need more time to prepare. If you talk to those guys that close to the game, you'll lose your concentration."[13]

Magic indicated, "He was right, and I stopped doing it."[14]

"Without proper self-evaluation," said John Wooden, who coached UCLA to nine NCAA championships, "failure is inevitable."[15]

Playing smart basketball requires that players understand their own strengths and weaknesses, which can only happen if players are brutally honest in sizing up their strengths and weaknesses.

Magic Johnson wholeheartedly concurs:

Every player has ... to ask, "What can I do to become a better player?" Then he has to go for that extra skill even if the task is awkward, difficult, and frustrating at the beginning. ... A lot of players fall into the trap thinking, "This is the best that I can do." They think that just because they enjoyed one good performance, even one good season, they [can] stop trying to improve ... so they get lazy.[16]

Bill Russell was systematic in evaluating his level of play. After each game he took some time, either in the locker room or while driving home, to go over the key elements in his play and grade himself. Even if he had a great game by ordinary human standards, he often gave himself a relatively low grade:

The best score I ever gave myself was [for] a game in Boston in 1964, which I considered my best year. I got between 30 and 35 rebounds, made a high percentage of my shots, blocked a dozen shots, started a lot of fast breaks, intimidated my opponents and made them lose their concentration, and said the right things to my teammates to keep us playing confident basketball.[17]

Sounds like an A+ coming up, right? Not if you're Bill Russell:

Despite all this ... errors stuck in my mind. I'd embarrassed myself missing free throws, looking like a shot putter; I'd missed five or six passes I'd seen but failed to make, and I didn't set five or six screens. ... All in all I couldn't give myself a grade higher than 65.33.[18]

"You never stop learning," say Jerry West. "As long as I played there was always someone who could show me new tricks."[19]

But Jerry had some tricks of his own, too. He was the first player I saw who allowed his man a half-step advantage, then when that player thought he was open for a jump shot, West came from behind to take the ball off his shooting hand. I remember seeing Hal Greer, the Sixers guard, go through with his shooting motion only to find that there was no ball to shoot!

Smart.

Bill Walton puts it this way: "You need an insatiable appetite to learn. That's really the ultimate test of leadership—your willingness to learn and to listen so that your positions are constantly refined. Things change. Smart people adjust their thinking based on what they know."[20]

Michael Jordan concurs. He says that physical talent takes you only so far: "For me, especially later in my career, the challenge … was all mental. I [had already] proved I could take off from the free throw line and dunk or lead the league in scoring. After that the challenges become more and more mental."[21]

Most players coming into the NBA have at least a small grain of doubt about their ability to make it. Their first goal is to prove that they can. I asked Larry Bird when he knew he was going to be a good player in the NBA. He said, "Before training camp began, I scrimmaged with the veterans [Dave Cowens, Cedric Maxwell, Nate Archibald, Chris Ford, Rick Robey] and I knew after the first day that I could play in the league."

Tony Parker, the Spurs mercurial point guard, had a different experience. Parker, only 19 years old and with playing experience limited to France when the Spurs drafted him in 2001, told me, "I had confidence that they [Spurs management] thought I was good enough to draft me in the first round. My concern was with my teammates. I felt I had to show them I could do the job. Timmy [Tim Duncan] hardly spoke to me until late in the regular season, when I had a big game against Gary Payton up at Seattle. After that he must have thought I was OK."

Parker went on, "Pop [Coach Gregg Popovich)] really got on me, but I knew he was only trying to make me better, so I didn't have a problem with that. Timmy was the guy I wanted to have believe in me."

And he did. I still have a picture in my mind of Duncan giving Parker a bear hug when the Spurs finished off Cleveland in the 2007 NBA Finals. Parker was the series' Most Valuable Player. Both Parker and Bird before him took that initial bit of self-confidence and used their smarts to become great players.

There's a common misconception that NBA players don't need coaching ... that the coach merely "rolls the balls out" and lets the players play. That couldn't be further from the truth. Larry Bird says he learned more about the game of basketball in one season of coaching than in all his years as a player:

> As a player, everything I did was based on reaction. And once I learned the fundamentals, I could see how to improve my game by practicing. In coaching ... [t]here are so many things going on, and you have to make these spur-of-the-moment decisions. ... As a player you are worried about your responsibilities within the game. As a coach, your responsibility is the entire game, including the five guys you put on the court.[22]

Bird told me that same story on more than one occasion. But Larry had the smarts to know what he didn't know, and he hired Dick Harter as his defensive coach and Rick Carlisle to handle the offense before his first coaching season at Indiana in 1997–98. He relied on them heavily in his first year of coaching. I attended a Pacers practice that season where Harter and Carlisle ran the whole workout while Bird watched from the sideline, only stopping the action on occasion to make a comment to a player. By the third season, Bird was more in charge of the team, but he still welcomed input from Harter and Carlisle.

Smart stuff by the Birdman.

There's been a surprising number of players who were thrust into NBA coaching positions without previous experience and a fair number of college coaches who came into the NBA unprepared for the differences in the two games.

Paul Silas became head coach of the LA Clippers in 1981, following his retirement as a player at Seattle. Paul had been a smart, productive player for 14 years in the NBA. But was he ready for the challenges of being a head coach?

I unexpectedly bumped into Silas in the workout room of a hotel in the preseason of his first year as coach. He had just come out of a sauna and was dripping sweat. He had one towel wrapped around his middle and another draped over his head. He looked at me for several seconds and said, "Why didn't you tell me it was like this?"

"Like what?" I asked.

"Coaching. It's an impossible, tough, [bleeping] job! I don't know how you do it all these years."

"Welcome to my world, Paul," I laughed. "You'll get used to it."

(And he did. Silas coached the Clippers for two more seasons and then had successful stints at Charlotte and New Orleans before finishing at Cleveland.)

Jerry Tarkanian had the same reaction to NBA coaching when he took the San Antonio job in 1992. Tark had a marvelous coaching record at UNLV before hooking on with the Spurs. I was the television analyst for the 76ers that season, and we were working an early season game in San Antonio when Tark agreed to tape an interview with me one morning after shooting practice. Before we went on camera, I asked Tark how it was going. He used the same terms Paul Silas had used years earlier: "I had no idea it would be like this. This is a different game."

In jest, I asked if he would finish the season. He paused and said, "I don't know. I just don't know." Two weeks later, Jerry Tarkanian resigned. The Spurs were 9-and-11 at the time.

Two different reactions to NBA coaching: Paul Silas learned how to succeed; Jerry Tarkanian gave up and returned to college coaching.

Most players, especially those from inner cities, learn the basics of the game unsupervised on playgrounds. Former Knicks shooting guard John Starks says that playing in the parks of Tulsa as a boy helped prepare him for the NBA:

The NBA season is a very grueling, draining season, and if a player doesn't have experience playing game after game, like I did in the parks, hour upon hour, then he's not going to have the mental toughness to play in the NBA. You can't be soft and be a dominant park player.[23]

Starks had an uneven path to the NBA. Undrafted, he wound up on a Knicks roster in 1990 after a couple of good seasons in the Continental Basketball Association and the World Basketball League. He worked his way on to the starting lineup under Coach Pat Riley and blossomed into an outstanding, mentally tough player on a Knicks team that went to the NBA Finals in 1994.

Jeff Van Gundy was an assistant coach on that team, and I watched him work out Starks before a big game that year. Van Gundy and Starks were the only ones on the court. Starks was in constant motion, making slash cuts across the lane, driving to the hoop, or spotting up for perimeter shots. Van Gundy passed Starks the ball at various points, and Starks shot, sometimes on the catch, sometimes off the dribble, but always taking the kind of shot he would get in the game. Van Gundy critiqued his every move and stopped the drill occasionally to make suggestions. Both were incredibly focused.

When the drill ended after about a half hour, Starks went to Van Gundy, gave him a high five and a hug and said, "Thanks, Coach. You're the best."

The point: the player worked hard to improve his game, and the coach helped him every step of the way.

Smart.

I was Reggie Miller's coach with the Pacers in his rookie season (1987–88), and I watched him develop a meticulous pregame routine to get himself ready to play. He came on the court about two hours before game time to loosen up and work on his ball handling and shot making. He worked very efficiently, practicing every shot he might use in the game—

drives to the basket, short runners, pull-up jumpers, long 3-pointers, and so on. He took quick-release shots that he'd get coming off screens. He worked both sides of the court with rapt concentration.

When the game began, I knew Reggie Miller was ready to play.

Playing smart *team* basketball, though, depends on the coach.

I played four years of college basketball against strong national competition, and I was playing for Harrisburg (Pennsylvania) in the Eastern Pro League when I started coaching at the high school level. I thought all that qualified me to coach. I figured I knew enough to *show* my young players how to play by scrimmaging with them and giving them a style of play.

I was dead wrong.

See, I wasn't *coaching* them. After my team was walloped by some very good, well-coached teams, I realized that I needed to start teaching and coaching my players, not just showing them how I played. It was a rude but necessary awakening.

That first year of coaching at St. James High School in Chester, Pennsylvania, was a real wake-up call for me. I don't remember the exact record—and I dearly hope that nobody else does, either—but we were well under .500. I determined then and there that if I was going to stay in coaching, I had better learn how to *coach*—that is, how to teach, how to make my players better, and how to prepare a game plan capable of winning.

So I did a complete overhaul of what I had been doing. I went to coaching clinics, picked the brains of other coaches, got tapes of NCAA and NBA games, and I watched what those coaches did. I changed my whole approach.

A good coach, at any level, in any sport, makes sure his players are well-grounded in fundamentals. Footwork, body position and balance, and basic skills become key issues. I had to learn how to teach step by step. I knew that if I wanted to be a good coach, I had to learn to teach.

Another part of the coach's job is to get information on the opposing team and their players in order to develop an effective game plan. I tried to see each opponent personally before my team played it. I did that at every level that I coached. In the NBA, I would also go to the arena early before a game and watch opposing players warm up. Athletes are great creatures of habit. They'll unconsciously use moves during the warm-up that are identical to those they'll use in the game. I'd give that information to my players to augment scouting reports, alerting my defenders on tendencies to look for and getting them mentally ready to compete.

I became a better teacher, my players improved on their skills, and my teams got better. I was becoming a coach.

Many NBA players credit specific coaches and parents with providing them with the motivation to learn the game and the knowledge to master it. Magic Johnson, for instance, was fortunate to have a father who was knowledgeable about the game and who took the time to transmit that knowledge to young Earvin when he was only a grade-schooler. He told his son that he needed not only to "think the game" but "feel" it as well and that the best skill he could have was "a basketball mind."

Magic's father, the son recalls, was a longtime fan but more grounded in basketball technique than most other dads:

> Before he'd take me out to the driveway, he'd sit down
> with me and we'd watch the NBA games on television. Dad
> made me see the importance of the little things in basket-
> ball, the fundamentals, even to players in the pros. Watch-
> ing Dave Bing [of the Detroit Pistons] ... with my father
> was how I learned the simple secrets of basketball. Dad
> pointed out everything down to the smallest detail—the
> footwork, the head fakes, the defensive stances, blocking
> out underneath the boards, things that separated the great
> players from the good players.[24]

Larry Bird credits two high school coaches for teaching him the fundamentals:

Jim Jones was the first to stress how important it was to use my left hand. At the time, I'm not sure I understood why that was such a big deal, but the better I got and the tougher the competition I played, I appreciated that advice. ... [He] was also the one who drilled the idea of "boxing out" into my head until I wouldn't dream of not doing it. ... Gary Holland picked up right where [Jim] left off. No wonder by the time I got to the pros everyone was talking about what a sound fundamental base I had.[25]

Bill Bradley, perhaps the most cerebral player ever to play in the NBA, also credits his high school basketball coach, Arvel Popp, at Crystal City (Missouri) High School, for teaching him lessons that served him throughout his college and professional careers:

Coach Popp, the only man who could ever be "the coach" to me, was like a monk, withdrawn personally and unsociable in town circles, unreachable by the power of the company, the church, the bank, or the mayor, rigid with discipline and sparse with compliments; inspiring to boys like me, cruel to those unprepared or unwilling. Never did he confuse his roles. He was not the college counselor, family advisor, tutor, athletic businessman or budding politician. He aspired only to be the coach. It was a calling. If in the years as a New York Knick there were thousands of words written about passing and teamwork and hitting the open man, it would all be true, but it would not be new. It would be "the coach's game," which by age seventeen was second nature to me.[26]

Almost all the great NBA players I've watched and talked with in nearly half a century coaching and calling games can recall with almost photographic clarity very specific lessons learned as teenagers from coaches you've never heard of, lessons that they drew on in building their careers.

From left, John Wooden, Arnold (Red) Auerbach, Ramsay, and Bill Walton in 1994 at an Academic Hall of Fame dinner honoring Walton.

Kareem Abdul-Jabbar says he benefited from a series of great coaches through high school and college who pushed him, criticized him, and pushed some more until in the process he became a great player:

> *The coaches I grew up around all believed that they had to get you out of your comfort zone in order to teach you something. You couldn't stretch your game without the effort, and sometimes the pain of it. ... Part of the reason I'd always want to improve my game was to shut them up and get them off my back.*[27]

Bill Walton says that John Wooden, his college coach at UCLA, convinced him that he had to learn to play away from the basket if he was to take his game to the next level:

> *I didn't believe it at the time, but it turned out that playing the high post that entire freshman season was the best thing in the world for me. It allowed me to develop skills that I would need as I moved up to each new level of competition. I became more versatile, which is the key to success in basketball and life. Had I not learned how to play away from the basket, my game would have stagnated.*[28]

I was asked to speak at a dinner honoring Walton as an Academic All-American in Washington, D.C. John Wooden was also in attendance. In my remarks I told how Walton had said at my first meeting with him as his Portland coach, "Coach, don't assume we know anything." He was saying, in effect, that the Blazers needed active coaching.

When Wooden went to the lectern later, he turned toward me and said in a feigned, mortally wounded tone, "Not anything, Jack? Nothing? Four years at UCLA, and Bill learned nothing at all from me?"

Of course, Bill learned all of his great fundamental skills under Wooden's guidance, and everyone in the audience knew it. But it was great banquet fare, and Wooden's comments brought forth a generous chorus of laughter from the black-tied crowd.

Players learn from each other by observing, asking questions, reading, watching video, and competing against better players. When Kareem Abdul-Jabbar was still Lew Alcindor at Power Memorial Academy in New York City, his high school coach, Jack Donahue, often took him to see Knicks-Celtics games at the old Madison Square Garden. A longtime fan of the Boston Celtics, Donahue always instructed him to pay especially close attention to No. 6 (Bill Russell) for the Celtics, particularly his rebounding, passing, and shot-blocking. Not surprisingly, No. 6 had an important effect on the young man's development as a center:

I learned how to use the outlet pass from watching Bill Russell. I also learned how to guard people and intimidate shots from watching him in those games. I don't block shots in the same way he did, but the concept was made clear to me then: help your teammates when they get beat.[29]

Kobe Bryant, whom San Antonio coach Gregg Popovich describes as a "basketball assassin," became the youngest player to score 24,000 NBA points early in the 2009–10 season. Kobe used that occasion to cite other players who had a positive influence on his game. Bryant (6'6") made special mention of the tips he got from Hall of Famer Hakeem Olajuwon during the previous summer that helped him expand his low-post game.

Chris Paul told me how Bryant quizzed him on Paul's unusual technique in the paint when both played for Team USA. Bryant is already one of the game's greatest players. He has five championship rings, but he keeps working to get better.

Smart.

Larry Bird once told me that in his rookie season he watched video-tapes of his own games as soon as he could after they were over—not to relive the highlights with a beer, but to study how he and his teammates had worked together on the court:

What I'd do is zero in on plays where I had the ball and see where my teammates were positioned. That way I could tell if I could have made a better play, or if there was some-one who was open that I hadn't noticed on the floor. It also helped me make sure my teammates were going to the proper spots on the court. You can't believe how many times I'd be sitting home replaying the game I had just played, and I'd watch myself come off as pick, and I'd see Danny Ainge wide open in the corner, and I'd say to myself, "Geez, how did I miss him?"

Larry Bird, another great player who never stopped trying to get better.

Smart.

A handful of players and coaches, through their powers of observation and creativity and their focused study of the game, changed the way basketball was played, both on offense and defense.

Russell changed the game with his impact on defense. There had never been a concentration on blocking shots until Bill came into the NBA in 1956. No player has done that better than Russ. Eleven championships in 13 years attest to the enormity of his skills.

Red Auerbach's incredible string of eight straight NBA championships at Boston we already know about. But let's not overlook two other Auerbach innovations—the small-forward and the sixth-man concepts—that remain a prominent part of the game today.

In the 1940s and 1950s, the conventional wisdom in basketball was to use the starting five—hey, they were your five best guys, right?—until either fatigue or foul trouble required going to the bench. But Red, always a couple of steps ahead of other coaches, had a different approach. Almost always, he kept one of his best players on the bench for the first six to eight minutes of the first period. He explained it this way:

> *When a game or half starts both teams get into a certain rhythm. After a little while, a little bit of fatigue sets in and everyone begins to lose just a little. My thought was, "If I send one of my two or three best players into the game at that point and he's completely fresh, he's going to be able to take advantage of people. He'll probably make some plays right away because his legs are fresh. In turn that gives guys a burst of energy and picks up the whole team."*[30]

Frank Ramsey (6'3") was the first player to employ Red's strategy at Boston in 1956, the same year that Russell joined the Celtics. Auerbach used Ramsey off the bench at forward, and Frank ran the legs off his bigger, slower matchup.

Since Red's time, the "sixth man" has become a familiar part of the game. Now every team has a designated sixth man who infuses his team with energy, is sometimes the team's leading scorer, and is on the court when the outcome is decided at the end of the game. That role has become so imbedded in the structure of the game that the NBA has, since 1983, given out a Sixth Man Award at the end of each season.

Red Holzman employed the Auerbach concept in New York when he moved a "tweener," 6'5" Bill Bradley, to small forward from guard. Nobody was happier than Bradley at the switch:

When I came into the league ... I had to play guard. Because I wasn't quick enough, I got burned often. When I returned to forward I was relieved. When writers asked Holzman how he could play me, a small 6'5" forward, against men 6'9" he told them that a disadvantage was often an advantage. What he meant was that when an opposing team saw the difference in height they often forced the action toward my man, thus disrupting the normal flow of their offense, and forcing my man to take a bigger scoring responsibility. Often their hopes of taking advantage backfired when my man missed shots, or passes went awry when they tried to get the ball to him. Meanwhile, on offense, I was quicker than the bigger man and could maneuver for shots easily.[31]

The bottom line? There has never been a championship team in basketball that didn't play smart.

Not one.

You can win championships with a team made up of players with minor deficiencies in physical skills here and there. But you cannot win championships with a team composed of players with impeccable physical skills if they don't play smart. Period.

Play smart.

NBA coaches (from left) Bill Cunningham, Ramsay, Gene Shue, Lenny Wilkens, Jack McKinney, and Cotton Fitzsimmons relax at a Nike coaching trip to Hawaii in 1980.

You know what? I think there might be a life lesson in there that goes beyond basketball.

2

LIVE IN THE HERE AND NOW

Focus … concentrate … pay close attention.

We start hearing variations on that theme our first day in school, if not before, and if we don't heed the admonition—if we *don't* pay close attention—we get our knuckles rapped by life.

The greatest demonstration of focus and concentration by a player I coached was turned in by Bob McAdoo of the Buffalo Braves in Game 3 of the first round of the 1976 playoffs. The Braves and Sixers had finished the season with the same record (46–36), and each team had won on the other's court in the playoffs to set up the "win-or-go-home" game.

Philadelphia led by two points with a couple of seconds remaining in regulation when McAdoo was fouled on an attempted shot. Mac needed to make both free throws to send the game to overtime. But when he went to the line to shoot, he looked at the basket, and it was moving from side to side. Mac wasn't having a dizzy spell. The basket was moving—literally. An overzealous Sixers fan was pulling on the guy wire backboard support, causing the whole backboard and the basket attached to it to move back and forth laterally.

Referee Jake O'Donnell had already given McAdoo the ball when Mac discovered the moving hoop. Mac stopped and returned the ball to O'Donnell and told him of the problem. Jake looked along the baseline, saw the culprit, and shouted to him, "Cut that out!" The chastened fan stopped pulling on the cable and returned to his seat. O'Donnell returned the ball to McAdoo and said, "Shoot 'em."

The backboard continued to sway. Not as much as before, but there definitely was movement. Mac hoped he could wait until it stopped altogether, but O'Donnell repeated, "*Shoot 'em!*"

So McAdoo readied himself to shoot, and with the basket still sliding back and forth, and the Philly Faithful at full throat, he calmly knocked down both free throws to tie the game and send it into OT. We went on to pull out a 124–123 win to advance to the Eastern Conference Semifinals.

Bob McAdoo had great range with an unorthodox jumper. He had a big first step on his drive to the basket. And he could jump over most defenders when he posted up. But what made Bob such a great clutch player was his ability to screen out distractions, anything from fan noise to swaying baskets. McAdoo led the NBA in scoring in 1974, 1975, and 1976 and was MVP in 1975. He later played on two championship teams for Pat Riley with the Lakers (1982, 1985). I was proud to sponsor Bob on his admission into the Basketball Hall of Fame in 2000.

I see Mac, currently an assistant coach with Miami, when I do ESPN broadcasts involving the Heat. He loves to talk about the Braves and, when prompted, about the time he hit the moving target ... twice.

To win in basketball, you must be able to bring an extraordinarily high level of concentration to a work environment that is frenetic, fast paced, wild, changing, and sometimes crazy. I've never landed a space module on the moon—at least not yet—but that's the level of concentration I'm talking about. Without it, there's no way you can keep your head on straight, make good decisions, and put yourself in a position to win.

That may seem obvious for players, but it's no less true for coaches.

Coaches must focus 100 percent of their attention on what's happening on the 4,700 square feet of hardwood in front of them. That's not an easy thing to do when there's a packed house of thousands of passionate fans yelling their heads off, especially if you're on the road, and they're screaming at you to screw up.

The demeanor of basketball coaches during a game runs the gamut from the placid UCLA legend, John Wooden, to the wild, shouting, gesturing rants of Red Auerbach. Yet as far apart as the on-court bearing of those two gentlemen was, they were both paragons of concentration and focus on what was happening in front of them.

Wooden always sat with arms folded, a game program wrapped in his hand, staring stoically at the action unfolding before him, seemingly oblivious to crowd noise and even to the frenzied action taking place just feet away from him. I always thought he looked like he was posing for an updated sculpture of The Thinker.

More than once I heard John say that he believed his principal responsibility was to prepare his players meticulously and thoroughly at practice and then let them play the game. Cheerleading from the bench? Not John Wooden's style.

(Not long ago I mentioned this image of his revered coach to Gail Goodrich, who played on Wooden's first NCAA championship team in 1964 and who is now in the Naismith Basketball Hall of Fame. Goodrich smiled and said, "That may have been true when Coach Wooden had Abdul-Jabbar and Walton, but with us, he was on top of every play.")

Stu Inman, Portland's director of personnel, was a great "Wooden watcher." Stu had coached at San Jose State College when the Wizard began at UCLA, and he told me that while Wooden appeared to sit quietly on the bench, he constantly chirped at officials throughout the game. So the great coach may not have been as detached as he appeared.

But focused?

For certain.

The demeanor of NBA coaches has changed dramatically over the years, most obviously in their reaction to calls made by game officials.

Back in the days when the Celtics were racking up NBA championships, Auerbach prowled the sidelines, rarely sitting down during a game and often running out on the court to suggest to refs that he had valid objections to calls. Although at times it did look like his head might explode, I don't think Red was ever out of control (well, rarely). I think most of the yelling and arm waving was done to get an edge for his team. And I never ever thought Auerbach lost his concentration on the game.

Alex Hannum (seven different teams over 16 seasons) and Red Holzman (best remembered for his 14 campaigns with the Knicks) also made sure referees knew it if either thought a bad call had gone against his team. Alex, an imposing figure (6' 8", 240 pounds), would stand and stomp on the floor with his size-16 shoes, an act that seemed to shake the court. Red would unleash a stream of expletives that turned the smoke blue in the old Madison Square Garden and could be heard above the crowd noise. But both maintained their focus on the game.

Butch van Breda Kolff and Kevin Loughery were coaching contemporaries of mine in the 1960s and 1970s, and I think all three of us "lost it" on occasion. Butch coached the Pistons and the LA Lakers after an outstanding stint at Princeton with Bill Bradley. I recall a game in Detroit when I was coaching the Sixers, and the Pistons got hit with what Butch considered a bad call. The teams were seated on either side of the scorer's table near midcourt, and when I heard Butch scream obscenities at the official, I glanced over in the direction of the Detroit bench … no van Breda Kolff. Then I saw him *striding across the top of the scorer's table*, still ranting at the officials, and broad jumping over my head onto the court to continue his harangue. Butch got two Ts for that display of athleticism.

Loughery could be equally volatile (although I never heard of him doing any scorer's-table strolling). Kevin had a full head of carefully coiffed gray hair that made him look like an investment banker, back in the days when that was a respected profession. But when he perceived that calls were going against his team, he would tear at his hair, throw his jacket (occasionally drop-kicking it in the general direction of an offending ref), and sometimes rip open his shirt. *Technical!*

I also had my share of tirades, and one season I led the league's coaches in technical fouls. An example? In a Sixers-Baltimore Bullets (now the Washington Wizards) game played at the University of Maryland's Cole Field House one year, the teams were seated on folding chairs along the side court. Early in the game, I had jumped up to question a call, and referee Jack Madden looked over and said, *"Don't jump up again!"* I nodded my head, "Okay, okay." But later in the game, a really terrible call went against us, and I jumped up. Then, remembering Madden's edict and not wanting to get a T, I tried to get back on my chair quickly. The problem was I hit the folding chair unevenly and it collapsed, with me on top of it. Madden heard the clatter, looked over, shook his head while trying to suppress a grin, and brought a horizontal palm down against a vertical palm: *Technical!*

Gene Shue was the Baltimore coach at the time, and he told me that he got the videotape of that scene, and before his next practice replayed my pratfall over and over for his players. Apparently the locker room was in hysterics. I told Gene I was glad to be of service.

There was a theory when I first started coaching in the NBA that the coach who had the first technical called on him won the game. I recall a casual conversation I had with veteran official Manny Sokol in an airport coffee shop. Manny described a situation in a recent game he refereed: "We were having a nice game. Neither coach was complaining, and …"

The idea bulb lit up in my head. What Manny was saying between the lines, as I interpreted it, was that if a coach doesn't say anything, it means he thinks the officials are getting all the calls right. And while that might be true much—okay, *most*—of the time, I felt more convinced than ever that a coach needed to let officials know in no uncertain terms when they missed one.

Call it a public service: I felt it was my responsibility to my team and an aspect of maintaining my focus on the game. Maybe it also crossed my mind that it might give me an edge at a critical moment near the end of a game.

Good in theory. But early in my first year in Portland I called a timeout, only instead of waiting for my team at the bench I walked out toward midcourt to complain to the refs about a call. Bill Walton intercepted me. "Coach," he said quietly, "don't you know we don't play well when you do that?" That stopped me in my tracks and made me rethink my responsibilities as a coach. The number of technical fouls called on me plummeted after that.

The key to handling disagreements with officials, I discovered after years of trial and error (with emphasis on the latter), was to present my opinion to the official while under emotional control and without raising my voice. Whatever you do, don't show him up. Just make the point and continue to focus on the game. The result: fewer technical fouls, better communication with officials, and happier scoreboards.

Officiating in today's NBA is far superior to what it was in my coaching days.

Games nowadays are controlled by three officials as opposed to two in most of the years I coached. Officials are better trained and supervised. They often confer on questionable calls before making a decision, and there is now league-approved limited usage of television replay to make sure that certain types of calls are made correctly. As a broadcaster with the advantage of seeing television replays after every whistle, I'm impressed by the high percentage of close calls officials make accurately. Of course, as an unbiased broadcaster, I have nothing personally vested in the outcome of games, so I can look at them more objectively. (Funny how neutrality can alter one's perspective.)

Not all current NBA coaches share my opinion about the quality of officiating. I recall visiting a coaching friend (who shall remain nameless) to offer condolences after a tough loss in a game I had broadcast. As I walked into his office, he fixed me with a baleful look and blurted out,

"How about that son of a bitch?" I didn't know which son of a bitch he was referring to and said so. "That bleepin' … !" he shouted. "He bleeped us!"

The truth is, I thought it had been a well-officiated game, but I certainly wasn't going to share that evaluation with my friend. I changed the subject, we chatted a bit more, and when I left, I decided that it would be better to avoid the loser's postgame locker room in the future.

Every NBA coach has his own way of handling the pressures of the game. Pat Riley, who retired in 2008 after 26 NBA seasons at the helm

Pat Riley

of the Lakers, the Knicks, and the Heat, stood in front of his bench, his arms folded across his chest, hair slicked back, and, in his Armani suit, looking like an ad for *GQ* magazine. Riles was the textbook definition of composure, coolly impervious to barbs from fans at away games, courteously appreciative of cheers at home, and always quick to call a play on offense or change the look of his defense.

I was a television analyst for the Heat during the first six years of Riley's tenure with the team. He would question calls occasionally, but I never once saw him lose concentration on the game and on how his team was performing. (It worked pretty well: five NBA championships and three NBA Coach of the Year awards in 23 seasons.)

Riley's game face was always firmly in place by the time he arrived at the arena. In Miami, he sequestered himself in his office near the Heat locker room for about an hour before it was time to give his pregame talk.

He used the time to make out "reminder cards" for the game that he would tuck away in his inside jacket pocket. During his time in Miami, he would allow me to come into his office during his "quiet hour" and get his personal insights into the game, which I would then use for my TV broadcasts.

Prior to one game, I knocked on his office door and walked in to see him taking a deep drag on a cigarette. I knew Pat smoked, but I also knew he was scrupulously careful not to be seen doing so in public. I had caught him off guard. He looked at me, smiled, and said, "You caught me, Triathlon Man." Riles then squashed out his cigarette, and we talked about the upcoming game. It was the first and last time I ever caught him in the act. (Riley stopped smoking altogether in 2006.)

You'd never be able to guess from their courtside demeanor that NBA coaches were in the same profession. For instance,

- During games, Phil Jackson sits in a specially constructed chair designed to ease his chronic back and hip problems. (The chair goes with him on road trips.) But if a Lakers player fails to carry out his defensive job, Phil is out of the chair as if catapulted.
- Denver's George Karl stands impassively, almost like a statue, near his bench.
- Indiana's Jim O'Brien is, fittingly, a pacer—constantly on the move, all the while shouting out instructions to his players.
- Doc Rivers of the Celtics sometimes sits, sometimes stands, and sometimes paces back and forth.

Among today's coaches, Stan Van Gundy is the most emotional. You don't have to check the scoreboard to know how the Magic are doing in a game. Just look at Van Gundy. When his team's playing well, he's at peace with the world and chats with an assistant sitting beside him. But when it's not …

If the Magic's performing less than magically, Stan is a contortionist, writhing on the bench or stalking the sidelines shouting to his players. At timeouts, he beseeches his players with a strident, raspy voice to make a point and then quickly draws a diagram on his coach's board to illustrate his point. The Magic players listen, take his critiques in silence, and then usually regroup for a final word by themselves before they leave the sideline.

Gregg Popovich, whom I regard as the best coach in the NBA, usually sits on the bench, absorbed in the action, frequently conferring with Mike Budenholzer, his top assistant. Pop occasionally stands and walks the sideline to question a call or have a quick word with a player, but he's typically under emotional control. His timeout talks with his team are direct, concrete, and positive. But if he senses a lack of effort or concentration, selfishness, or a failure to follow the game plan by a player … well, that guy had best run for cover. Coach Pop is all over the cause of his ire like General George Patton, and it doesn't matter who it may be. I've seen him jump on Tim Duncan or Tony Parker as well as a substitute off the bench. And his language would be bleeped even on late-night TV.

But when he's expended all of his ammo on that emotional salvo, Pop calms down and returns his focus to winning another game. That's something he's done with impressive regularity, as evidenced by his four championships in a long NBA career, all with the Spurs.

The one thing these and all other good NBA coaches have in common? Their intense concentration is on the here and now, on what's taking place on the basketball court in front of them.

When I coached, I found that I concentrated best while kneeling on one knee in front of my team bench and near the sideline. That position seemed to bring me into the action. I was into every bounce of the ball, almost as if I were playing. And on one occasion I *did* become a player— an illegal one at that—when I inadvertently intercepted a pass.

Coach Jack Ramsey coaching the Portland Trailblazers, 1977.

There I was, in my customary kneeling position in front of the Portland bench, when an opposing player, trapped in the backcourt, leaned over the sideline, attempting to pass the ball up court. His pass came right at me, and I instinctively put my hand up and found the ball stuck there! Play came to a screeching halt. Referee Jake O'Donnell again was incensed. He whistled me for a technical foul and said, "I should throw you out of the game." I told Jake that I hadn't intended to catch the pass; it had just happened. I apologized, and he let me stay in the game. I made sure I never became a "sixth man" again.

But I continued using that kneeling position close to the sideline as long as I coached. It allowed me to block out the fans from my side vision, at least some of the crowd noise, and any other distractions that might occur. I called plays and changed defenses from that position, usually communicating one on one with my point guard, whom I counted on to direct his team.

I'll never forget a game in which one of my communications was intercepted. It happened near the end of the first half in a playoff series with the Lakers. I called a play to be used on the ensuing possession while an L.A. player was shooting a free throw at the basket nearest the Blazers bench. Lakers superfan Jack Nicholson was in his usual seat next to the visiting team's bench. I was so focused that I didn't see Lakers guard Norm Nixon sidle up to Nicholson just before the free throw to ask what play I had called. Nicholson told him.

My assistant Jack McKinney had witnessed the exchange between Nixon and Nicholson and told me what had happened as we walked off the court at halftime. I said to Jack, "We'll fix Mr. Nicholson when we come out for the second half."

Nicholson was in his seat when I approached him as the players warmed up for the second half. Walking over to him with an angry look on my face, I reached down, grabbed the lapels of his jacket, raised him out of his seat, and got right in his face: "If you *ever* tell the Lakers what I say to my players again, I'll take your head off."

Now, I'm a huge Jack Nicholson fan, and I'd chatted with him many times at past games. For the first time that I'd ever seen, Nicholson was flustered. "Jesus Christ, Jack," he sputtered, "I wouldn't do anything like that. What do I know about basketball?" With that, I released my hold on his jacket and broke up with laughter. He laughed, too, but with a hint of relief. I then refocused for the game and got ready for the second half.

That's the way players prefer their coaches to be, of course: focused and ready. They want us to be to be poised and under control. They have enough to think about without the distraction of their coach going bonkers on the bench. That's not to say that a coach shouldn't get after a player or his entire team if he detects lackadaisical or sloppy play. But he has to pick those moments carefully, and his exhortations must be precise and— you guessed it—focused.

Needless to say, the same goes for players. Phil Jackson says that a player must become "so completely absorbed in playing the game that he is unaware of anything not directly concerned with it."[1] Pat Riley believes that the more you play the game the more you became aware that "there can be only one state of mind as you approach any profound test: total concentration."[2] Oscar Robertson gets to the same place with just three words: "Basketball *is* concentration."[3]

John Wooden once pointed out the futility of allowing the mind to attach itself to thoughts about what happened in the past or to leap forward to think about what might happen in the future:

You have control only over the present, right now. Let me prove it to you. I ask you to do this: change the past. Even the smallest, most incidental, least important thing that happened in the past. Go ahead and show that you can change it. The future? Again, I ask you, change now something in the future. Can you? Of course not. Your control exists now, in the present, right here.[4]

In 1896, the year the first professional basketball game was played, a fellow who didn't know a basketball from a bass fiddle—Mr. Rudyard Kipling—put it this way in his poem "If":

If you can keep your head when all about you are losing theirs … you'll be a Man, my son!

Or maybe even an NBA player or coach.

Yes, the first professional basketball game was played in 1896. Not many people know that.

As we all do know, Dr. James Naismith was asked to come up with an indoor activity for the YMCA Training Center in Springfield, Massachusetts, whose students were training to be P.E. teachers. The result was basketball, with the first game played on December 21, 1891 (final score: 1–0). The game spread rapidly in YMCAs across the Northeast. The problem was, Naismith intended his invention to be a game of finesse, not brute strength, but things got pretty rough pretty fast, and some YMCAs started banning it. In 1896, a couple of teams in Trenton, New Jersey, were refused permission to play in the local Y. Not to be deterred, they rented a local Masonic hall, charged admissions, and split the proceeds: $15 per man, with the captain of the winning team hauling down $16. One thing led to another, and now we have the NBA.

But I digress …

Mental preparation starts early on game day. Players and coaches have different techniques for sharpening their focus and different times for "getting ready."

There are many players in the NBA that you simply can't talk to on game day—and you shouldn't try to. They are so zoned in on what they have to do after the first tipoff that they cannot abide any distractions—from anybody. For example, Avery Johnson, who played 16 seasons with six different teams, is as affable and outgoing a person as you've ever met, but on game day he was wound tighter than his alarm clock from the time it woke him up. AJ had his game face on before he brushed his teeth. Nobody could penetrate his intense focus, not his coach, his teammates, the press—not even his family.

And I would hazard a guess that half, if not more, of NBA players echo his approach on game day. They try not to allow outside vectors of any kind enter their consciousness on game day. They're focused totally on what they and the team have to do. The pregame nap and meal (typically four hours before game time), the trip to the arena, and their time with the team trainers for therapy and taping are all preplanned to the minute.

Many players won't participate in day-of-game interviews. San Antonio's Tim Duncan usually doesn't talk to *anyone*. In the locker room he prepares by watching a tape of a previous game with the opponent. Then he goes on the floor and spends half an hour—30 minutes, not 26 or 32; exactly 30—practicing the shots he figures he'll get in the game. Then it's back to the locker room for meditation before he returns with the team to warm up for the game. TD is in his personal cocoon. It's not that he's unfriendly, but if you approach him, he'll shake hands, but usually that's it.

I'd always had a good relationship with TD since he came into the league in 1997. So, before Game 7 of the Detroit-San Antonio NBA Finals in 2005, I decided I would try, with Coach Pop's permission, to pry into his private basketball world a little bit before the game. I was covering the series for ESPN Radio, and I thought that Tim had been playing tentatively against Ben Wallace and Rasheed Wallace. I waited at the side of the court until Tim paused in his shooting routine to towel off, then approached him and asked—off mike, off the record—"Tim, can I give you a thought about tonight's game?" He nodded in the affirmative, so I said, "The Pistons don't have anybody who can carry your jock. Don't even think about it. Just go out and kick their ass." Duncan smiled and said, "Thanks."

End of conversation.

Will Perdue, who was also working the series for ESPN, watched that scene from his broadcast location above the court and told me later, "I don't know what you said to Duncan, but he made eight straight shots after that." TD also made a key baseline jumper to assure the Spurs the victory and another NBA title.

Did my brief comment trigger that performance by Duncan? Probably not, but the old coach in me would like to think it had something to do with it.

As a coach, I needed to get *myself* mentally prepared to help my team get mentally prepared to play. Before meeting the team on the morning of a game day, I got a good physical workout in the gym or swimming pool to get all the cobwebs out of my mind and ready myself for game day practice. I had to be ready before I could check to make sure they were ready.

The so-called "shootaround" practice takes place at midmorning and is the best time to help prepare your team physically and mentally for the upcoming game that night. I required an hour of concentration from my players. I started each session by showing video segments of the opposing team, pointing out their strengths and weaknesses. Then I walked my players through the opponent's game tendencies on the court and showed them how we could counteract them. I went over the responsibilities of both starters and reserves. Next, I gave a short synopsis of what the team needed from each of them to win the game. Finally, we went through about 20 minutes of competitive shooting games. End of session.

After the shootaround, I would take a half-hour nap and then eat a light meal. Most players followed more or less the same routine. I would arrive at the arena about two-and-a-half hours before game time. After writing the game plan on the locker room chalkboard, I would carefully watch the players as they came in, noting their moods and levels of concentration. I engaged them in light conversation and tried to be aware of what might be going on in their lives away from basketball, alert to any personal issues that might have an impact on their game performance.

I expected everyone to be dressed and ready to play exactly one hour before game time. At the 30-minute mark, I'd give them a 10-minute review of the game plan with specific objectives clearly defined. Then, about 20 minutes before the opening buzzer, it was out to the floor to warm up. My assistants and I stayed in the locker room to check out last-minute details and make sure we were on the same page. Then, with about 10 minutes left until starting time, we'd head out to the court to observe both teams going through their final warm-ups. Finally, a brief team huddle and … *let's go get 'em!*

There are 30 teams in the NBA, each with its own style of play—its "game"—requiring intense concentration to execute effectively. Sometimes the differences are subtle, sometimes they're obvious. For instance,

- No team today runs the floor as much and as well as the Phoenix Suns. That's because they have the Houdini-like Steve Nash to handle the ball and quick-footed shooters like Jason Richardson and Jared Dudley always racing to get open looks.
- Every team has a low-post game, but no team puts the ball in the hands of its post man as often as San Antonio. You would, too, if your go-to man in the post was named Tim Duncan.
- The Lakers use the triangle offense, but they expand it to make sure Kobe Bryant is involved in just about every possession.
- Every team uses the 3-point shot as a weapon, of course, but no team relies as much on it as Indiana, where Coach Jim O'Brien gives it high priority in his team attack.
- Every team has a sequence in which the team's best shooter works off baseline screens on either side of the lane to get his shot, but if you watch closely (and often) enough, you'll pick up slight differences from one team to another.

And so it goes on defense, though subtle differences in team strategies and tactics are somewhat harder for the average fan to pick up. Some teams pressure the ball full court for part of a game, while others are satisfied to just contain it at the top of the defensive circle. Some do a lot of half-court trapping; some do none at all. Most force the ball to the baseline, but others force it to the middle of the court. Those differences combine to make each team play a defensive game that is all its own.

You must have the talent to win, of course, but you must also have the utmost focus, concentration, and confidence of every coach and player on the team. At Saint Joseph's College, where I first started out over half a century ago, my teams employed a lot of zone presses and fast breaks. I drilled the team on those concepts from the first day of practice on October 15. The players bought into the system and had confidence that it could make them winners.

I still remember my 1962 team captain Jim Lynam—later my assistant at Portland, then head coach of the Clippers, and longtime NBA assistant coach—drawing an imaginary line with his foot at halfcourt and saying to a teammate before the opening game of the season, "My man doesn't get the ball past here." With our pressing tactics, St. Joe's was never out of a game, which put us in line for some remarkable come-from-behind wins. We went to postseason tournaments in 10 of the 11 years that I coached there, in large measure because my players fully understood and had great confidence in what we were doing as a team.

When I set out to formulate a style of play for the Philadelphia 76ers after taking over as head coach in 1968, a major overhaul was in order because for the three preceding seasons the team had revolved around Wilt Chamberlain, and now he was gone. There wasn't enough team speed to have a dominating fast break, but we did have forwards who could score (Chet Walker, Billy Cunningham), a good high-post center (Luke Jackson before a major injury), a premier shooting guard (Hal Greer), and a pair of capable point guards (Wally Jones, Archie Clark). I spent a

1967 World Champions

The 1967 NBA championship-winning Philadelphia 76ers.

lot of time during the summer months reviewing game films of the previous season, noting especially the styles of other teams. I had to come up with a *team game* before training camp began.

Under my predecessor, Alex Hannum, the Sixers had taken full advantage of Chamberlain's power game. They'd also run a lot of set plays, many designed at getting shots for Greer. Without Wilt, my plan was to use a more free-flowing transition attack with fewer set plays. I also put in the zone press defense, which hadn't been used before in the NBA.

That combination worked well in preseason games, but before the regular season began, Greer asked me, "When are you going to put in some set plays?" I told him that I liked what I had seen of our offense so far but would add set plays as needed. Hal's body language told me that it wasn't the answer he wanted to hear, but he didn't say anything. (And as it turned out, I did put in some "specials" for Greer and Cunningham that helped the Sixers win some close games down the stretch.) The zone press surprised teams and helped the Sixers win 55 games and make it into the playoffs. Although we lost to Boston in the first round, I was satisfied with the overall season, and I especially liked the concentration level of the team.

Throughout my four seasons with the Sixers, I was constantly having to adjust the game I wanted to play because of the declining skills of aging players. And, after that first season, I sensed a waning of concentration on team goals and a growing focus on individual achievement. I resigned after the last game of the 1971–72 season.

My next stop was Buffalo, a young franchise beginning its third season in the NBA. Before signing the contract, I had a meeting with owner Paul Snyder and GM (and old friend) Eddie Donovan. I'd heard of Snyder's practice of storming into the locker room after a loss to berate the team and the coach. I told them I would take the job only if I were in full charge of the team—and that there be *no* postgame visits to the locker room by Snyder except by invitation. Snyder said that he was glad to hear that: "You're the kind of coach that I want. I want a coach to take charge." I deposited that statement in my memory bank.

My Braves didn't exactly get off to an auspicious start: we finished 21–61 in 1972–73, one less W than in the previous season. Certain that we'd never win with the existing personnel, I beseeched Donovan to make wholesale roster changes. Eddie did a great job. He acquired nine new players to join holdovers Bob McAdoo, Randy Smith, and Bob Kauffman. The principal newcomers were our No. 1 draft choice, point guard Ernie DiGregorio, and forwards Jim McMillian and Garfield Heard, acquired by trades. I knew we now had the horses to be a very good fast-break outfit, and during the summer months I worked on how to implement it.

During training camp that fall, my focus from day one was to establish a fast-break offense. I wanted to run the floor on every possession, even after an opponent scored. Training camp went well. The players took to the system, and by the beginning of the regular season, everyone's concentration, focus, and enthusiasm levels were exactly where I wanted them to be. I sensed that this was going to be a turnaround season for the young Braves. And it was.

Ernie D. was a marvelous fast-break passer, and with McAdoo, Kauffman, and Heard pulling down rebounds, and Smith and McMillian running the wings, we went from next-to-last in scoring the previous year to the highest-scoring team in the NBA (111.6 ppg.). We doubled our win total from the previous year, finishing the season with a 42–40 record and a berth in the 1973–74 playoffs. McAdoo led the league in scoring, and DiGregorio was named the Rookie of the Year. To this day, Mac still claims that "nobody ever ran like we did" that first season we were all together.

Unfortunately, Ernie D was injured early in the following season and never again played up to his rookie level. And although McAdoo continued to lead the league in scoring, the team didn't run the fast break quite as well or as often. We also lacked the defensive ability needed to become a true contender. Our fast-break offense was good enough to get us into the playoffs but not good enough to contend for a championship.

The Braves were a fun team to coach. There was great camaraderie among the players, who never missed an opportunity to get on each other. Once, after a shouting match I had with Snyder outside the locker room that the players overheard, I traveled separately from the team to the West Coast in order to scout a college player. When I rejoined the squad for practice, the players quieted down when I walked into the locker room. Randy Smith came over and said, "Are you okay, Coach?" I assured him I was. Smith said, "You're still with us. That's the main thing." Our team spirit became even stronger.

After that I was sometimes brought into the locker room banter. There was speculation aloud among them about who would win if Snyder (short and stocky) and I went at it. Smith said, "I don't know, Coach. He was a wrestler in college." I assured them I could handle him. Fortunately for all parties, we never put the matter to a test.

There were, I must admit, a few occasions when the team's concentration at shootarounds was lax, and locker room levity found its way onto the court. During one of those times, I cut practice short and sent the players home with a warning: "If we play like this tonight, we'll get our asses kicked." The guys came to the game that night with their minds focused on what they had to do, and we won.

We made the playoffs the next two seasons, but my original three-year contract was up, and I was worn down by increasingly frequent disagreements with Snyder, so I left in 1976 to take the coaching job at Portland. Despite a 37–45 record the year before, the sixth straight losing season in as many years in the league, the Blazers—I honestly believed this—had the potential to both run and defend. I really relished the new challenge.

Ramsay and assistant Jack McKinney observe the action from Portland's bench, 1976. (Roger Jensen Photo)

I was pumped.

That first summer after I took over the Blazers, I spent many long hours with my assistant, Jack McKinney, working out the basics of what I called "the turnout," a transition attack in which the wingmen crossed under the basket as the ball was quickly advanced up court. If no fast break materialized, and no immediate open shot was obtained, the ball then went to our third-year center, Bill Walton, and a series of set play options opened up. It was a multifaceted, quick-paced game plan, and I felt it fit perfectly with the Blazers personnel.

In an early preseason meeting with Walton, I talked about my baby, the turnout. "What's a turnout?" Bill asked. I outlined the action for him, and he quickly grasped the idea. Weeks later, after he stopped in to watch a rookie camp workout, I asked him what he thought of the young prospects. He replied, "I don't know, Coach. They're not too smart. They don't even know what a bleeping turnout is."

I also felt good about our team defense. We had quickness and tenacity at the perimeter (Lionel Hollins, Dave Twardzik, Johnny Davis, Bob Gross, Larry Steel), strong rebounding and shot blocking up front (Walton, Maurice Lucas, Lloyd Neal, Robin Jones), and capable reserves (Herm Gilliam, Corky Calhoun).

Lucas, whom we acquired in the dispersal draft when the American Basketball Association and the NBA merged in 1976, became our designated intimidator. In two seasons in the ABA, Luke had earned a richly deserved reputation for being a mean, aggressive, physically tough player.

Maurice Lucas, ready to fire an outlet pass in a 1976 road game. (Al Hall Photo)

That rep started in his rookie ABA season (1974–75) when Luke got into a fight with the much bigger (5 inches taller, 25 pounds heavier) Artis Gilmore. Lucas swung a haymaker at Gilmore, caught him on the jaw, and knocked him to the floor. Everybody in basketball heard about it.

During the summer of 1976, prior to Lucas' first season with Portland, I drove to see him at Dave Bing's basketball camp in the Pocono Mountains in Pennsylvania where he was working. We talked about the offense and defense I planned to use and his role with the team. "I want you to be our enforcer," I told him. "You already have a tough-guy reputation. Be very aggressive the first time around the league. Bang guys around. Get into fights if you have to, but establish a physical presence. We'll pay the fines."

It was music to Luke's ears. Before the opening tap, he would flex his biceps and glower at the opposing players. Then, on the toss, he'd pop his matchup with an elbow, giving the guy a little taste of what he had to look forward to for the next 48 minutes. We benefited mightily from his intimidating physical presence. Plus, he had the best skills of any big forward in the league.

At the very beginning of training camp, I sensed the players were tired of losing. They felt they had a legit shot at winning. Concentration in the two-a-days was razor sharp. It wasn't long before the offense and defense were in sync. Our game was coming together.

When a team becomes unified, a lot of good things happen: more overall aggressiveness and better "help awareness" on defense and quicker, better-coordinated player movement on offense, with a nice, seemingly effortless rhythm and flow. Everything fits when team chemistry is just right.

We had it all in 1976–77, when we went 49–33 and beat the Sixers in the Finals (4–2) to win the NBA championship. From six straight losing seasons to the top: it still gives me goose bumps to think about it.

And in the following season, we looked like mortal locks to return to the top: 50–10 with 22 games to go. But injuries to Walton, Neal, and Gross tore us apart. We went 8–14 the rest of the way. We finished with the best W-L record in the NBA, and as defending champions we had a bye in the first round of the playoffs, but we got knocked out in the Western Conference Semifinals by Seattle, 4–2.

I know how pointless and even unprofessional it is to play "what if" games, but I couldn't help thinking back then, "What if those three key guys hadn't gone down with injuries?"

What if…?

Athletes have special times when everything they do is perfection. They are in a world of their own, where the game appears to slow down, and their movement is almost illusionary. In basketball, that player gets open for shots consistently, and the basket seems as large as the Pacific Ocean. He can't miss. It's called being "in the zone." This condition occurs more often in great athletes, but it visits lesser performers too.

I had one experience in that state when, after the college season of my sophomore year at St. Joe's, a teammate, Norm Butz, organized a team to play in a Knights of Columbus tournament in Philadelphia. In the first game, I was shooting the ball well and had 20 points going into the fourth period. We were winning the game handily, and Butz brought the players together and said, "Jack's having a big game. Let's get him shots." From that point, I was the only shooter and continued to knock them down. I don't recall exactly how many points I ended up with—somewhere in the 30s, a big number in those days. It was a sweet feeling.

The Blazers got two such in-the-zone performances from two players, Herm Gilliam and Bill Walton, in the Western Conference Finals in 1977. We won the first game handily in Los Angeles shortly after the Lakers had finished a tough series with Golden State. In the second game, however, they were ready, and we were struggling. In the second half, I put Gilliam, a good shooter who could fabricate shots, into the game. Gilliam had an incredible second half, scoring 20 points, 14 of them in the fourth quarter. He hit one big bucket after another, from anywhere on the court. Herm wasn't a starter, because he was inconsistent. But in that Lakers game, he was in the zone, and we rode him for all he was worth. We won that game and went on to sweep the Lakers. It might not have happened without Herm Gilliam being in the zone in Game 2.

Bill Walton found the zone in Game 4 of the same series:

It was as if everybody was playing in slow motion. I felt I was the only one playing at regular speed. ... When you're playing well, you want the game to go on forever. Nothing else seems to matter. ... You're in the zone. You can't hear anything. All you see is the ball and the basket. You see your teammates and their every move. You see your opponents and their every mistake. It is an incredible feeling, one that you don't want to see come to an end.[5]

Great players pay frequent visits to the zone. Michael Jordan spent most of his career there. But MJ would usually give some indicator to acknowledge that he was playing at an extra-special level. At times he would just shake his head as if he couldn't believe it himself. Other times he'd blow on the fingers of his shooting hand after knocking down a series of jumpers, indicating his hand was too hot for him to handle. Once I saw him close his eyes when shooting a free throw. Of course the shot went in.

To have one's own player in that idyllic state is great for the coach. Get that player the ball, give him space on the court, and let him do the rest. Sit back and admire. But if it's an opposing player with the hot hand, the best way to keep him from torturing your team is to deny him the ball. Sounds easy? Uh-uh. It's a monumental task.

It takes great focus, athleticism, and determination to keep a hot player from getting the ball. He must be overplayed, chased around screens, and played body to body. The whole team must be aware of his position on the floor at all times; they have to be ready to switch, double team, and harass on every possession. If a team can do that, it can turn the game around. A guy who's been driven out of the zone will often start forcing shots that turn into easy scores for the other team.

Hot doesn't last forever.

The game on the floor often turns on how you play the game in the mind. Mo Lucas was the master manipulator of my championship Blazers team. Luke wore a fierce look and banged opponents around early in games just to let them know they were in for a tough night. "Half of my matchups are afraid of me," Luke once said, "so I know I'm going to have an easy time with them. It's the other guys that I've got to get ready for."

Bill Russell, who played on more championship teams (11) than any player in NBA history, was a grand master at mind games. He took particular delight in causing opponents to lose focus and play tentatively, which he could do successfully because he was the greatest shot-blocker and intimidator in the basket area ever to play the game. Most of the time, his mere physical presence was enough to psych-out opposing teams.

In a game at Boston during my first season coaching Philadelphia, Chet Walker, a Sixers forward with good pump fakes in the post, received a pass at the baseline and started to back his defender down. He was in good position to shoot, but then he stopped to see where Russell was. By the time he discovered Russ was on the bench taking a short rest, the defense closed in on him and took away his shot. Russell understood exactly what had happened, and his amused cackle-like laugh could be heard around the court.

Trash talking, a key aspect of the mind game, can work brilliantly to distract a player from doing his job. Not everybody does it. Not everybody does it well. And the best trash talkers don't do it all the time. They pick and choose and determine when they can disrupt a player's concentration.

As good an intimidator-by-presence as he was, Russell wasn't shy about talking a little trash when he thought it might give him and his teammates an edge. Bill tells this story of himself:

> *Sometimes I'd make a speech out in the jump circle. ... I'd say to the other team, "Ain't no layups out here tonight. I ain't gonna bother you with them 15-footers cause I don't feel like it tonight, but I ain't gonna have no layups." Or I'd lean over to one of the forwards and say, "If you come in to shoot a layup off me you'd better bring your salt and pepper because you'll be eating basketballs."*[6]

This happened to Hot Rod Hundley once against the Celtics: "I got by Cousy and was coming down the lane. Russell jumps over and yells, 'Don't even think about it, Rod.' I said, 'I'm not' and kept going, dribbling back out to the top of the key."[7]

Trash talk? Or physical intimidation based on experience?

Does it matter?

Larry Bird was one of the best at taking his opponent out of his game. When Chuck Person was a Pacers rookie in 1986–87, he talked trash constantly, even when playing Bird and the Celtics. Make that *especially* when playing Bird and the Celtics. At first, Larry simply refused to acknowledge Person's presence. In one game early on, I took Person out, and he continued to talk trash to Bird from the bench. Larry came over to me and said, "Put him back in, Coach." Bird wanted to work him over, show him who was boss. I didn't do it. There was no point. I talked to Chuck after the game and told him that if you talk trash to Bird, you just motivate him more. We didn't need that.

If there were a Trash Talkers Hall of Fame, Michael Jordan and Larry Bird would be the first two inductees. (And be sure to save a spot for Kevin Garnett.)

Larry Bird describes how adept Jordan was as at working on an opponent's mind:

> *Michael did some of the same things I used to do, like walk up to a guy on the other team and tell him, in a low voice, exactly how he was going beat him. So now the defense knows what he's going to run, but Michael gets the ball, does exactly what he told the guy, and beats him anyway. Believe me, having done it to people myself, it's absolutely devastating. I am sure a lot guys in the league hated me. I didn't care. That was good.*[8]

Teams can intimidate, too. The Detroit Pistons in the late 1980s and early 1990s consciously used their "Bad Boys" image to get inside the heads of opponents. Joe Dumars says that when the Pistons were on the road, local reporters pounded home team players relentlessly with questions about how they expected to survive against physical, aggressive, downright nasty defense played by the Bad Boys—Bill Laimbeer, Rick Mahorn, Dennis Rodman, Isiah Thomas, and company. Sometime games were over before they started. No question about it, the Pistons' back-to-back championships (1989 and 1990) owed much to the mind games they played as a team.

I can't think of any master trash talkers in today's NBA—at least outside of Kevin Garnett, who's been talking trash since he could dribble a basketball. That's why I was surprised when I read about Kobe Bryant and Ron Artest going at each other verbally in a Lakers-Rockets game late in the 2008–09 season. I had the Lakers in a game broadcast soon after that and asked Kobe about it. He dismissed it: "Just monkey chatter."

Later, I asked him to expand on that statement. He told me, "I've played against Ron for a long time. That was the first time he tried that on me. He should know better." And yes, Artest *should* have known better. Shortly after his attempt to disrupt Bryant's concentration, Kobe went on a tear, scoring 18 of his 37 points in the last quarter to break open a close game and lead the Lakers to a 102–96 win.

The moral: if you're going to talk trash, be sure you're better than the guy you're talking it to.

The reason I've stressed the importance of intense concentration and focus in coaches formulating a game plan is because I think many of the most knowledgeable fans and certainly some of the more casual observers of the NBA would be surprised by the amount of planning and practice required to form a tailor-made, artfully constructed game for their teams. Here's a comment I've heard way too many times: "I guess there isn't much to teach players by the time they become pros."

Both groups seem to think the job of an NBA coach begins and pretty much ends with maintaining team spirit, with keeping keep up team morale. Sorry, folks: NBA coaches are teachers, planners, visualizers, builders … a lot of things, with cheerleading coming in last.

Ramsay posing for St. Joseph's in 1949.

Because I was the only coach at Philadelphia in the preassistant days, I did the team scouting, set up the conditioning program for the players, made up the game plan, and organized and directed the practices. Oh, yes—and I coached the games.

Before the economy crunch of recent years, NBA coaching staffs typically went on a quiet retreat for several days before training camp where they brainstormed the team offense and defense and reviewed personnel. Now, they do the same thing, but they stay at home and meet at the team's practice site. I have attended some of those sessions with the teams that Jim O'Brien has coached (Boston, Philadelphia, and Indiana). I can tell for sure there is a super-high level of concentration among all of the participants, and I'm willing to bet that's the same all around the league.

Teaching and learning a team's game requires voracious concentration. The drill work required for learning the various parts of the offense and defense demands focus and energy. Excellence of execution is necessary for the game to stand up against opponents, whose objective is to force you out of that game. If the opponent succeeds, he wins.

The game we put together in Portland before the beginning of the 1976–77 season was so sound that I felt no team could beat us if we stayed focused on the here and now. That was a great feeling. Driving home after routing the 76ers in an early season game, I recall thinking to myself, "I'm coaching the best basketball team in the world."

And you know what? I was.

3

SEE IT, FEEL IT, DO IT

Jason Kidd pushed the ball hard up court in a 2009 playoff game between his Dallas Mavericks and the San Antonio Spurs. His head was up, his eyes looking for gaps in the Spurs' tough transition defense. With a sudden burst of speed, he angled sharply to the basket and went into the air for the shot.

Or so it seemed to Tim Duncan, who stepped over to block the attempt. Piece of cake for TD, who at 6'11" has a seven-inch height advantage over the Dallas point guard. It would have been, too, if Kidd had shot the ball.

Instead, hanging in midair, he finger-tipped a no-look pass to Mavs 2-guard Jason Terry, who had drifted free and clear into 3-point territory on the opposite side of the floor. Terry drained the shot, and while retreating to defend, he pointed to Kidd in acknowledgement of his pass.

Ho-hum. Just another day at the office for Kidd, just another "how did he do that?" play-action move by the 37-year-old veteran who seems just as quick and fluid and in command on the court now as when he first came into the league in 1994.

The next day at the Dallas practice session, I spoke to JKidd about that play and others that he generates on the run. No gesture, no verbal communication, just getting the ball to exactly the right spot at exactly the right moment to exactly the right person. I want to tell you, I've been around pro basketball for a lot longer than Jason Kidd's been alive, and even I was mighty impressed: *How did he do that?*

"I have very good peripheral vision," JKidd told me in what can only be described as a Hall of Fame understatement. "I try to keep everyone, teammates and opponents, within my sight range. I can sense where openings are likely to occur, and I know where my teammates like to get the ball. I try to get it to them there when they're open. Jet [Terry] and Dirk [Nowitzki] are great perimeter shooters. Josh [Howard] can put it on the floor. They're our best scorers. I look for them. When I find them, they take care of the rest."

"So you're the coach on the floor?" I asked, knowing the answer.

"Something like that," he replied. "Rick's [Coach Rick Carlisle] okay with it. He calls set plays that we're to use in halfcourt, but he wants me to take as many of those freelance chances to score as we can get. You need those to win in this league."

I admire Kidd for his undiminished dedication to winning and his ability to keep himself in great physical condition after 16 grueling years at what I think is the most demanding position on the court. He brings his unselfish, creative, intuitive game with him wherever he goes. Kidd has yet to play on a championship team, but he did reach the NBA Finals twice with New Jersey (2002, 2003). I can't think of a single player in the league who deserves a championship ring more. I hope he gets one before he unlaces his basketball shoes for the last time.

Jason Kidd isn't the only NBA player with those virtually magical intuitive skills, of course. Kobe Bryant (Lakers), Dwyane Wade (Miami), LeBron James (Miami), Deron Williams (Utah), Chris Paul (New Orleans), Chauncey Billups and Carmelo Anthony (Denver), and Manu Ginobili (San Antonio) also possess the same high basketball intelligence that enables them to perceive, interpret, and evaluate the action around them in an instant.

And there's a flock of young Turks whose latent skills are quickly developing to the level of those veterans: Derek Rose (Chicago), John Wall (Washington), Rajon Rondo (Boston), Aaron Brooks (Houston), Russell Westbrook (Oklahoma City), Brandon Jennings (Milwaukee), Tyreke Evans (Sacramento), and Darren Collison (Indiana) spring to mind. Keep your eye on them.

A genuinely intuitive player operates on instinctive or gut feelings and seems to have a sixth sense about what happens on the court. He always seems to be ahead of the game. He sees the whole floor and everyone on it. He sees the game in slow motion. He's always under control, and he's always making split-second decisions, constantly reading the high-speed action instantly and correctly. Among an ever-shifting set of options, he has an uncanny knack for making the play that's best for his team. It's a natural aptitude enhanced by experience.

During the 2009 playoffs, I broadcast many of the Lakers games on ESPN Radio and conducted frequent interviews with Kobe Bryant. I was impressed by the number of times Kobe spoke about seeing the whole floor, how the game seemed to unfold before him, how he anticipated the action before it happened, and how that enabled him to make a scoring pass or knock down a critical shot. Kobe and Pau Gasol, another player with breathtakingly high intuition, engaged in frequent touch passes to each other that hit at the heart of opposing defenses. They were on the same wavelength, the same intuitive beam.

I talked to one of the young members of this elite club, Rajon Rondo, after an early season Boston victory at San Antonio in 2009. He had played a steady game (12 points, 12 assists) but hadn't often looked to score himself. After the game, I asked him why. "My job is to create offense," he told me. "I'll score when I need to, but mostly I'm trying to get shots for my teammates."

Rondo's doing a heckuva job of it. On a team of veteran stars (Kevin Garnett, Paul Pierce, and Ray Allen), Rondo runs the show on the floor. And what a show it is! He's lightning quick, keeps good control of his dribble on penetrations, has great hops, seems to have eyes in the back of his head, and makes easy-to-handle passes in traffic.

That intuitive sense is also on display on defense, where he hounds his matchup, forces turnovers, disrupts opposing offenses with his "reads," and is a surprisingly good rebounder for his size (6'1"). Rondo was the starting point guard on the Celtics 2008 championship team and had the stamp of approval of his coach, Doc Rivers, and Garnett, the team leader from the beginning of that season.

Contrary to the opinion of some, I wasn't in attendance when Dr. James Naismith hung the first peach basket in 1891, but I'm sure that players have shown intuitive skills ever since the game began. I did play briefly with future Lakers star and Hall of Famer Jim Pollard on an AAU team, the San Diego Dons, between Navy assignments at the end of World War II. Jim saw everything that happened on the court, had great passing skills as a forward, and was the first player I saw who spent a lot of game time above the rim. He had an almost eerie sense of the game, seeming to do whatever his team required at a particular moment, often creating advantages on the fly.

Previously, I had played with George Senesky at Saint Joseph's in 1942–43, and I regarded him as the best I'd seen and played against (in daily scrimmages) up to the time I met Pollard. George was the nation's leading collegiate scorer that season and the Helms Foundation Player of the Year (1943). But Jim Pollard was head and shoulders above Senesky in overall skill, and especially with his sixth-sense awareness. The man really opened my eyes to the vast possibilities in basketball.

Bob Cousy was one of the grandmasters of intuition on the basketball court, and he couldn't have come along at a more critical time for the game.

Today, basketball is one of the "big three" professional sports, but in the first decade after World II, it was struggling for survival. Many of the early basketball franchises had been formed to help fill in arena calendars when hockey teams were on the road. So it was in Boston, where the Bruins reigned supreme in "the Gahden." But in 1950, local boy Cousy— he'd played college ball for nearby Holy Cross—changed jerseys and helped change Boston sports history.

It almost didn't happen. Celtics bossman Red Auerbach wasn't a big Cousy fan. Red thought that Cousy was too fancy and that pro players would eat him alive. So Red spurned him in the 1950 NBA Draft, and Cousy was taken by the Tri-Cities Black Hawks, who promptly traded him to the Chicago Stags. But the Chicago franchise folded before the season began—as I said, these were rocky times for pro basketball— and in a dispersal draft, Cousy's name was drawn from a hat by, you guessed it, the Celtics. (I wish I could have seen Red's face.)

As we all know, it didn't take long for Cousy's marvelous intuitive instincts to win over Auerbach. He was named to the NBA All-Star first team in his second year in the league (1951–52), and once Bill Russell arrived in 1956, the Celtics dynasty was off and running.

With Russell blocking shots and grabbing rebounds, and Cousy passing the ball *exactly* where it needed to go, the Celtics developed a withering run-and-gun attack. Cousy seemed to have eyes in the back of his head, flipping no-look, behind-the-back passes to teammates for layups or wide-open jumpers. He also had a soft touch with pull-up runners that kept retreating defenders off balance.

A magician who employed a basketball instead of a top hat and wand for his sleight-of-hand. They didn't put it that way on Cousy's Hall of Fame plaque in 1971, but they should have, because it was true.

Bill Sharman, a Hall of Fame guard who played alongside Cousy, says he was constantly dazzled by the way Cousy used his imagination and creativity on the court. Sharman said that Cousy was a lot like Magic Johnson, in that he was an innovator, and his first instincts were to get a good shot. On the fast break, he was an artist, inventing something new— he was way ahead of his time.

Speaking of Sharman, I never coached against him during his playing career, but Sam Jones once told me that Bill was a fierce competitor who would fight at the drop of a hat, a trait that ran contrary to the "nice guy" image he had later as a coach. After his retirement as a player in 1961, Sharman became a coach, first with the San Francisco Warriors and later with Los Angeles, where he coached the Lakers (led by Jerry West and Wilt Chamberlain) to an NBA title in 1972.

Widely regarded by his peers as one of the most creative coaches in our profession, Sharman invented the game day shootaround that's now SOP for all NBA teams. In training camp before the 1971–72 season, when Sharman announced his plan, Chamberlain made it clear that he wanted no part of it. Pat Riley, who was on the same Lakers team, related to me Wilt's response: "I only play once a day. So you decide if it's going to be at 11 in the morning or 7:30 at night."

But Sharman was able to coax Wilt to give the 11 a.m. workout a try, and soon thereafter the Lakers kicked off a 33-game winning streak. Once they were rolling along on what still stands as the longest winning streak in NBA history, not even Wilt dared absent himself from the morning shootaround.

In chapter 2, I wrote about how Ernie DiGregorio in his rookie year contributed to my Buffalo Braves' transformation from league doormat to winning team. The key to that contribution? DiGregorio's use of intuition and imagery. One example of Ernie D.'s legerdemain that will forever stick in my mind occurred in a preseason game against Boston in 1973, half of a doubleheader in New York at Madison Square Garden. The Knicks were coming off a championship season, and their fans rooted for us against their bitter rivals. The Celtics typically didn't get too excited about preseason games in those years, but their players knew Ernie from his Providence College days where he had gotten a ton of media attention. I expected them to come after us hard, and they did.

But because of all our offseason moves, we were ready for them, and at halftime we were ahead by 20 points. Bob McAdoo was knocking down shots from 7th Avenue, and Ernie D. was putting on a passing clinic. In the locker room at halftime, the Celts must have said, "Let's take it to DiGregorio," and the first time he brought the ball up in the second half they trapped him at halfcourt. Ernie D. dribbled through the trap the first time, but the next time he got stuck just over center court, still dribbling with his back to the basket.

Suddenly, Ernie D. picked up the ball, his back still to the basket, and fired a two-hand pass back over his head to an unguarded Gar Heard at the basket for an uncontested layup. The Garden fans collectively gasped and then went wild. To a man, the Celtics players were incredulous: *"Did he just do what I think he did?"* I know I was asking myself the same question on our bench.

The Celtics' trapping defense was over for the night, and we beat them by something like 40 points. This was only the Braves' third year in the NBA, and that win, even in a meaningless preseason game, was a huge confidence builder. We went on to lead the NBA in scoring (111 ppg.), win 42 games, and earn a spot in the playoffs.

Like all great intuitive players, Bill Walton had an amazing knack for visualizing the whole floor. That ability made him the greatest passing center of all time. He knew where his teammates were on the court because he was the hub of the team offense, and his intuitive sense enabled him to pick apart opposing defenses. Walton made a ton of great passes in the two seasons that I coached him—his signature move was an outlet release while still in the air after grabbing a defensive rebound—but the ones I marveled at the most were those in the half-court offense that ended with layups for his teammates. Whoever got open got the ball—period.

One such pass that's as fresh as yesterday in my memory was one he stuck by Elvin Hayes' ear to a cutting Bob Gross for a layup. NBA defenders are so quick, and Hayes was one of the quickest big men of all time, that Bill *had* to have a highly developed sixth sense to make such a pass. I couldn't tell you the game, much less the year, but I'll never forget the pass.

Larry Bird had a great sense of where the ball was going to be all the time, which enabled him, despite his relative slowness afoot and limited leaping ability, to beat everybody to it almost every time. His strong intuitive sense made him an excellent team defender. Bird is the first to admit that the moment-to-moment decisions he made on the court had little to do with reasoning and analysis: "As a player, everything I did was based on reaction."[1]

Those who played with and against Bird recognized the power of his intuitive abilities on the court. Magic Johnson believes that he and Bird were able to play strong defense because each had an intuitive sense of how plays were going to develop on the defensive end of the court:

A team defensive player sees the whole picture. [Bird] understands the team's plays. He relies on instinct and intuition. He reads the floor and anticipates what's going to happen. That's why the two of us came up with so many steals. We had point guard instincts in big-man bodies.[2]

Magic is right on target. When both he and Bird first came into the league, I thought they would both be victimized by quicker players at their positions. I anticipated that Magic (6'9") would have big problems with smaller, speedier guards; and the same would happen to Bird with his matchups at small forward. They both adjusted, and because of their court savvy and intuition, turned a negative into a positive. Both could sniff out opponent tendencies and invariably get into position to deflect or intercept a pass, draw a charge, or force a bad shot.

The 24-second clock, instituted in 1954, mandates an up-tempo game. Thank goodness. No one in his right mind would want to go back to "ye good olde days" when basketball crept along with "freeze-and-foul" strategies that produced such monstrosities as the Lakers-Pistons game on November 22, 1950. Final Score: 19–18.

Fast-paced, up-and-down, run-and-gun basketball is perfectly suited to today's superbly conditioned athletes, and no team put that style to better use than the Phoenix Suns under Mike D'Antoni (2003–2008). He perfected the style after the Suns, at his urging, reacquired Steve Nash in 2004. Nash had been drafted originally by Phoenix in 1996 and then traded to the Mavericks in 1998—to run the show. The key word there is *run*.

A dynamic point guard who plays with a Bob Cousy flair, Nash has extraordinary floor vision and passing skills to complement his great focus and intuition. During their four seasons together, the D'Antoni-Nash high-speed racers had a combined 232–96 W-L record and made it to the playoffs all four times, with D'Antoni earning Coach of the Year honors in 2005. Their style of play even inspired a book by veteran *Sports Illustrated* writer Jack McCallum about the 2005–06 NBA season with a title that really tells it all: *:07 Seconds or Less: My Season on the Bench with the Runnin' and Gunnin' Phoenix Suns*.

Speed thrills; we all know that. But the Suns' success during the D'Antoni years was built on more. If a team isn't stocked with players with good basketball instincts, and led by a floor leader with a high basketball IQ—somebody like a Steve Nash, say—then speed produces just so much helter-skelter, not Ws.

D'Antoni packed up and moved east to take over the New York Knicks in 2008, where his coaching philosophy has been less successful. The closest D'Antoni has been to the NBA playoffs during his first two seasons at Madison Square Garden is the widescreen TV in his rec room. Meanwhile, Steve Nash and his fellow Sun thoroughbreds stayed back in Phoenix with Nash still in the saddle.

The obvious conclusion? If you're going to run, you need horses.

The Utah Jazz, in the John Stockton-Karl Malone era, played a beautiful combination of fast-break and ball control basketball. John and Karl played together for 18 seasons, longer than any star duo in NBA history. They had an almost eerie gift for nonverbal communication, which translated into an uncanny ability for making scoring plays in seemingly impossible situations.

Stockton was an incredible passer. He was only 6'2", but he had shovels for hands, great passing technique, and wraparound vision. Malone knew that if he ran the floor hard, and ran great angles, that Stockton would deliver the ball exactly where he wanted it. Stockton would throw a ball into an open area in transition even though Malone wasn't there when the pass was thrown, and Karl somehow managed to get to the right spot to receive the ball and score. In halfcourt, Malone would go under the basket and come to the post, and Stockton would deliver the ball the moment he arrived. In the entire history of the game, Stockton and Malone connected on more passes for scores than any other two teammates.

You can look it up.

Phil Jackson, after he was named head coach of the Lakers in 1999, met with Shaquille O'Neal and Kobe Bryant individually to explain to them the demands of the triangle offense he wanted the team to play. He told Shaq that the ball would go to the post on as many possessions as possible. The post player in the triangle is as much a passer as shooter, and Shaq embraced the concept totally.

Kobe was a different matter. He wanted to fast break as often as possible, then use the post when the game was in the halfcourt. An up-tempo style suited Kobe much better than a slow-paced game. Phil told him that he didn't rule out fast breaks altogether, but the first objective was to get the ball to Shaq in the post and play through him. Kobe was not thrilled with the concept but agreed to give it a chance.

Jackson wisely loosened the restrictions of the offense as the season progressed to give Bryant some of the freedom he wanted, and the Lakers thrived. O'Neal (29.7 points and 13.6 rebounds) and Bryant (22.5 points and 4.9 assists) had great years. More important, the Lakers posted the league's best regular-season record (67–15) and beat Indiana in the NBA Finals. O'Neal was named Most Valuable Player for both the regular season and the NBA Finals.

Kobe and Shaq were simply brilliant together. They read each other's moves to near perfection. Kobe, the team leader in assists, fed Shaq lobs at the rim that O'Neal put away with thunderous dunks. Shaq, the Lakers' second best in assists, consistently found Kobe for layups and open jumpers with deft passes from the post. The two were in sync, their intuitions on full display.

The results of their bonding? Three NBA titles in the five seasons they were together on the Lakers.

Intuition plays such a powerful role in basketball because of the very nature of the game. Phil Jackson believes that when players *don't* use their imagination or their creativity they're inviting thoughts to get in the way of actions. By doing so, they fail to respond intuitively and don't take advantage of situations that present themselves on the court: "Players get into the habit of watching themselves watch the ball game. They see a loose ball and instead of just reacting and diving for it, there is a tenth-of-a-second pause. That brief hesitation can be fatal."[3]

One opposing player whom Jackson and I especially admired for his ability to respond without wasting that tenth of a second on thinking was Dave Cowens, the powerful Celtics center-forward (1970–71 through 1981–82) who was elected to the Hall of Fame in 1991. Cowens is a super example of a player who will instantly commit himself to action, but that's not a quality an athlete can train himself to master. It's more the result of a player opening certain channels so that impulses don't have to go up to the head before an athletic decision is made. Stimulation should be the only thing that causes an aggressive athlete to act.

I tried to acquire Cowens for the 76ers soon after Boston drafted him in 1970. I called Red Auerbach and offered him Luke Jackson and Archie Clark for the rookie Cowens. Auerbach paused and then answered, "I probably should do it, but I'm afraid these Boston Irishmen would run me out of town."

A Celtic for 10 years, Dave knew only one way to play: all out. He pursued every missed shot at both ends of the floor. He dove for loose balls and either blocked shots or took charges on defense. He told me once that when he got five fouls in a game, he played even more aggressively because he reasoned that the officials didn't want to foul him out. And no one ran the floor harder than Big Red.

As Phil Jackson said, "Dave Cowens never pushed the pause button."

The value of intuition as it relates to offensive creativity and defensive team awareness is obvious. Less obvious, perhaps, but equally important is the role intuition plays in rebounding.

The two most prolific rebounders in NBA history were Wilt Chamberlain and Bill Russell. Wilt was powerfully built (7'1", 275); Russ was willowy (6'9", 215). Chamberlain averaged 22.9 rebounds a game for his career; Russell 22.5.

Chamberlain towered over his adversaries, hung out in the basket area, and sucked up just about all the opponents' missed shots that he didn't block. Wilt never gave blocking out a thought.

Russell had to find a different way. He studied the trajectory of shots and sensed where a missed shot was likely to go after hitting the rim or backboard. And Russ was the ultimate shot-blocker. He told me he thought he may have averaged double-digit blocks in his rookie season in the NBA. (The league didn't keep that statistic at the time.)

Later in the NBA, Moses Malone (1976–1995) and Dennis Rodman (1986–2000) became highly skilled chairmen of the boards through a combination of great intuition and fierce determination. Moses (6'10") lacked offensive skills in his early years and would literally throw shots at the basket and then go get the miss for put-back scores. Rodman (6'7") didn't have the height to outreach other paint dominators, so he had to outsmart and outelbow them to get to balls.

According to Rudy Tomjanovich, who coached them both, Malone and Rodman drew their strength from amazingly developed intuition and instincts. What really set Malone apart from the beginning, Rudy says, was his amazing instinct:

> *Some people call it a nose for the ball. Moses always seemed to wind up where the rebound was coming off. He would study the shot in the air, judge how it would hit the rim, and maneuver himself in to the likely area of retrieval. This process would only take a fraction of a second. Moses would simply react quicker than the other guys on the floor.*[4]

Later, Malone developed a soft shooting touch to polish his game, and he won three MVP awards before sailing into the Hall of Fame (2001).

Rodman had the best anticipation for where the missed shot would bounce of any player I ever saw. He also was amazingly quick in getting off the floor. He bounced off the hardwood as if he were on a pogo stick, making multiple jumps to the ball if need be, often tipping it to himself so the few inches he gave away to most of the guys he matched up against were never a serious disadvantage. He was also brilliant at gaining inside position at both boards. Probably his greatest gift was a sixth sense that enabled him to be in the right place at the right time. Tomjanovich says Rodman was "a lot like the Phantom of the Opera. He's there … then he's not."[5]

Phil Jackson, who coached Rodman when the Bulls won three NBA championships in the 1990s, saw the same instincts in Rodman that Tomjanovich observed: "The Bulls never would have won those last three rings without Dennis Rodman. With his leaping ability and uncanny sense of knowing where the ball would bounce off the rim, he snatched rebounds from taller, bulkier opponents."[6]

I once sought Dennis out to interview him after he had a big game for the Bulls and finally found him in the workout room, spinning at 90 rpm on a stationary bike. I recorded the interview while he pedaled, and he wasn't even breathing hard.

There's no rebounder in today's NBA who approaches his job quite like those four did theirs. Now effective rebounding depends on blocking out one's matchup with good footwork to obtain inside position, then making contact with him, knees slightly flexed and ready to thrust to the ball. Tim Duncan (San Antonio) is the best example of solid rebounding technique in today's NBA.

Intuition sometimes trumps form. For example, Clyde Drexler dribbled with his head down, and the first time you saw him play, you were thinking, *this guy can't have much floor vision.* Bad call. Clyde always knew exactly where every one of his teammates was on the floor—and exactly where each of them was going to be *next*—and those superior basketball instincts enabled him to make great passes to them time after time.

It seems that anytime I write about the passing skills of ball handlers in today's NBA, my mind turns first to Steve Nash, another player who operates on gut feeling and who has a spooky sixth sense of where his teammates will be. His teammates, in turn, know that if they make good cuts to certain spots on the floor, Steve *will* get the ball to them. They have absolute trust in his 20-20 floor vision. Nash often delivers picture-perfect passes without appearing to see his receivers. I can't count the times I've seen Steve drive to the basket, go into the air as if to shoot, and then at the last nanosecond flip the ball behind him to Amare Stoudemire for an uncontested shot. How does Nash know that Amare is going to be there? Intuition.

High-level intuition.

We really can't talk about intuition or having a feel for the game, of course, without talking about the greatest player of all time, Michael Jordan. Michael believes that he made the best decisions on the court when he focused his mind on dealing with what was happening in the present moment, when "his heart and soul" were in the here and now. "Not knowing" enabled him to operate intuitively:

> *The best thing about living that way is that you don't know what the next moment is going to bring. And that was the best thing about the way I played the game. No one, not even me, knew what I was going to do next. If I had to pick one characteristic about my game that would be it. I performed my best when I didn't know what was coming.*[7]

So *that* was MJ's secret weapon—not knowing what he was going to do next.

Now he tells us.

4
PRACTICE, PRACTICE, PRACTICE

Look, I can't promise it'll get you to Carnegie Hall, but I *guarantee* that focused practice on the things that really matter is an important key to getting control of your life and making the most of your talents.

Want an example? Take me and the triathlon.

I first became interested in triathlon competition back in 1978, when I was coaching in Portland. I was 53 years old, and I thought myself to be in pretty good shape. I had taken part in all three tri components—swim, bike, and run—but none of the three in competition mind you, much less together. I had swum (mainly in below-the-surface strokes) as a frogman in the Navy, had taken many distance bike rides with friends, and had run for conditioning in basketball. So I signed up for an Olympic-distance triathlon: 1-mile swim, 25-mile bike, and 9-mile run (actual run distance for an Olympic triathlon is 6.2 miles). As I said, I was in pretty good shape, and I was competent in all three skills, but I knew that wasn't nearly enough to compete in a triathlon. I needed help.

A neighbor and former Olympic swimmer, Don Shollander, put me in touch with his old coach, Tye Steinbach, and I began pool workouts with him in Portland. I joined a group of cyclists who took 20-40 mile trips through the Oregon hills on weekends. (I'll never forget the amused looks of my newfound biking friends as they took in the kickstand and wheel reflectors on my heavy, recreational Schwinn. I got rid of both by

Ramsay finishing the mile swim at a 1985 triathlon in Oregon.

Week 2 and bought a lightweight speed bike by Week 3.) Finally, a local international track coach, Roger Smith, agreed to help me with my running form. (To tell the truth, I didn't think I needed any help in that department. Boy, how wrong I was.)

My new coaches gave me tips on how to improve my form, speed, and stamina in their disciplines. My stamina improved noticeably, and I thought I was making good progress. But then a local TV station videotaped a few of my workouts, and I watched myself perform. What an awakening!

I couldn't believe what I saw on the TV screen. This person—yours truly, hard as it was for me to accept—was painfully slow and still showed major form defects in each of the categories. I swam with my lower body riding too deep in the water, which produced significant leg drag. I sat too erect on the bike, not tucked like I should have been to reduce wind resistance. And I ran with my left foot crossing in front of me, rather than moving straight ahead in synch with my right.

Each violation of good form led to a loss of speed and an increase in effort. No wonder my stamina was improving: I was working much harder than I needed.

Next step: study the best performers live and/or on tape in each category and get a mental image of them as they competed. In the process, I discovered that swimmers rode high in the water, with their upper torsos almost above the surface and their feet just breaking the water in a steady flutter kick. I learned that cyclists sat in a letter C position, their heads low over the handle bars, and I saw that runners' feet hardly touched the ground as they ate up yardage with each straight-ahead stride.

I watched these top swimmers, bikers, and runners in action, then I watched some more, consciously visualizing myself performing like them with each stroke in the water, each revolution of the bike wheel, each stride on my run. My improvement was gradual but steady. By race day, I had improved enough to be "in the pack" of 300 competitors throughout the event. I finished third in my age group. (There were about a dozen other 50-somethings, as I recall.) As I sprinted across the finish line, I felt a surge of pure, blissful euphoria.

I stayed active in triathlon competition for another 20 years, always using basic visualization techniques during my training to improve my performance. Those techniques also helped me greatly in rehabbing from my surgeries. And today, I still "see" myself—as if looking down from the sky—on my daily swims off the Florida coast in the Gulf of Mexico. It's a great feeling, and I am 100 percent convinced that it makes me a better swimmer.

As a young athlete, I occasionally heard vague suggestions by a coach to "see yourself" as I practiced this or that skill, but that's where it ended, with no specific guidance for how to do it. It wasn't until I became the coach of the Portland Trail Blazers in June 1976 and met Dr. Bruce Ogilvie that I learned about the enormous potential of visualization and applied it to my coaching and my own competitive activities.

Bruce was a pioneer in the field of sports psychology. He was the first in that specialty to recommend psychological testing of athletes as an aid in their selection and improvement. Nowadays, of course, psychological testing is commonplace, but Bruce led the way. All NBA teams put players through a battery of psychological tests before signing them. Back then, it was radical—borderline revolutionary—and looked on with a mixture of incredulity and derision by some teams. Stu Inman, Portland's personnel director, had brought Ogilvie on board when the Blazers were being put together in 1970, and Bruce had instantly established his credibility with both management and players.

In my first rookie camp with the Blazers, I recall that Jack McKinney and I thought our fourth pick in the 1976 NBA Draft, Jeff Tyson, showed promise of making the final team roster. But at a meeting with McKinney and me before practice one day, Bruce said, "I don't know what your plans are for Tyson, but I wouldn't count on him. He hasn't made a commitment to play basketball at this level."

That statement surprised us, because Tyson had played hard and well up to that point. But before that day's practice, Jeff came to my office and said that he had decided to leave training camp in order to enter medical school.

Chalk one up for Dr. Bruce!

Bruce tested the full roster at fall training camp. His findings led him to conclude that there were significant psychological differences among the players that could influence how they interacted with teammates and even their willingness to be coached. It was information that I was glad to receive. Bruce also asked me for permission to work on the visualization concept with the players. I agreed and sat in on the first session that he conducted with each player.

At the meeting, Bruce laid down the general framework of the meaning of visualization, how it took place, and the results he had seen achieved by its practice. Bruce told each player that he could help him to improve his game in specific areas—but not because he was a "basketball man." He told them up front that he didn't know anything about basketball skills: "That's up to you and the coaches." "But," he would say, "I can help you see what you need to do."

Bruce then asked the player to name the skill he wanted to improve. The first response from almost everyone was usually along the lines of "I want to be a better shooter"—remember what was most important back on the playground?—either from the field or the free throw line.

"Too vague," Bruce would say as he shook his head. He pressed hard to get the player to be specific about the *single* shooting skill he wanted to focus on.

"Okay, my 20-footer from the baseline," a shooter would say. Blocking out for better rebounding position might be a big man's skill search. Whipping a pass with his left hand to a guy driving from his right was a point guard's wish. "That's the ticket," the Doctor of Visualization would say: "Let's go to work."

Bruce then asked the player to relax completely, using yoga breathing to get him there, and transport himself to a place where he was most comfortable and at peace. Then he asked the player to recall an occasion when he had his greatest performance in the specific skill he wanted to improve. Bruce asked the player to zero in on that game and visualize the feelings he had as he played it—the specific feelings. Next he had the player close his eyes and see himself performing his skill perfectly.

"See yourself on the back of your eyelids, making one shot after another from the baseline ..." "See yourself getting position and grabbing every rebound ..." "See yourself making that pass from your off hand that leads to an easy basket, and then another, and then another ..."

Bruce asked the player if he could *see* that happening in his mind's eye. Each claimed that he could. Bruce told him that repeated visualizations would improve his skill area and that the best time to apply the technique was when resting ... like before a pregame nap.

I watched these sessions from a corner of the room and sensed that while many of the players bought into Bruce's theory, others displayed guarded interest, and a few just weren't buying the concept. (Mo Lucas rolled his eyes at me as he left the room, and I felt that Bill Walton was reluctant to reveal any psychological area of himself.) But most bought into Bruce's program, and I think it helped us become winners.

Actually, it helped us *a lot.*

An athlete uses visualization to picture in his mind's eye the performance he wants to achieve. Sounds simple enough. And for some, visualization comes easy. But others need to be instructed on to how to employ it.

Bruce Ogilvie varied that instruction, depending on the player. For instance, while in the meeting room, Bruce had one player lie on his back, close his eyes and totally relax, and then visualize himself perfectly executing the skill he wanted to improve. I heard Bruce tell another player while on the court, "I don't care how you shoot it—just see the ball *going into the basket* as you release the shot."

To Lloyd Neal, while being defended at the basket (but actually standing alone on the court with Bruce), Bruce said, "You're going to get the rebound and put it back up after I shoot this ball off the rim. Can you see yourself getting it?" Lloyd nodded in the affirmative. Bruce shot the ball off the backboard. Neal grabbed the rebound and made the put-back five consecutive times over his imaginary defender.

To help Bob Gross improve his free throw shooting, Bruce s-l-o-w-l-y walked him through the entire act of shooting one … but with eyes closed and without a ball to start with. He had Bob imagine the texture of the leather and the weight of the ball before bringing it up to shooting position. The next step was to visualize an *exact* target and then go into his shooting routine, which began with a deep breath intake, a slow exhale, a slight flexing of the knees, and ended with a fluid propelling of the imagined ball along its visualized arc.

"Feel the ball leave your fingertips," I can still remember him saying, "and let your hand finish high and straight toward your target." Finally, "Watch it swish through the net."

Gross, and others working on improved free throw shooting, were encouraged to repeat this visualization drill over and over until they had fully absorbed it. (Today, we'd say "owned" it.) Bruce advised players to play this scene out in their heads during their off-the-court rest periods, using the inside of their eyelids like a movie screen.

On the court prior to practice sessions, Bruce would have the player initiate the process with a ball, going through the same shooting mechanics with his eyes open. Bruce stressed the need of visualizing the totality of the free throw—don't forget the swish!—before *each* shot.

I felt the visualization technique had merit and used it in my coaching on the practice floor after Bruce left the team at the end of training camp. "See yourself," I'd say as I urged a player to concentrate and execute a specific skill. I corrected technique when necessary and then forced repetitions until the proper form became ingrained.

One of the best subjects turned out to be none other than Mr. Bill "Stay Out of My Head" Walton, especially at the free throw line, where he'd had limited success in the past.

No basketball skill lends itself more to the employment of visualization techniques than free throw shooting. On the line, the player is all alone performing an isolated task. And here Bruce's visualization training seemed to bear the most fruit. Compared to the previous season, for example, Gross' percentage from the line improved from .683 to .851; Bill Walton's went from .583 to .697; and Lionel Hollins' from .721 to .749. I believe that visualization was a factor in helping them to boost those percentages.

In other individual stats, Walton improved his rebound average from 11.4 to 14.4 and his blocked shots from 1.6 to 3.25 per game. He led the NBA in both categories. Was visualization a factor? I believe it was. So does Bill.

Our overall team shooting from the field also moved up, from .469 to .481. But here the number of new players on the team and a different offensive game plan makes an objective comparison impossible. That being said, I have a gut feeling that visualization had a positive effect.

In today's NBA, I don't see many teams spending formal time to instill the practice of visualization on a team basis, at least not the way I did employing Bruce Ogilvie's talents. But every coach I talked to while writing this book uses visualization in some part of his individual and team preparation.

Gregg Popovich of the Spurs told me that he and his staff work individually with some players on visualization. In trying to help Tim Duncan become a more consistent free throw shooter, Pop told me, "We set up a series of consecutive videos that show him with perfect form and accuracy from the line. This allows him to watch himself successfully shoot free throw after free throw, while visualizing himself duplicating those techniques."

Pop also said that he has worked over the years with Tony Parker, his explosive point guard, to get him to react more consistently on his penetrations into the paint: "I've talked to Tony a lot about visualizing beating his man, then seeing in his mind defenders that pop up in his path, and then seeing himself make the right decision to shoot or pass." As he visualizes the various scenarios, Parker either makes the basket himself or makes a scoring assist. Parker has developed into the toughest player in the league to defend in the paint. Pop feels the visualization work helped Parker in that process.

Parker agrees: "That visualization drill that Pop had me do really helped me make much better decisions with the ball. I'm shooting a higher percentage and not turning the ball over as much."

Of all the positions players, point guards probably have the most to gain from visualization training. They have the ball more than any other player and have the responsibility for the success of the team's offensive execution. Among point guards in today's NBA, I rate Steve Nash (Suns) as the most creative at initiating team offense, Chris Paul (Hornets) as the best passer in traffic, Deron Williams (Jazz) as the most powerful penetrator, and Parker as the top finisher at the hoop. All concur that visualization is a key part of their game preparation.

Kobe Bryant concentrates on his personal game plan for each opponent, and visualization is a part of that process. Kobe sees in his mind how defenses—"I've seen them all"—have played him in the past and is ready to attack them in a way that benefits his team the most. I rate him as the best floor general among all current NBA players.

Coach Pop puts it another way: "Kobe is an assassin."

Some of the all-time great players employed *de facto* visualization in some form in game preparation for years, well before it acquired the name and certainly before it was part of any formal *team* program.

Take Hakeem Olajuwon. I established a friendship with Hakeem when he was still a player at Houston University, and after he entered the NBA in 1984, I never missed a chance to chat with him as an opposing coach or broadcaster. Hakeem is an extremely humble person off the court, and he often asked me at the beginning of his NBA career if I had any helpful suggestions about how to improve his game.

What do you say to someone who was one of the league's best big men from the moment he slammed down his first power dunk? Well, the only shortcoming in his game in the early years was his passing; it wasn't until Hakeem's eighth NBA season (1992–93) that he had more assists than turnovers.

And so I talked to him about learning to "read" defenses better. Olajuwon says that he would lie in bed at home during the day of a game, drift off into sleep, and visualize, evidently in a dream state, what he would do on the court:

> *All season long I go to sleep before every game and picture myself playing against the other team. I see myself challenging every shot, making them miss, snatching every rebound, dominating. I see that. When I wake up the game is in my head, my confidence level is high. I have a feel for the game that evening. When I get to the court I am happy to be there because all the things I saw in my mind now can happen.*[1]

Sometimes Olajuwon had difficulty getting himself into a sleep state before a game. On those occasions, he says, he didn't play as well:

> *There are also some times when I don't concentrate enough before the game, when I try to picture the team I am playing against and I can't. I'm not prepared mentally. I haven't done my homework. Those are the games in which I struggle. I try to adjust, to see the play, but sometimes I struggle through the whole thing.*[2]

It wasn't surprising to me, considering how zealous he was about improving his game, to read that Larry Bird spent serious time visualizing all aspects of his game. And I think you'll agree that it worked out pretty well. But for some reason, visualization didn't do much for his shot blocking, the Birdman's least developed basketball skill. Bird never averaged one block a game in a season. (Hey, nobody's perfect, not even Larry Bird.)

Larry's pregame shooting practice has been well documented. His focus and concentration were always at the highest possible level. Many times from the opposing bench I watched him bring those qualities to everything he did to get ready, even pregame layup drills. Larry's face always bore a grim mask of determination while so many others, on his team and mine, drifted through layups with faraway looks in their eyes.

Bird once told me that one of his toughest challenges was to block out distractions in the locker room before games so that he could get game ready. To use visualization before a game with teammates milling about, talking, and joking took immense focus and concentration. The Birdman had both aplenty, which is why he was ready for every game I ever saw him play.

To this day, Bird believes that players should always go through a mental rehearsal before a game: "See yourself executing all aspects of your game perfectly. Hear the crowd roaring for you. Practice being a winner."[3]

In the summer of 1991, I had the opportunity to coach Bird and Magic Johnson in a charity all-star game in Indianapolis. It was a meaningless exhibition, but that didn't affect the intensity levels of the two great players once it was underway. They were both lighthearted in the locker room beforehand, but when the ball was tossed to start the game, it was like a switch was turned on. They were all business. Both gave 100 percent—nothing less than I expected—and both seemed to take special pride in connecting on no-look passes. It was visualization on the fly.

Who won? Who remembers?

Michael Jordan with Jean and Jack Ramsay at MJ's Senior Flight School, Las Vegas, 1999.

But I do remember that it was great to see.

Bill Fitch, coach of the Celtics from 1979 through 1983, says that with Larry Legend it was as simple as point and click: "Larry's mind takes an instant picture of the whole court, and he sees creative possibilities."[4]

Yes, Bill, but remember that Bird had already taken that picture and had seen those creative possibilities *before* the game.

Initially, Michael Jordan was a tad suspect of the visualization techniques that Phil Jackson introduced to the Chicago Bulls. Jordan says he "looked out of the corner of my eye" to see if all the other guys were "into" the visual concentration sessions that Phil prescribed. He found that they were and that they worked for him, too.

But Michael had used a form of visualization long before coming to the NBA. It was second nature to him. He never realized it was something that others had to learn: "I go back and forth thinking about the game. ...

I start picturing the way I want to play. … I visualized how many points I was going to score. How I was going to score them. How I was going to play and break down my opponent."[5]

Although Jordan is best remembered for his amazing offensive play, we mustn't forget his ability to shut down the opposing team's big guns and high scorers, guys like Clyde Drexler, Reggie Miller, and Joe Dumars. Before a game, Jordan would conduct a careful mental review of a player's strengths and weaknesses, then visualize how he would play against him: "I would envision his favorite spots on the floor. How he liked to receive the ball. It's like I would watch this little game unfold in my mind. Then I made decisions based on what I saw."[6]

Jordan went to that technique especially after an opposing player had enjoyed a good scoring game against him. (A rare occurrence, but it happened.) As a broadcaster, I always looked up the number of points his matchup had scored against MJ in their previous meeting. If he had scored big, I knew that Michael would intensify his effort in this game. He would be all over the player from the opening whistle, using his visualization of that player's tendencies to put his every touch at risk.

Jordan also made adjustments in his game plan when necessary: "It didn't always play out exactly how I saw it, but most of the time it did. The process of seeing success before it happened put me in a positive frame of mind and prepared me to play the game once it started."[7]

Bill Russell was not only the best big-man defender ever, he was also—in my book—the most cerebral player of all time. It didn't hurt that Russ was blessed with superior hand-eye coordination and had catlike responses to the actions of opposing players. I recall a series of pictures published in a newspaper soon after Russell came into the NBA (1956). It showed a player with the ball in shooting position and Russ with his hand in a challenging position with both feet on the floor. The next photo showed the player going up to shoot, Russ with his hand closer to the shooter, feet still on the floor. The final image showed the ball in the air and Russell, vertically straight, several feet in the air, blocking the shot as it left the shooter's hand.

Russell says that visualization helped him with his shot-blocking skills and that it developed over time:

What changed for me, what made this imaginative process creative, was when I began to see in my mind's eye the moves I would need to defend against these players. Each move I then came up with was an invention of mine, something that had not existed before.[8]

So far, I've only talked about NBA superstars who practiced visualization. Does that mean the second-tier stars, the role players, and the bench backups spurn visualization? Not at all. The quality of play in the NBA is such that to get there—and stay there—a player must use everything in his tool kit that might conceivably give him an edge.

Take John Starks, a fine 2-guard and ferocious competitor who won one Sixth Man of the Year Award (1996–97) but made just one All-Star team in his 13 NBA seasons (mostly with the Knicks). Before games, Starks would seek out a quiet place where he could have privacy to visualize what he was going to do on the court that night:

I used to go into the little trainer's room [in Madison Square Garden] where we used to get checked for injuries and close the door and turn off the lights. I'd lie on the trainer's table and it would be completely dark in there, and I'd get myself focused. ... For fifteen minutes before it was time to go out on the floor, I'd go in there and block everything out and visualize what I wanted to do on the court.[9]

Starks also prepared visually by watching other players on television. He watched Michael Jordan on TV and relied on visualization from those televised games when he played against Jordan in the NBA: "I knew Jordan's game like a book from watching him so much on television. I'd played him like 1,500 times in my mind."[10]

Starks seemed to revel in his matchups with MJ, and while I never saw him shut Jordan down—I never saw *anybody* shut Michael down—John always competed hard and never backed down. MJ respected players who came at him. Starks and Joe Dumars ranked high on that list.

You won't be startled to learn that Phil Jackson, later a highly successful Zen-disciple coach for Chicago and the Los Angeles Lakers, was an avid practitioner of visualization way back in his playing days as a backup forward on the Knicks' 1973 championship team. Phil followed a routine similar to that of Starks:

> *I would sit quietly for fifteen minutes or twenty minutes before the game in a secluded part of the stadium—my favorite is the New York Rangers' locker room [in Madison Square Garden]—and create a moving picture in my mind of what was about to happen. I'd call up images of the man I was going to cover and visualize myself stopping his moves. ... The idea was to code the image of a successful move into my visual memory so that when a similar situation emerged in a game it would seem, to paraphrase Yogi Berra, like déjà vu all over again.*[11]

A gangly 6'9" stringbean, Phil was all shoulders, elbows, and knees, and he was a masterly defender. He could defend low-post big men with more heft and height, and he could stay with smaller guys with more speed who tried to drive past him. His ability to visualize an opponent's moves helped him keep bigger and quicker players from beating him.

Lakers swingman Michael Cooper, the 1987 NBA Defensive Player of the Year, says that before each game he would zero in mentally on the player he'd be guarding that night: "Then I visualize how my determination to dominate my opponent will ultimately help us win the game. I always think positive. I knew that, in this league, a positive attitude is all important."[12]

Cooper says that he was taught to visualize by his Pasadena High School coach, George Terzian, who told him he must learn to "see the gym":

[Coach] wanted us not only to see the entire court and the other nine players on it, he wanted us to see the bench, the stands and the scoreboard. At first it was hard to do while concentrating on the game and your opponent. After a month of practice though, I began to see more and more of the court. By the end of the season, I realized that I could "see the gym." This discipline has aided me ever since, through my college and professional careers. Seeing the "big picture" helps with everything I do.[13]

Cooper also used visualization to improve his shooting, particularly at the free throw line. In the first four of his 11 NBA seasons, Cooper shot 78 percent from the line; in his next seven, he was successful 86 percent of the time. Why the improvement? Because he started *seeing* it: "I focus my eyes on the back of the rim and visualize the sight of the ball going cleanly through the basket as I block all other thoughts and sounds."[14]

Pete Maravich, a marvel at creating scoring plays on the fly at Louisiana State University and later for the New Orleans Jazz, used visualization to help him shoot more accurately. He learned how to do it from his father, Press Maravich, who was his college coach.

Pete and his dad had a wonderful relationship both as father and son and as coach and player. Press worked hard with Pete on the basics of the game from the time he could first bounce a basketball, and the father dearly loved the way his son played the game. I remember sitting alongside Press watching Pete in a high school all-star game. Pete completed an incredible play in which, on the fast break, he faked a pass to a teammate while in the air, took the ball around his body, faked the shot, then laid off a scoring pass to another teammate who was running the floor behind him. The crowd went wild, and Press nudged me and said, "The kid's the greatest, isn't he?"

Here's Pete on his use of visualization to improve his shooting:

Dad introduced me to the concept of image shooting, or conceptualization. He told me to image a little man who played basketball all the time. When I shot the ball, the little man shot the ball. The only difference was the little man never missed. After hours of shooting, I developed an instant picture of the little man shooting the ball going through the hoop. Eventually, before every shot I attempted I pictured the ball through the hoop before it left my hand. Dad designed the technique to give me confidence before every shot.[15]

As brilliant as Pete was as a passer-scorer, I never considered him a team leader (sorry, Press). To me it seemed that his first instinct on the court was to create a sensational play rather than do something less flashy that would help his team win. I sensed that his teammates resented him in Atlanta and that when surrounded by a less talented supporting cast in New Orleans, he felt compelled to put on a "show" for the fans every night. The bottom line: Pistol Pete was a great *individual* talent, but he had no championship rings to show for his 10 seasons in the NBA.

Magic Johnson was another matter altogether. Magic was *all* about team, *all about* winning. Pat Riley, his Lakers coach during the "Showtime" era of their combined careers, often commented on Magic's obsession for winning. "I never saw anyone like Buck," Riley would say to me. "He just never let up, whether it was practice or a game. He *had* to win."

Johnson had incredible—okay, I'll say it—*magical* floor vision. He was the best I ever saw at seeing the whole floor and creating the exact play needed for a score. It might be a three-quarters-court bounce pass, something that very few players would even attempt and even fewer could pull off. It might be a simple bounce pass at the end of a break when everybody in the house figured he was going to take the shot. It might be a no-look pass to a trailing teammate. Whatever it took, Magic had it in his tool bag.

Johnson says he consciously employed visualization *during* games:

To me, everything was clear. It was like a book where everything was explained down to the smallest detail and illustrated with pictures that were clear and strong. But to a lot of people, the game was too fast and too complicated to see. The pictures were blurry. That's unfortunate because if people would learn to visualize the game, to see it and think it the right way, then everything on the floor becomes crystal clear. It becomes a whole new game.[16]

Today, visualization as a technique for improving performance is commonplace in every locker room that I visit before NBA games. Videos of individual players, their teams, and their opponents are on the TV screens so players can study themselves in order to learn how to perform better. We're not talking ESPN highlights here; we're talking active pregame classrooms. And it's happening with every team in the league, not just those in the championship hunt.

"Players today are accustomed to playing video games in their leisure time and are tuned into that medium," says Pacers coach Jim O'Brien. "We prepare videos for each player, showing his best performance against our immediate opponent. He sees only positive results and visualizes himself doing those things in the game ahead."

Every NBA team goes through this process. And the second-tier teams prepare at least as hard for every game as do teams deeper in talent. They have to, or they'll get blown out every game. They can't afford turnovers, defensive breakdowns, or missed high-percentage shots. So they prepare, prepare, prepare. I think in retrospect that my best coaching jobs were getting Buffalo to 42–40 (1974) from 21–61 the previous season and Indiana to 41–41 (1987), compared to 26–56 the year before I got there.

In my pregame preparation of teams that I coached, I stressed the visualization of anticipated trends of opposing players and teams. I asked my players to project what they could do against their matchups to gain an advantage. I asked them to visualize their making a key stop, or a pair of free throws in a tight situation, or getting the right position to pull down a rebound against a taller opponent. I found it extremely helpful.

Rudy Tomjanovich says that when he was an assistant coach with the Rockets during the 1979–80 season, head coach Del Harris brought the team together periodically for "positive visualization" sessions:

Before one game Del asked us to close our eyes and visual-
ize ourselves playing tough defense, then grabbing rebounds
in traffic. After that he told us to visualize making our shots.
Then Del said, "We've had some problems lately. Now, see
a bag. We're putting all the bad stuff in the bag and walk-
ing to a bridge with water below. Drop the bag over the
side. It hits the water with a splash and disappears. Our
problems are gone. You can open your eyes now, guys."[17]

Open your eyes.

Visualize.

You'll be amazed at how much more you can see.

Lionel Hollins hitting the game-winning shot to decide the 1977 first-round
playoffs against Chicago. (Roger Jensen photo)

5

BELIEVE IN YOURSELF

We were two weeks into my first training camp as coach of the Portland Trail Blazers in the fall of 1976. The Blazers were beginning their seventh NBA season without ever having a .500 record, much less a playoff appearance. Losing seemed like a permanent condition in the Pacific Northwest.

But I sought out the job after leaving the Buffalo Braves (two years later, the San Diego Clippers) at the end of the previous season because there was an intriguing array of talent already assembled in Portland. Center Bill Walton was starting his third NBA season. Power forward Maurice Lucas and gritty point guard Dave Twardzik had been acquired after the collapse of the American Basketball Association earlier that summer. Bob Gross, Lionel Hollins, Lloyd Neal, and Larry Steel were solid holdovers from the 1975–76 Blazers. Veterans Herm Gilliam and Corky Calhoun, recently obtained from Seattle and Los Angeles, respectively, joined rookie draftees Johnny Davis and Wally Walker as well as Robin Jones, a free-agent center who had played in Europe.

It was a group bubbling with high potential.

I pushed them hard from day one to learn the basics of a different style of offense and a pressure-type defense. I was gratified with their response. We knew there was a lot of work to do, but the two-a-day

Commissioner Larry O'Brien presenting the 1977 NBA championship trophy to team owner Larry Weinberg, Dr. Jack Ramsay and Bill Walton.(Roger Jensen Photo)

Bob Gross jumping over Dan Issel (44), Ted McClain (12) and David Thompson (33) in a Western Conference semifinal game against the Denver Nuggets. (Roger Jensen Photo).

Rookie Johnny Davis played like a veteran after Dave Twardzik was injured in the 1977 playoffs. (Portland Blazers Archive photo)

Walton floats to the basket while Sixers players look on during the 1977 NBA Finals. (Roger Jensen Photo)

Dave Twardzik attempting a shot against Kareem Abdul-Jabbar. (Roger Jensen Photo)

Dave Twardzik drives past San Antonio's Mike Gale as Spurs star George Gervin looks on, 1977. (Roger Jensen Photo)

Bill Walton shoots a sky hook over 7'2" Artis Gilmore in the 1977 Chicago playoff series. (Roger Jensen Photo)

practices had gone very well. I was excited. At the end of the first week, I said to my assistant, Jack McKinney, "We're going to be pretty damned good." He agreed.

Suddenly, at the end of our second week of camp, everything came together in a scrimmage. Both teams were playing in-your-face defense. Missed shots were viciously rebounded. There were put-back scores or outlet passes to quick-footed runners to start fast breaks. Players moved without the ball in the half-court offense and were in

Lloyd Neal calmly picks out the open man against a Sixers double team of George McGinnis and Steve Mix in the '77 Finals. (Roger Jensen Photo)

exactly the right spots to receive passes fired with pinpoint accuracy. It was beautiful to watch.

After about 10 minutes of that display, I whistled the action stopped and gathered the team around me at midcourt. I waited until every player's eyes were on mine.

"We can win if we play like that."

I said the words slowly and calmly as I looked around from face to face. Some players nodded in agreement; all kept looking in my eyes.

"I don't mean just having a winning record," I went on. "I mean we can win the whole thing … the NBA championship."

I waited for the words to sink in, keeping eye contact with the players. I could tell they knew this was no routine pep talk. They knew I was dead serious. It was the beginning of a sense of team confidence.

It was the first step to Portland's upcoming championship of 1977.

Strong egos make players strive to be the best that they can be. They work tirelessly to sharpen their skills because they hate to lose and love to win in equal measure. In team sports, they realize that they can't win by themselves, and so the test of a truly great player is whether he brings out the best in his teammates and makes his team better. For these players, there is nothing quite as satisfying as sharing the joy that comes from a hard-earned team victory.

I've witnessed many championship performances from players who had the confidence and courage to step up in crunch time and deliver a winning field goal, make a scoring pass, pull down a much-needed rebound, or shut down a star player when that stop meant winning the game.

The best performance of that kind by one of my players in a key game was turned in by Bill Walton in Game 6 of the NBA Finals against Philadelphia in 1977. Bill seemed to be everywhere on the court at once, dominating both ends of the floor. He finished the game with 20 points, 7 assists, 8 blocked shots, and 23 rebounds. You read right—*23 rebounds*. On the final play of the game, Walton tapped George McGinnis' missed shot toward the backcourt to teammate Johnny Davis. That preserved our 109–107 Blazers victory and gave us the NBA championship.

In their preseason reviews, knowledgeable pundits didn't list us among the league's elite teams, much less consider us as favorites to go all the way. But during the course of the season, Walton's self-confidence lifted us all up. As a result, that Portland team, which had never before had a winning record in its seven-year history, became NBA champs.

The greatest player of all time, Michael Jordan, demonstrated tremendous confidence every time he set foot on a basketball court. No surprise there, right? Of all the great MJ performances I have witnessed, both from courtside and the broadcast booth, I believe the one that most demonstrated his confidence came in Game 5 of the 1997 championship against the Utah Jazz. Michael had been stricken with food poisoning the night before that game, and it was a "game decision" regarding his ability to play. (That's code for saying you don't know whether a player's going to be able to take the court until he does.)

But MJ, although dehydrated and feeling nauseated, simply would not sit out that game. I was doing the radio broadcast for ESPN, and I watched in awe as Michael labored through the game, bending over from the waist, hands on his knees, and gasping for breath at breaks in the action, then magically pulling himself together when play resumed. He *would not* surrender to his physical weakness. He *would not* let his team lose.

That day Michael played 44 minutes, scored 38 points, and had the confidence in himself to demand the ball to take—and make—the game-clinching 3-point shot. Then, utterly exhausted to the verge of collapse, Jordan was helped to the locker room by his teammates.

Want another profile in confidence? Flash-forward to Game 7 of the second round of the 2008 NBA playoffs, Celtics vs. Cavaliers. Boston's Paul Pierce was matched up against Cleveland's LeBron James. Intimidated? Not exactly. Pierce came out firing, hitting shots from all corners of the court. Pierce was in the zone, that idyllic place that all shooters love to visit. He made 13 of 23 attempts from the field (including 4 of 6 3-pointers), and 11 of 12 from the free throw line for a total of 41 points. Pierce's confident demeanor enabled the Celtics to eliminate the Cavs and advance to the NBA Finals, where they beat the Lakers for the title.

Pierce after the game: "I knew I had to have a big game, and everything fell together for me. My shot really felt good. I had confidence the ball was going in every time I shot it."

No way can players rack up performances like that if they don't believe fiercely in themselves. But that doesn't mean they come about that confidence alone. Coaches and teammates can help players reach that level of absolute confidence by giving them positive feedback. Doc Rivers called plays for Pierce that took advantage of his hot hand, Rajon Rondo made Pierce his first option in transition fast breaks, and Kevin Garnett set some bone-jarring screens to free up Pierce for open looks.

Team basketball at its best, based on confidence that Paul Pierce would deliver. And he did.

Coaches and players know that self-confidence is a by-product of successful work on the practice court. Confidence grows out of many successful repetitions in practice under simulated game conditions.

A player's confidence spikes when his coach makes a special effort to show that he appreciates his skill and dedication. Sometimes a pat on the butt and a "Good job, big fella" is all that it takes. Sometimes a private session is necessary to bolster a certain type of player's confidence. I also used videotapes of outstanding performances of a player, stopping the action to point out especially good examples of his right choices and good execution.

Everybody feels better about themselves when they know what they're doing is appreciated. Basketball players are no exception to that fundamental law of human nature.

Smart coaches also use the media to single out players when they perform well. Praise sent their way via the media can boost self-confidence. But the praise must be warranted. Players are the first to know when they haven't performed up to par; false accolades can make them distrust their coach's judgment and undermine team morale.

In other words, it's absolutely imperative that the coach be honest with his players. I know, I know—Coaching 101. But you'd be surprised (or maybe not) to learn how often that basic premise is ignored. I always told my players *exactly* how I saw things. I told them when they played well, and *exactly why* I thought they played well, with concrete examples. I also told them when they played below acceptable levels, and I showed them on videotape and on the court what I was talking about. Players appreciate a coach's honesty, even when it's hard to take.

I'm talking about good players here, the kind you want on your team.

An example? Take the meeting I had with Scott Skiles (now head coach of the Milwaukee Bucks) after the 1987–88 season when I coached the Indiana Pacers. Skiles had just completed his first season with the team, and I told him his performance had been unsatisfactory. He was too slow as a point guard, uncertain with his left-hand dribble, and a liability on defense. (I know, "Other than that, Mrs. Lincoln, how did you enjoy the play?" But I wouldn't have been helping Scott or the team had I softened my message.) I said that he needed to get himself in much better condition and to improve his game skills if he hoped to stay in the NBA. The Pacers had an excellent summer conditioning program under the direction of Dean Brittenham, and I made it clear to Scott that I expected him to "volunteer" for it.

Skiles was definitely *not* pleased to hear my evaluation. He later told me that he was "really pissed" as he drove home. But he did take part in the conditioning program, and he did work hard on those parts of his game that I had singled out in our little fireside chat. He was a much-improved player when we reassembled that fall. His career took another positive jump a year later after the Orlando Magic plucked him away from us in the NBA Expansion Draft. Scott still holds the NBA record for single-game assists (30), set in December 1990 in a game against Denver. He was named the NBA's Most Improved Player that season.

Years later, Scott told me that my meeting with him was the best thing that ever happened to him as a player and that he still maintained a consistent, rigorous exercise routine, a fact that I'm sure does not go unnoticed by his Milwaukee players.

Gregg Popovich helps instill self-confidence in his San Antonio team by creating a family atmosphere. Since my first day in professional basketball, I have not encountered a franchise quite like the Spurs. Pop makes every player feel that he's important to the franchise. He has an excellent coaching staff that works hard and effectively with every player.

But here's what's really special: every player and coach in the Spurs franchise must engage in some activity that benefits the community. That, in turn, binds them to the community. Most NBA teams require players to become involved in some kind of community activity, but no team gets the total involvement of all of its players and coaches like the Spurs.

The players trust Popovich. They have confidence that he'll get them through the inevitable rough spots of the long NBA season. "Pop will work it out," Tim Duncan told me regarding the Spurs player rotation prior to the playoffs in the team's 2007 championship season.

Coach Pop goes over his anticipated substitution pattern with each player before every season. For instance, Manu Ginobili is the Spurs' best clutch player, but Coach Pop mostly brings him off the bench, even though he knows Manu would prefer to start. At the conclusion of his preseason heart-to-heart with Ginobili, Manu tells Pop, "You do whatever you think is best for the team. I'm okay with whatever you decide."

That demonstrates utter confidence by Ginobili in his coach—and in himself.

San Antonio is not a glamour location like LA or New York or Boston, but players like to play there. They like the franchise, the owner (Peter Holt), the general manager (R. C. Buford), the coaching staff, and—most important—each other. The family atmosphere gives them a comfort zone in which they can relax more and play their game.

The result? Four NBA championships from 1999 through 2008, the best success rate in the league during that time frame.

The toughest, most confident players in the NBA just *will not give in*. And they carry their teams with them.

Michael Jordan was the best I ever saw at displaying this trait, but Kobe Bryant is right there with him. MJ exuded confidence and trusted selected teammates, like John Paxson and Steve Kerr, to complete big plays when the occasion demanded. Michael never thought of failing. Six rings, remember?

Bryant, now in his early thirties, has the same mind-set: "I've been playing the game for so long, I know I've done it before. It's a kind of calm that you have, knowing you'll succeed."

In the 2009 NBA Finals, Bryant made shots from everywhere on the court against a stubborn Orlando team, and when the Magic defense ganged up on him, he found Lamar Odom and Pau Gasol for layups or Derek Fisher for open jumpers. He richly deserved being named MVP of the Finals.

Among current NBA closers—and there are great ones like LeBron James, Dwyane Wade, Chris Paul, Paul Pierce, Steve Nash, Manu Ginobili—I rate Kobe the best.

Confidence is contagious.

Phil Jackson has his team captain(s) speak to the squad at the end of the last practice before a game. I was an onlooker as Derek Fisher addressed his Lakers teammates before Game 5 of the 2009 NBA Finals against the Orlando Magic: "There will come a time in the game tonight when we can take their will. My question to you is, 'Will we do it?'"

They did it, and then some, blowing out the Magic 99–86 on Orlando's home court to give the Lakers their 15th NBA championship (second only to Boston's 17) and Phil Jackson his 10th. Phil's now won more championships than any coach in any major American sports league.

Of course, even the most confident players have poor games now and then. Hey, stuff happens. But players with strong egos put a bad game behind them quickly—*after* they figure out what went wrong. They'll learn from their mistakes and then dismiss the game from their minds, almost like it never happened.

Manu Ginobili, when he has a rare subpar performance, asks the Spurs video coordinator immediately after the game to give him a disk containing all his minutes. Manu takes that disk home and critiques his performance that same night. Coach Popovich tells me that he never needs to say anything to Ginobili about a bad game: "Manu's very hard on himself. He'll go over that game before the next practice and correct whatever he has to. I don't worry about Manu."

Phil Jackson is aware of how easy it is for players to lose confidence in themselves. And he explains what must be done in typical Phil-Speak: "The key for any team is to find something, anything to believe in to ward off the demons of self-doubt."[1]

I remember a Bulls-Heat game during Chicago's championship run in which Michael Jordan, at his peak then, didn't take a single shot during the entire first period. After the game, which the Bulls won going away (and Jordan ended up with his usual 20+ points), I asked him why it took him so long to get his scoring game going. His answer: "I can get my points any time. Scottie had been struggling with his game lately, and I wanted to get him off early."

Jordan had the confidence to feel he could score anytime he wanted. He also sensed a slight erosion of Pippen's psyche. MJ took care of both issues.

Jackson was the first coach I know of to employ meditation consistently as a tool to relax players, sharpen their focus, and instill confidence. On occasion, he has his players stretch out in a darkened room where there's no talking, no noise, and no disruptions. The objective is to relax and visualize a perfect performance in the upcoming game.

Jackson's Bulls and Lakers players whom I have spoken to all agree to the benefits derived from meditation. Lamar Odom told me before a 2009 playoff game, "PJ got me started on it when I first came to the Lakers. Now I do it by myself before every game."

Later, after the game, I asked Odom how he felt approaching the free throw line in a close-to-the-vest finish. He said he did a "little meditatin', talked to my mom [who'd recently passed away]. She told me to take my time, and I'd be all right."

Odom made both free throws, and the Lakers won.

Confidence.

Former Blazers psychologist Bruce Ogilvie described that meditative process as "watching yourself play the perfect game—you make every shot, make the scoring pass, shut down your man, grab every rebound—seeing the game play out on the inside of your eyelids as you're resting."

I never used meditation as a team exercise, but I did suggest Ogilvie's method to players who struggled with their free throw shooting. And I have an improved golf swing as a result of my personal use of the technique.

Bill Bradley believes there is a direct correlation between skills developed in practice and self-confidence: "The harder you work, the sooner your skills improve. Then the virtuous circle takes over. As your skills grow, you get a rush of self confidence, which spurs you to continue working, and your skills increase all the faster."[2]

During Bradley's career with the Knicks, he would relax following the long NBA season until about mid-August, and then he'd commence his preseason conditioning program in New York City. A couple of nights a week that program involved driving down to Philadelphia to play in the Baker League, a summer league that always attracted a few NBA players—Hal Greer, Chet Walker, Billy Cunningham, Earl Monroe, and Wilt Chamberlain were Baker League irregulars—looking to stay in shape along with non-NBA types hoping to catch the eye of scouts combing for hitherto undiscovered talent.

I was coaching the Sixers at the time, and I regularly went to Baker League games looking for quality players who'd been skipped over in the NBA Draft. I loved watching Bradley in that setting. Opposing players were very physical with him, hoping to intimidate him. But Bill kept his cool, never backed down, and dished it right back. Each week his game got better. By the time the Knicks began training camp, Bradley was physically and mentally ready for another NBA season.

As an example of Bradley's point about confidence being built on long hours of practice, Senator Bill offers us Larry Bird: "He walked into the locker room before the first NBA All-Star 3-point shooting contest [in 1986] and announced, 'Which one of you guys is shooting for second place?' That kind of confidence comes from constant practice and total concentration on what you're doing."[3]

Bird confirms that his confidence was built on pregame preparation—and not just his own:

The kind of confidence I'm talking about is the kind I feel when I know I have done everything I can to prepare for the game, when I believe in the abilities of my teammates, and when I trust and respect the judgment of my coaches.

When I feel the confidence of knowing these things, I don't care what team we're going to play. I know that the team and I are going out on the floor and will play to the best of our potential. And that's enough to get me psyched for a game.[4]

The Celtics star always followed a pregame mental drill designed to send him into combat in the right frame of mind:

I sit in the locker room before a game and feed my mind with information that makes me feel confident. I think about how hard I've worked in practice; I think of the games in which our team worked together and pulled out a big win; I think of some of the key changes our coach made that won games for us in the past. I roll those things around in my mind. I feel confident. I walk out on the floor, quietly and confidently. I play my game full blast.[5]

Few of his Celtics teammates had Bird's level of concentration, of course. Kevin McHale and Dennis Johnson were more typical: lighthearted, loud, and talkative in the locker room. I once asked Bird how he managed to keep his mind on the game in sometimes-raucous surroundings. "Easy," he said. "I just turned my chair around and faced my locker, so my back was to them. When I did that, they usually got the message and quieted down."

Success builds success—and self-confidence.

Jerry West says that "the more you come through, the more you're apt to keep coming through." The man who earned the nickname "Mr. Clutch" says that as his career progressed "it became easier and easier to score in clutch situations because my confidence grew. I didn't care who was guarding me or what the defense was, I could get the ball in the basket."[6]

Not all players want the ball in crunch time. West from Cabin Creek, West Virginia, always did.

You don't think of Charles Barkley *ever* lacking self-confidence, at least not from the time he took his first step as a toddler. But Sir Charles acknowledges that the 1984 Olympic tryouts when he was a junior at Auburn gave his ego a special boost. Even though he didn't make the USA team that year, Barkley played against such future NBA stars as Michael Jordan, Patrick Ewing, Chris Mullin, John Stockton, Sam Perkins, and Joe Dumars. "Being able to play with and against those guys was a big turning point for me in my career," Barkley says. "That kicked me to a whole different level."[7]

When Barkley returned to his Auburn campus, Coach Sonny Smith asked him about his experience. Barkley's response: "I told him I knew then that if I worked on my game, worked all summer and had myself ready, I'd be able to play with any player in the country," Barkley recalls. "I knew I'd be able to do well in the NBA because these guys I'd already held my own against at the trials were going to be the stars of the NBA."[8]

When Blazers scout Bucky Buckwalter returned from observing those Olympic tryouts, I asked him what player impressed him the most. He answered without hesitation: "Charles Barkley. He kicked everybody's ass, including Patrick Ewing's."

Hakeem Olajuwon says that his confidence rose dramatically when, as a young player at the University of Houston in the early 1980s, he gained the respect of Moses Malone during summer workouts. Hakeem recalls it being a great learning experience for him to go up against Malone, the NBA's most dominant big man:

He showed me the respect of playing hard against me. That gave me confidence, mentally and physically. I began to feel that if I can play with Moses, then college should be easy; there's no big man who can play like Moses. Then Moses started talking about me to the reporters. When they asked, he started telling them about my footwork, my speed on the court. He said I could run like a deer. He told the reporters I could dominate college basketball easily.[9]

For Atlanta Hawks rookie Spud Webb (5'6"), beating teammate Dominique Wilkins (6'9") in the slam dunk contest at the 1986 All-Star Game caused his self-confidence to soar. When the second half of the season began, Spud says, he was a changed man:

> *Where before I had been withdrawn, playing sometimes unsure of myself, now I was totally confident. Even though the slam dunk was sideshow material, completely apart from my professional game, the win gave me some unexpected confidence. Suddenly, I was fearless, and back to my old reckless, hard-charging ways.*[10]

I truly admired Spud. He was listed at 5'6", but I thought that was generous. He weighed only 133 pounds, and maybe that was after a good meal. But there he was, game after game, penetrating the paint against opposing 7-footers, and sometimes *dunking* the basketball. He was like the Energizer Bunny, only with more hops. Spud had fans all over the league who loved to see him perform, and I was one of them.

Webb was at a clinic that I did for the late Wayman Tisdale at his basketball camp in Tulsa, Oklahoma, in the summer of 1987. Spud's part of the instructional period was to demonstrate ball handling and passing skills. He did a great job with that, but when he finished, the campers clamored "Dunk! Dunk! Dunk!" Finally, with a little more coaxing, Spud obliged with a 360-degree, twisting, turning, two-handed crusher!

The attendees, mostly high school teenagers, went wild. They couldn't believe what they had just seen.

Before I left to return to Indiana, I told Spud how much I respected his game. "I love playing, Coach," he answered. "For me to play in the NBA is like a dream come true. I've proved I can play ... and I believe in myself. Now I just try to help my team [the Atlanta Hawks] any way I can."

You're a good man, Spud Webb.

A free tip should you ever become a coach: when a player looks you in the eye and says he believes he can do something, let him try.

In a Sixers-Sonics game at Seattle during my first year coaching in the NBA (1968–69), Billy Cunningham was matched up against a rookie, Garfield Heard. During a first-period timeout, Billy looked me in the eye and said, "I don't mean for now, but if we need a hoop late in the game, I can beat this kid every time." And he did. Billy C. was always loaded with confidence, and just about always he delivered.

Michael Jordan says his confidence level jumped up a notch in 1982 when, as a "snotty-nosed kid," he hit a big shot to beat Georgetown in the NCAA championship game:

That started my career. Why? Because I had confidence. No one could take that away from me. I was in that situation and I came through. ... You can always go back to that moment. You have confidence because you have done it before. ... I don't weigh the negatives and positives and hope the positives win. I just go back to past successes, step forward and respond.[11]

As successes continued to multiply, and his confidence grew stronger and stronger, Jordan came to the point that he wanted the ball when a game was on the line—every time: "You're thinking, give me the ball. I'll shoot it. No problem. If you make the shot, then everybody will be shaking your hand. If you miss, you've done it before, so what? You've got room for error. But your expectation is success because you've had the success in the past."[12]

MJ was a master at getting his Bulls teammates to believe that they could not be beaten, especially in big games when the chips were down. In the 1993 NBA Finals, the Bulls were forced to travel to Phoenix for Game 6 against the Suns after losing Game 5 in Chicago on their home court. The Bulls were still up 3–2, but they knew they'd let a great opportunity to wrap up the championship slip through their fingers. A perfect opportunity for self-doubt to creep in, right? No, said Michael Jordan. *Hell, no!* Here's how then-Bulls broadcaster Tom Dore describes the way MJ handled matters:

Michael walked on the plane going to Phoenix and said, "Hello world champs." He's got a foot-long cigar, and he's celebrating already because he knows the series is over. He knew, going into Phoenix, that they were going to win. It wasn't a question with him, and I think that's what the team had. They just had this arrogance. They weren't mean about it. They just felt like they were going to win.[13]

When Jordan returned to the NBA at the end of the 1994–95 season after his aborted attempt at playing professional baseball, I watched him work out about two hours before a game in Miami against the Heat. The season was winding down—the Bulls had 17 games left to play before the playoffs began—and MJ was hoping he had enough time to get his game back to its best level.

From the effort he put into those two hours, you'd have thought he had something to prove. And, given the standards Michael set for himself, he did. I had never seen Michael work out like that before a game. He was in a full sweat when he left the floor. He later scored 31 points as the Bulls won 98–93. After the game, I asked him about the pregame practice he had done.

"Dr. Jack, I'm just trying to get myself ready for the playoffs," he said. "This is harder than I thought. I thought it would be like riding a bicycle, jump on and ride just like before. But it's not."

And for Jordan, it wasn't. The Bulls were ousted in the second round from the playoffs by Orlando that year. Jordan spent the following summer with his personal trainer, Tim Grover, dedicating himself to getting into top physical and game-skill condition. Once that happened MJ's swagger was back, and the Bulls were at the top of their game.

Jordan and the Bulls were off and running once more, adding three more championship rings to their collection (1996, 1997, 1998).

That's a total of six, if you're scoring at home.

Clyde Drexler says a team leader must actively work to demonstrate his confidence to his teammates: "If you are looked upon as a go-to-guy and you don't have confidence, your teammates see that and it takes away from their confidence, too. I probably took it to the point of overconfidence, just to make sure my teammates continued to feel confident. That's an important part of the mental game."[14]

Drexler wasn't the easiest player to coach. He thought that any offensive sequence in which he wasn't the first option was a waste of time. But he was skilled and had great confidence in himself. It was my job to find a way to maximize his talent to the team's greatest good.

At about midseason in his second year (1984–85) with the Blazers, I had a sit-down with Clyde to see how I could get his best effort on offense without disrupting our team game. As I drew up a new play that allowed him to catch, shoot, drive, or pass from the free throw line or low post, his eyes lit up. "Now that's something that I'll make work," he said. And he did.

Drexler led the team in scoring (17 ppg.) and averaged 5.5 assists and 6 rebounds; we made the playoffs with a 48–34 record, but then we got swept by Phoenix in the opening round. Clyde continued to develop as a player, though, and finally, 10 years later (1995) with the Houston Rockets, he got what he deserved: an NBA championship ring.

Sometimes a confidence boost comes from an unexpected source. Just before his rookie season with the Warriors tipped off in 1965, Rick Barry says he was feeling doubts about his ability to make it with the big boys, when out of the blue he got a jolt of confidence from an unexpected source—a guy from downstate with a different color jersey, Jerry West:

We had been playing some exhibition games against Los Angeles and we're on a flight with the Lakers to Las Vegas to play another. I had been playing erratically and was worried about my chances. Jerry West sat down next to me on the flight and said, "Hey, Rick, if you don't mind my saying so, you're too tense, trying too hard. It's something we all go through when we first break in. But I've seen you play and I know you can play in this league. All you have to do is loosen up and play your game and you'll do all right."[15]

Barry says he couldn't believe his own ears:

Here was a great star and a player on a rival team trying to help me, trying to give me confidence in myself. ... It wouldn't have meant as much coming from my coach or a teammate or a friend, but for a great star on another team to boost me was something else. I thanked him and I thank him to this day. He sort of set me free. I felt what he said was true, but his saying it made me believe it.[16]

I regard Barry as one of the greatest clutch players ever. It's interesting that his self-confidence in the NBA was born by such a chance occurrence. Rick was perceptive enough to take West's words to heart and jump-start his game at the professional level.

Momentum is huge in basketball, maybe more so than in any other sport.

When my Blazers team went up against the Sixers in the 1977 NBA Finals, we lost the first two games at Philadelphia decisively. On the plane trip back to Portland, my assistant, Jack McKinney, and I hashed over what our next step should be. We talked about a possible lineup change, about using our trapping defense more often, and about various other adjustments.

Then, as the plane flew through the night, it dawned on me that what we really needed to do was to just play *our* game at its best level. I felt we were a better team than Philly but that we hadn't demonstrated that in the first two games. We'd been sluggish and out of sync on offense, and our defense lacked aggression.

At the next practice back home, I told my players that we weren't going to change anything ... except *how* we played. I told them I wanted them to play "our game"—tough, aggressive defense and a quick-breaking, sharp-cutting, accurate passing offense. I showed them video clips of the regular-season game in which we'd beaten Philly by 40 points. I assured my guys that all we had to do to win was play at *our* level.

And that's exactly what we did. We won Game 3 by 22 points, then Game 4 by 32, and then headed back to Philadelphia with the momentum in our favor and our confidence restored. We won Game 5 there and then beat the Sixers back in Portland to become NBA champs.

We've had many reunions of that championship group, and the players still talk about that team meeting when we agreed that all we had to do was play "our game."

"When momentum comes," says Walt Frazier, "it's contagious. Guys get involved; they start to strive and thrive." But things can change in a hurry, especially when a team gets cocky and deviates from its game plan. But all need not be lost. When an opponent has the momentum going in its favor, you can shift it back—sometimes—with tough defense, as Frazier relates:

> *Your defense becomes your best offense by forcing turnovers, capitalizing on transition and contesting every shot. When the other team misfires, it does not get a second opportunity. . . . A couple of shots from the baseline that bounce out to the top of the key [can] set up fast breaks the other way, and all of a sudden that 20-point lead is gone.*[17]

Larry Bird agrees that tough D offers you the best shot at tilting momentum back your way: "When you see a break, a steal or a blocked shot that turns into a fast break and two points, you can shift gears. When the momentum shifts your way, you will be ready to react and ride it like a wave as fast as it will take you."[18]

There's no way you're going to turn the momentum of a game around, Bill Bradley says, if you have a negative mental attitude:

> *In most contests there are good and bad moments; the flow is inevitable. Yet some players and some teams can't seem to come back from a bad break. When a team makes a few*

dumb plays or gets a few bad calls, its play often deterio-rates. Teammates will glare at each other; occasionally hostile words will pass between them. By the fourth quar-ter, they're starting to prepare for their postgame excuses. Defeat is inevitable. When things go bad for such teams, no one steps in to change the momentum, and then they get even worse.[19]

I remember a Lakers-Buffalo Braves game in LA in the early 1970s when my Braves rallied to close a double-digit Lakers lead to two points late in the fourth period. The action was at the end of the floor in front of our bench when the Lakers called a timeout.

Our guys were pumped as they approached the bench. I shouted to them, "We got 'em! We got 'em!" The Lakers players were slower going to their bench, and I caught Gail Goodrich looking at me with a resigned expression on his face. As it turned out, we did "have 'em," and our young team came away with a big road win. The momentum had shifted in that game, and the Lakers couldn't do anything about it.

You hear the term *heart* used frequently in sports to describe some-one who has displayed great ability to succeed in pressure-packed situa-tions. Heart is more than confidence. All NBA players have confidence, or they couldn't have made it to the professional level.

Players with heart won't be denied. They make game-winning shots with defenders hanging all over them. They come from nowhere to block an opposing player's critical shot. They find an open teammate for a layup when they've been boxed in a tight double-team. They make the steal their team must have to get a possession in dying seconds of big games.

The song "You've Gotta Have Heart" is very apropos.

Championship teams gotta have 'em ... players with heart.

Michael Jordan loved guys who could deliver in the clutch, who could stand up under pressure, guys like Steve Kerr and John Paxson, his teammates on those great Bulls championship teams (1991–93, 1996–

98). Not superstars—there was only one on those Bulls teams—but guys who never shied away from pressure. "These guys played with heart," says Michael. "Heart is what separates the good from the great."[20]

An example? The first of many that come to my mind took place in Game 6 of the 1993 NBA Finals, Bulls vs. Suns, Chicago up 3–2 in the series. The Suns have a two-point lead with 10 clicks on the clock; Bulls' ball out of bounds. The Suns need a stop to force a Game 7. The in-bounds passer can't get the ball to Jordan, the logical choice for a final shot, and has to pass it to Scottie Pippen. MJ's still not open, so Scottie passes to Horace Grant on the baseline. Grant has no shot, so he kicks it out to Paxson, who calmly drains a 3-pointer.

Bulls 99, Suns 98. Bulls three-peat as NBA champions.

Heart? I think that was John Paxson's middle name.

During the Celtics' championship years in the 1950s and 1960s, Sam Jones was the player who consistently demonstrated the most heart at the end of close games. Bill Russell says that during a timeout Red Auerbach would look around at faces, trying to decide what play to call. It was at such moments, Russell says, that even the better players in the NBA would start coughing, tying their shoelaces, or looking the other way. Not Sam Jones, as Russell points out:

At such moments I knew what Sam would do as well as I knew my own name. "Gimme the ball," he'd say. "I'll make it." And all of us would look at him, and we'd know by looking that he meant what he said. ... Sam would be all business, but there'd be a trace of a smile on his face, like a guy who was meeting a supreme test and was certain he'd pass it. "You guys get out of the way," he'd say. ... In LA Jerry West was called "Mr. Clutch," and he was, but in the seventh game of a championship series, I'll take Sam over any player who ever walked on a court.[21]

Reggie Miller was another player who always wanted the ball in the final seconds of a close game:

I've always loved being the go-to guy. The way I look at it, you have a fifty-fifty chance. You can be the hero or the goat. But with me, considering the amount of work I've put into my shot, I tell myself, "You've got a seventy-thirty chance of making the shot." I'll take those odds any day.[22]

Reggie came into his own after I left the Pacers, but he developed into a clutch-shot killer and seemed to take special delight in tormenting the Knicks with heroic, end-of-game displays of incredible shooting.

Finally, let's listen to Jerry "Mr. Clutch" West talk about his nickname:

I thrive on pressure. It excites me and brings out the best in me. When it comes to the clutch, I want the ball; I want to make the shot. I want it bad. I don't think anyone else has as good a chance of making it as I do. I know I can make it. I think others have confidence in me, which gives me confidence in myself.[23]

Well spoken, Mr. Clutch, but I still have to say that for me, the toughest player at the end of close games to coach against was Larry Bird. Jordan hadn't yet started winning with Chicago, and today's NBA stars weren't born yet. Larry seemed to make whatever play had to be made for his Celtics to win close games. Maybe it would be a fall-away jumper from the deep left corner over two defenders in Boston, then running toward the dressing room with both fists clenched above his head before the ball settled in the net. Maybe it would be a perfect pass in the closing seconds of a playoff game when he was being double-teamed. Whatever it took for his team to win, the Birdman had it in his repertoire.

Confidence?

Heart?

Larry Bird had more of both than anybody I ever coached against.

6
KICK SOME BUTT

In 1977, the year my Portland team won the NBA championship, we played Chicago at home in a decisive Game 3 in the first round of the Western Conference Playoffs. Lose that game and we're out of the playoffs. We had a two-point lead (100–98) and the ball with 36 seconds left on the clock. We needed another bucket, but three of my best players— Bill Walton, Maurice Lucas, Bob Gross—had fouled out. I called for a timeout and watched my players as they came to the bench. Lionel Hollins was the only one who looked at me. The other guys were looking at the floor, or into the stands, but not at me. I grouped them around me and said, "Lionel, it's you."

Lionel nodded in the affirmative, still looking at me straight on. I drew up a side court screen for him so he could drive to the hoop or pull up for his jumper. He got the inbounds pass, came off the screen, drove to the free throw line, and buried the jumper.

Ball game.

We added a couple of more hoops when the Bulls turned the ball over in their anxiety to score, but we won the game because Lionel Hollins, under maximum pressure, had stepped up and delivered.

Now, Lionel wasn't having a good shooting game that day (4–15 at that point), but over the season, he'd demonstrated his self-confidence and competitiveness over and over. I made my decision based on his willingness to tell me through his body language and his eyes coming over to the bench that he was ready to make the shot.

In the team celebration later that evening, Herm Gilliam asked me why I'd chosen Lionel to take the critical shot: "He wasn't exactly shootin' the lights out, Coach."

"He was the only one who looked me in the eye, Herm," I responded. "That was enough for me."

"Every good player," Charles Barkley once said, "has a little bit of an asshole in him."

Sir Charles, never one to mince words, explained that being good-natured and friendly on the basketball court doesn't produce winners. You have to have a hard edge. Barkley says that you have to view the opposition as the enemy:

> *It's about competing. It's about hard work and kickin' butt. For forty-eight minutes it's about you and eleven other guys and doing what it takes to win, by any means necessary. That's all that matters. Everybody on the other team is your enemy—my enemy.*[1]

Barkley was a fierce competitor on offense. I regard him as the toughest player for his size (6'5") ever to take charge in the paint. His ability to score from the post, put back rebounds, and generally dominate in the lane was amazing. Unfortunately, Charles never attached the same importance to defense. In my view, it may have prevented him from playing on a championship team. And I told him so.

My first job as a game analyst on television was with Barkley's Philadelphia team. I told viewers when Charles was slow getting back on defense or giving his matchup too much shooting space. I extolled his great plays on offense, of course, but I didn't shy away from mentioning his deficiencies on D.

Prior to a game one night, Charles called to me from the other side of the Sixers locker room and said, in a voice just a decibel or so below a yell, "Jack, you're killing me on TV about my defense."

The locker room got very quiet, and the other players turned to listen to what my response would be. "Charles," I said, "I tell what I see. I tell it when you make great plays on offense, and I tell it when you loaf on defense. That's my job."

Teammates out of Charles' line of vision were smiling and nodding in agreement.

Charles responded, "I can't do both."

I said, "Your friend Michael Jordan does."

More head nodding from teammates.

This time, no response from Charles.

A true competitor prepares himself through hard, rigorous training, both physical and mental. He looks forward to meeting a tough opponent, one who will bring out the very best in him. Although they're engaging each other in something called a "game," the true competitor feels it in his gut as a battle for survival. And he lives for that feeling.

Looking back on my life as a high school basketball player in Milford, Connecticut, and Upper Darby, Pennsylvania, I know I didn't prepare myself adequately to compete. I wanted to win, of course, but I didn't do the necessary training and drill work on my own to lift my game to match that of better opponents. I'm not sure why. Maybe I was just a confused teenager behaving like your typical confused teenager.

College ball was different. A stint in the military (1943–1946) during World War II between my freshman and sophomore years at Saint Joseph's College (now Saint Joseph's University) radically altered my perspective on preparation and training—for basketball and just about everything else in life. When I turned 18 in 1943, I enlisted in the Navy's V-12 program for prospective officers. I was sent to Villanova University for a year of academic work, then to Columbia University's Midshipman's School before being commissioned in December 1944 as an ensign in the Navy.

I was hot to get into the action, so I volunteered for the Naval Combat Demolition Unit. Never heard of the NCDU? Well, it was the forerunner of the Navy SEALS. Now you probably see where I'm going with this.

The training at Fort Pierce, Florida, was physically intense and psychologically demanding, astonishingly so, more than I could ever have imagined in my wildest nightmares. Days began at the crack of dawn or earlier. On a typical day, after a quick breakfast, we'd be taken in a landing craft to a point a mile from shore and dropped off. Our mission: swim to the beach. The imperative "Don't be last!" always hung in the back of my mind, but I was actually more intent on being the first to reach shore.

After finishing our morning dip, the really tough part of the day started up with competitive fitness drills. ("Don't be last!") Following a quick lunch, we spent afternoons learning about explosives. (We were training to become members of an underwater *demolition* team, remember.) Every day our instructors would bark out some version of the same message: "Pay attention! No second chances on this job if you bleep up!"

You got the drift pretty quickly. I know I watched and listened very, *very* carefully. On completion of our eight-week training period, I was assigned to lead a platoon in UDT-30. (*UDT* stood for Underwater Demolition Team.) I wanted my platoon to be the best in our team, and I wanted UDT-30 to be the best of the 30 Underwater Demolition Teams in the Navy. The competition among the teams was fierce. Every man was highly focused. Morale was superb. This wasn't a game we were playing. We were preparing for war.

The job of the UDTs was to prepare the landing sites for assault forces that came ashore in Japan on D-Day. That meant that at dawn prior to the invasion, our teams would approach to within 500 yards of the beach in small attack boats and then swim, mostly under water, to the landing area. We would note on small slates hung from our necks any obstacles just under the water's surface such as railroad tracks pointing seaward, large hexagonal blocks of cement, barbed wire, large wooden "cribs" filled with cement blocks, big rocks, and other impediments that the enemy had planted in the sand to stop our incoming landing craft. When the recon was completed, our swimmers would return to the drop-off area, where we'd be picked up and taken back to our ships.

After compiling and analyzing the recon information, teams would return to the area at night to load explosives on or around the obstacles and activate time fuses. Then back to our drop-off points and back to our ships. As you can imagine, exact timing was essential.

UDT-30, along with the Navy's 29 other demolition teams, left San Diego in early August 1945 and headed west on destroyer transports to prepare for the invasion of Japan. Most of the guys on my team were in their late teens or early twenties. Scared? Not yet. We were too excited about our mission.

We had hardly begun our voyage to Japan when the U.S. dropped the atomic bomb on Hiroshima (August 6) and then Nagasaki (August 9), and the invasion that we'd been trained so hard for was put on hold. When Japan surrendered on August 15, it was canceled altogether. We returned to California and were reassigned to other duties. Sounds crazy, because the war was over, but my guys were keenly disappointed. We felt like we'd prepared hard for the biggest competition of all, only to have the other team fail to show up.

I never forgot the competitive lessons learned during my training with the NCDU. I applied them to my athletic endeavors when I returned to Saint Joe's. I applied them while playing six years in the Eastern Pro League following graduation; throughout my years of coaching high school, college, and professional basketball; and in amateur triathlon racing competitions.

Over the years, I learned firsthand that great competitors have the ability to perform consistently at the highest level and to make decisive plays when the game is on the line. But most important, they never, ever, *ever* give in. John Wooden, whom I regard as the greatest of all basketball teachers, explains how to identify competitive drive in a player:

> *Real competitors love a tough situation. That's when they focus better and function better. At moments of maximum pressure, they want the ball. ... The more difficult the game, the more they improve. True competitors derive their greatest pleasure out of playing against the very best opponents, even though they may be outscored. The difficult challenge provides rare opportunities to be their best.*[2]

A playoff game in 1977, when my Portland team went up against the Bulls in the old Chicago Stadium, bore out Wooden's premise perfectly. The pregame noise level was deafening as we were waiting to be introduced. Bill Walton, a prized pupil of Coach Wooden's at UCLA, leaned over and shouted in my ear, "This is the greatest, isn't it, Coach?" Bill loved the challenge of a big game.

Among the greatest competitors in today's game, I rate Kobe Bryant, Kevin Garnett, Manu Ginobili, LeBron James, and Dwyane Wade as the top five when a game is on the line. (Notice I used alphabetical order, guys. So please, no angry text messages.)

But, as the cliché goes, those guys stand on the shoulders of giants. Giants like George Mikan and those who follow.

George Mikan

The NBA's first big man (6'10", 245) and its first superstar, Mikan led the Minneapolis Lakers to four championships in the early 1950s and was the personification of a great competitor. Mikan had a power game, scoring with hook shots with either hand and with something brand-new to the game—the dunk. There was no stopping him. "Mr. Basketball" (a nickname he richly deserved) dominated the paint like no one before him. In fact, he was almost single-handedly responsible for the NBA's decision in 1951 to double the size of the paint, going from a six-foot lane to 12 feet (Knicks coach Joe Lapchick quite properly called it the "Mikan Rule") and later to the 16 feet it is today in the NBA.

But it wasn't his scoring ability that led *Sports Illustrated* to name Mikan the best player of the first 50 years of pro basketball. It was his fierce competitiveness.

Legendary Knicks coach (and old adversary of mine) Red Holzman once related a "Mikan moment" from the playoffs between the Lakers and the Rochester Royals in 1951 that exemplifies Mikan's tough mind-set. Red, the Royals' point guard, liked to come from the weak side to steal the ball or tie up unsuspecting big men. He hadn't had much success in the regular season pulling this off against Mikan, who typically held the ball high, clamped between his two large hands, and kept his elbows fully extended. But early in the opening game of the series, Red saw his chance, darted across the lane, and picked Mikan clean to set up a fast-break score for the Royals. Big George gave Red a scowl and shook a finger at him, as if to say, "Don't try that again."

Red saw another chance late in the close game and went after it. This time, Big George saw him coming and leveled him with an elbow that momentarily knocked Red out. When Red came out of his daze, he saw Mikan approaching him with his hand extended. Red shook his hand thinking it was a sporting gesture by Mikan. But as George came up close, he said, "I told you not to try that again, you SOB." Holzman took the hint and gave Mikan his requested space. Mr. Basketball had made his point loud and clear. (Even so, the Royals had enough to win that series without further larceny from Holzman and went on to win the franchise's only NBA championship.)

Jim Pollard, another member of that great Lakers team, confirmed what Holzman found out when I spoke with him at a Hall of Fame induction in the early 1990s. "I think George would have killed if necessary to win a game," Pollard said with a smile. "He just could not bear to lose, and he was the same at practice. I made sure I was always on his team in scrimmages."

I met George Mikan several times after his playing days were over and he'd served as the ABA's first commissioner. He was always affable and gracious, belying the strong, competitive fires that burned within him as a player. But on those occasions, I never tried to steal the ball from him either.

Bill Russell

Basketball's best competitors have an unyielding spirit that asserts itself in the most difficult situations. Bill Russell, whom I rate as the game's greatest center, typified that definition as well as any player I ever saw. Russell did whatever was needed to give his team a chance to win.

Need an example? I recall a game in Boston when my Sixers team had a two-point lead with less than 30 seconds left in the game. Sam Jones, the Celtics' best clutch shooter, missed a side court jumper, and we got the rebound with less than 24 seconds left to play. We kicked the ball out to Archie Clark, who was all alone near midcourt. Archie should have dribbled out the clock, but instead, he drove toward the basket for what he thought was an uncontested layup. From out of nowhere came Russell. He blocked Clark's "uncontested" layup, grabbed the rebound, and in the same motion fired a long pass to Sam Jones in the right corner. Sam didn't miss twice. The game went into OT, and the Celts won. I don't know how many players would have made the effort that Russell did on that play. Maybe none. But Russell's great competitiveness wouldn't let him give up on the play.

When Bill retired as player-coach of the Celtics with the incredible record of playing on 11 championship teams in 13 years (1956–67 through 1968–69), he told me that he wasn't interested in becoming a bench coach. A year later, he signed on as coach-general manager of the Seattle SuperSonics. When I saw him later that year in Buffalo, I said, "Bill, I thought you didn't want to coach?" He said, "I didn't, and I told that to [Sonics owner] Sam Schulman. But he thought I was just negotiating and kept coming back with a higher offer each time I said no. He finally reached a number I couldn't refuse."

Then Russ threw back his head and let out one of his signature throaty cackles.

Gospel: of all big men who ever worked the paint, Bill Russell was the greatest defender of all time. Period. Russ had an uncanny knack of timing his leap to block an opponent's shot. He almost always got the shot on the way up and then tipped it to his teammates to initiate a fast break. A special skill? Maybe, but I think it had as much, maybe more, to do with the man's unquenchable competitive drive.

The NBA didn't keep a blocked-shots stat during his career, so I asked Russ how many blocks he thought he might have averaged per game. He said that he had no idea. I said I thought it had to be double digits. Russ laughed: "Maybe in the first couple of years, but after that they stopped taking the ball to the basket on me."

Then, as an afterthought, he said, "But I do remember getting Luke Jackson [of *my* Sixers team, thank you very much] five times on the same possession." Another cackle.

A former teammate at Boston, Bailey Howell, once told me how the rest of the team waited to hear Russell throw up in the rest room before a big game. The other players, dressed and ready to go on the floor, would smile, knowing they would get a big game from Russ that night. Another measure of his competitive spirit, though the NBA didn't keep stats on that, either.

Russell didn't like to practice. He played all 48 minutes most nights and didn't like to expend energy at practice. Howell told me that if the team lost a couple of games in a row, a couple of the veteran players would go to Russ and say they thought the team needed him to practice that day. He would oblige, grudgingly, and almost always the Celts would start to win again.

Bill to me at the 2008 NBA Finals: "Dr. Jack, you're one of the few guys in the game I like. I don't know what that says about either of us."

Loud cackle.

Wilt Chamberlain

Wilt Chamberlain had an enormous impact on the game of basketball. Back when he was at Kansas, his Jayhawks wiped the floor with a good SMU team, after which Blackie Sherrod of the *Dallas Times Herald* headed his Sunday column with a memorable (and spot-on) lead: "If they let Wilt Chamberlain play basketball, they ought to let the Grand Canyon play ditch."

A superb physical specimen, Wilt was an enigma. He could dominate a basketball game like no other player, but he was also surprisingly insecure. He seemed always to be trying to prove himself anew, as if he hadn't already done so with his first power dunk in the NBA.

For instance, Wilt was very stats conscious. He seemed to decide in advance of a season on which particular statistic he was going to focus. He led the NBA in almost every category at some point in his career—scoring, rebounding, assists, field-goal percentage, and minutes played. Acquiring stats seemed to be Wilt's No. 1 priority. He never fouled out of a game, not ever, in high school, college, or the NBA.

Philadelphia's legendary statistician, Harvey Pollock, had his stats crew keep unofficial records that he would occasionally give to local beat writers. He remembers having a member of his crew keep blocked shots on occasion—it wasn't an official league stat at the time—and distinctly recalls Wilt racking up 25 blocks in a single game. Yes, *25*. That was before opposing players learned to steer clear of the big man when he had his game face on.

Chamberlain always seemed to know what his personal numbers were without looking at the stat sheet. I don't know this for a rock-solid fact, but it was rumored that he once approached the statisticians at halftime of a game, scanned the sheet, and demanded, "Who's keeping rebounds?" When the rebound keeper identified himself, Wilt said, "I have 12 rebounds, not 10. Put it down ...*12* rebounds." Stats man: "Okay, Wilt." Wilt stayed at the table until the statistician changed the number.

Chamberlain was a notoriously poor shooter from the line. When I was GM of the Sixers, Wilt shot 44 percent (1967) and 38 percent (1968). In that second season, I told our coach, Alex Hannum, that I thought I could help Wilt to shoot better free throws. Alex told me to go ahead and wished me luck. Wilt agreed to give it a try, and we met on the court early in the afternoon of a game day.

I instructed him on a two-hand underhand delivery, with the ball held evenly on the sides, arms extended straight downward. Then, with a slight knee dip, release the ball with slight reverse spin over the front of the rim. Wilt grasped the technique quickly and before long was making 8 out of 10, then 10 out of 10, then 20–24 out of 25. After about 40 minutes, I said, "Wilt, you've got it! You can do this." His response: "Yeah, I'm making them now, but wait 'til the game. I won't make them in the game."

He was right.

I will always remember Wilt best for a game that to this day still sticks in my mind—and craw: Game 7, 1968 Eastern Conference Finals, Sixers vs. Celtics. Trying to defend our 1967 NBA championship, we'd established a 3–1 playoff lead over the Celtics. Then we lost at home and at Boston to force a decisive Game 7 in Philadelphia.

The game was tight through the first half, although Wilt was struggling against Russell. (Who didn't?) Then, in the second half, Wilt did not attempt a single field goal ... not one. Chamberlain, who had once scored 100 points in a game, and who had once averaged 50 points a game for a season, *did not take one single shot* in the second half of a decisive Game 7 in the NBA Playoffs, a game that his team lost, 100–96.

Asked by reporters for an explanation after the game, Chamberlain said that his coach had not told him to shoot.

No, he didn't.

Alex Hannum defended Wilt publicly for not shooting in that game, but privately he told me, "I can't take the big guy anymore." Soon after the season, Alex left the Sixers to become coach of Oakland in the ABA.

Wilt appeared keenly interested in the selection process to replace Hannum. He stopped by the Sixers office frequently to ask how I was progressing. Then, at a meeting with owner Irv Kosloff and me, Wilt proposed the idea of him as player-coach, with me as his assistant to take care of the Xs and Os. I liked the idea. I reasoned Wilt would play very hard because his name was on the line and also to show that he could do what Bill Russell was doing at Boston.

Wilt said that he was going to the West Coast for a week. We agreed to meet again on his return. Koz and I agreed we'd go along with Wilt's suggested plan. But when we met again after Chamberlain's return from the coast, Wilt announced that he was no longer interested in being player-coach of the Sixers. Instead, he demanded a trade to a West Coast team or threatened to jump to an ABA team.

I was stunned ... and angry. When Wilt had left the room, I said to Koz, "To hell with him. Let him go." We made a deal—one that will forever live in infamy among die-hard Sixers fans: Wilt for Archie Clark, Darrell Imhoff, and Jerry Chambers—and that's how Wilt Chamberlain became a Laker for the rest of his career.

Now, with Philadelphia's superstar departed for the West Coast, I faced a really hard job in finding a coach. Finally, as the start of the season rapidly approached, Kosloff asked me to take the job for a year to give us a little breathing room while we continued to search for a new coach.

I agreed, and that fall I began my first of 20 seasons as a head coach in the NBA.

Oscar Robertson

Oscar Robertson grew up in a disadvantaged family in Indianapolis, where he attended the all-black Crispus Attucks High School. His Attucks teams won back-to-back state titles and 45 consecutive games during Robertson's years there. After high school, he went on to the University of Cincinnati and set out immediately to dominate the collegiate game.

The Saint Joe's team I coached played Robertson's Bearcats in his first full season (1958). Shortly before we played them, I went to Madison Square Garden in New York City to scout Cincy's game against Seton Hall. What I saw took my breath away. Robertson scored 56 points—two points more than the entire Seton Hall team—in a spectacular, spellbinding performance. He scored on 22 of 32 attempts from the field and made all 12 of his free throws.

Oscar made the game look easy. He was able to get wherever he wanted on the court with the ball, most often into the 15-foot area. Once there, he either drove to the hoop or pulled up for short-range jumpers. He released that shot from slightly behind his head while sticking his elbow in the face of his defender. How does a defender challenge a shot like that? Not without drawing a foul or losing a tooth. Or both.

On defense, Robertson seemed to be everywhere at once, stealing balls, deflecting passes, and rebounding missed shots. From there, Oscar was a one-man fast break, pushing the ball up court on the dribble, then either assisting open teammates or scoring himself. Needless to say, the New York sports media, always on the lookout for the next big thing, raved over this new phenom of college basketball.

In preparing my team for the game against Cincinnati, I geared our defense against Robertson. I had a one-on-one matchup with my best defender, double-team traps when he put the ball on the floor, and multiple zones ready for the Big O. We may have contained him a tad. He didn't score 50 points, but Robertson still dominated the game and assured his team of the win. Much later, after his glorious playing career was over, Oscar says this of himself:

I was an intense competitor. My face could be calm and smooth, just as it could contort. I talked to the refs. I was competitive. The truth is, most of the time, when I looked mad, I was mad at myself. I knew I should have been doing better. But I was a rough player. I knocked guys around and got knocked right back.[3]

Somewhere along the way, Red Holzman said, "Oscar acquired a competitive spirit that always made him fight to be the best. He was a young man with a mission. No one was going to take that away from him without a fight.... I always felt he played like someone desperately trying to prove something. He always seemed to be responding to some inner challenge, and everyone was a threat to whatever he was seeking."[4]

After I retired from active coaching, I was asked to coach one of the teams in the 1991 Legends Game played during All-Star Game weekend in Charlotte, North Carolina. Frank McGuire, the legendary college coach who also made his NBA mark with the old Philadelphia Warriors, coached the other team.

Frank and I had decided beforehand to match up similar age groups to reduce the possibility of overexertion by the more senior players. Oscar, clearly one of the most senior members on either team, was on McGuire's squad. Both teams had more "young" players that year, so I named a starting lineup of that group and sent my list to McGuire so that he could start a comparable age group. McGuire complied. However, when he told his team who was starting, Robertson told McGuire that if he didn't start, he wouldn't play. Oscar, then in his early fifties, simply couldn't accept being anything but a starter. So, in order to accommodate Oscar, I also started an older player, the former Celtic great Sam Jones, and the game went on.

Jerry West

A country boy from rural Cabin Creek, West Virginia, Jerry West gave new meaning to the term "all-purpose player" at the University of West Virginia. In his senior year, West, a 6'3" guard, averaged 29.3 points, *16.5 rebounds*, and 4.3 assists from his 2-guard position. My Saint Joe's Hawks met West Virginia in West's junior year in the 1959 NCAA Eastern Regional playoffs held at Charlotte, North Carolina. I had an exceptional defender in Joe Spratt, who matched West in size, quickness, and determination. Spratt did a great job, and midway through the second half, my Hawks held a double-digit lead on West Virginia.

But with about eight minutes remaining in the game, Spratt fouled out. West immediately took over the game, scoring 19 of his 36 points. He played like a man possessed—scoring, rebounding, getting steals, handing out assists, doing everything but reffing the game. The Mountaineers won in the final minute, 95–92. West Virginia advanced to the NCAA Finals that season (1959) but lost to the University of California, 71–70. West was named tournament MVP.

West teamed with the great Elgin Baylor on the Los Angeles Lakers beginning in 1960 to become the second-highest scoring tandem in league history. In 1961–62, they combined for 69.1 points a game, second in league annals only to the 72.3 point total compiled by Philadelphia Warriors teammates Wilt chamberlain and Paul Arizin in 1962, the year that Chamberlain himself averaged a phenomenal 50.4 points a game.

West made so many game-winning shots that he became known as "Mr. Clutch." Look closely at the NBA logo. That guy dribbling the ball? Jerry West.

While I did Miami Heat telecasts during Riley's tenure there, we sometimes chatted about "the old days," and I asked him about the 1972 Lakers, who ran off a 33-game win streak on their way to the NBA title. Wilt, Gail Goodrich, Happy Hairston, Jim McMillian, and West formed the starting lineup. A reserve on that team, Pat talked about how much fun the winning streak was. Pat said that when they got to the Finals, Jerry, who'd been to the Finals seven times without a ring to show for it, thought something—a jinx!—would happen to deprive them of the championship, even though the Lakers were by common agreement the best team in the league. Then when the Knicks won Game 1 in L.A., Jerry was sure of it. Riley told me, "I never saw him so nervous."

Only when the Lakers won the next four straight and put the "jinx" to rest did Jerry relax.

Rick Barry

Like all great competitors, Rick Barry used the challenge of an opponent to bring out his best. For instance, many NBA players avoided taking the ball to the basket against Boston when Bill Russell ruled the defensive paint, but Barry would never be denied.

Teammate Nate Thurmond, himself a Hall of Fame center, described how Barry competed against the Celts and Russell when Rick first came into the league in 1966:

He wasn't about to let anyone get the best of him. I remember once Bill Russell blocked one of his shots in Boston. Of course, Russell did that to everyone.... I knew it wouldn't discourage Rick. I knew it would make him determined. I said to myself, "Russ baby, you're gonna have to do it ten times more if you hope to make it stick." ... Sure enough, Rick went right back at Russell. Again and again. He kept going at him and going at him. Even Russell couldn't handle him. No one could.[5]

Bill Bradley

First at Princeton, then with the New York Knicks, Bill Bradley had limited speed and even less jumping ability, but he was a great shot-maker and passer and played with a point guard's mentality from the forward's slot. Over and over again in practice, Bradley worked on the shots he knew he would get in the game until he had them down near perfect.

The result? In an NCAA tournament game against my Saint Joe's team in 1963, Bradley made 12 of 21 field-goal attempts and dropped all 16 of his free throws. We won in OT only after Bradley fouled out.

Along with absolute determination and discipline, Bradley believed that competitive drive was the mental quality that enabled players to endure the pain of getting into condition to play a demanding game. Here's how he explains it:

You can't lead the fast break or tear down twenty rebounds in a game if you can't run and jump without fatigue. Getting into shape and pushing the body to new levels every day is a mental activity. When you believe you can't do another lap or another pushup or another abdominal crunch, your mind forces you to go ahead. When your wind is short and you have a pain in your side from running, only the mind can get you to withstand the pain and go on.[6]

When you lose because you haven't made the mental effort, Bradley concludes, you have no one to blame but yourself.

Bradley was drafted by the New York Knicks in 1966 and, after a year at Oxford University as a Rhodes Scholar, he began his NBA career in the 1967–68 season. He started out as a 2-guard but had difficulty defending quicker matchups and getting a shot for himself. He played in only 45 games and averaged 8 points. Not an auspicious beginning. The next season, Red Holzman switched Bradley to small forward, and his career took off. Bradley beat out Cazzie Russell to break into the starting lineup. He played in all 82 games, averaged 12.4 points, and the Knicks became an immediate title contender. In 1970 they were NBA champions.

Although Bradley played alongside great players like Willis Reed, Walt Frazier, and Dave De Busschere on the Knicks championship teams of 1970 and 1973, I considered Bradley the team's most valuable player because of his selfless attitude, his ability to move without the ball, his persistent screen-setting that got his teammates easy hoops, his clutch shooting, and his feisty, help-out defense.

Holzman was probably closer to the mark when he pointed out Bradley's competitiveness. Red often spoke to me about Bradley's toughness and willingness to play when most players would have been sick in bed:

> *Bill had a tremendous ability to play with pain and discomfort. Once in San Diego we had a lot of players either sick or hurt. In the locker room Bill looked green and feverish. He threw up a couple of times. "Maybe you should go back to the hotel and sleep it off," I advised Bill. "No, Red, I'll be all right. You can start me." The game started and Bill played. Bill vomited about six times on the court – "Woosh, Woosh." Players were ducking to get out of the way. He was sick but he was playing great. Although we were short on manpower, his extra effort made up for it, enabling us to win.*[7]

John Havlicek

John Havlicek, the great Celtics forward from 1963 to 1978, could run forever and not show any indication of fatigue. I mean, the man hardly worked up a sweat during a game, his color never changed, and he never seemed to be breathing hard. Hondo kept himself in superb physical condition and challenged opponents to compete with him in running the floor.

Bradley describes how this Hall of Famer wore down his opponents and sapped them of their competitive drive:

My toughest opponent, John Havlicek, was a true genius when it came to using conditioning as a weapon. His goal was to get his opponent to give up, to stop overcoming fatigue and stop pushing himself. Havlicek saw it as a matter of who gives up first. [8]

A Bradley-Havlicek matchup was always a classic. Neither even knew the meaning of "give up." Every possession was an illustration of an intense physical and mental challenge. Basketball purists came to their games just to see them battle each other for a fleeting opportunity to score. I tell you, it was beautiful to watch.

Havlicek once told me that he attempted to destroy his opponents mentally through sheer physical discipline: "You'll pass out before you're overworked, but most people don't know that. They think they're overworked, so they stop. They could have kept going, but they didn't. They weren't beat physically. They were beat mentally."

I asked John how this amazing dedication to conditioning got started.

"When I was a kid," he said, "I didn't have a bicycle and my friends did. So, when we went someplace, they rode their bikes and I ran alongside them. I got so that I could keep up without really being tired."

Remember that the next time you think about blowing off a workout at your gym.

Spud Webb

Anthony Jerome "Spud" Spud Webb, who played point guard for Atlanta through the late 1980s, stood all of 5'6" and weighed 130 pounds—not exactly your standard NBA dimensions. But the size deficit didn't keep Spud from playing with ferocious intensity. I admired him for his no-nonsense style, his overall aggressiveness, and especially his willingness to take the ball to the rim against the league's giants. Spud describes his mind-set when he came into the league:

> *One lesson you learn quickly in the NBA: nobody gives a rookie anything. You've got to prove what you can do, and show how tough you are right from the beginning, or the veterans will eat you alive.... No matter who I was playing against, no matter how famous he was or how tight a friend he was, I had to go out and beat him for my team. Even if it was my brother, I'd try to kill him.... [Y]ou've got to have killer instincts. Get your guy down and bury him.*[9]

Not exactly what you'd expect to hear from someone going head-to-head—well, head-to-chest—in a hard, physical game in which he was spotting everybody nearly a foot and a hundred pounds. But with that attitude, Spud Webb turned himself into a winner.

Calvin Murphy

Another feisty, small (5'9") point guard, Calvin Murphy played college ball at Niagara University before coming to the NBA in 1970. Murph was lightning quick and could stop and pop with the best. He averaged just under 18 points a game for his career at San Diego and Houston, and he was voted into the Basketball Hall of Fame in 1993. But to me, it wasn't just his scoring touch that made Murphy such a valued player. It was his toughness, his nonstop competitiveness.

Rudy Tomjanovich, Murphy's coach, calls Calvin "one of the fiercest competitors I've been around." Rudy elaborated: "I'll never forget one time in Atlanta when he had the flu and spent most of the day vomiting. Calvin didn't want to let the team down by staying in his room. He decided to give it a try and wound up being our leading scorer, making the game-winning shot at the buzzer."[10]

Murphy never backed down from a physical confrontation. Portland players recounted to me an incident when Murph and Sidney Wicks, the Blazers 6' 9" forward, got into it in a game the year before I became coach. The story that I got was that Murphy tattooed Wicks about five times to the head and body before Sidney landed a punch.

Once, after I took over as coach, Murph challenged Maurice Lucas, our team's enforcer, to duke it out as the teams left the court at halftime. Luke brushed aside the challenge and said to me later, "I know all about Murphy. I'm not crazy enough to get into it with that little guy."

Wise decision.

Willis Reed

Competitive drive is typically accompanied with a willingness to tolerate pain and to play despite it. NBA Hall of Famer Willis Reed was the prototype of such a player. "[He] had an incredible ability to tolerate pain," Red Holzman said of his pillar of strength. "Willis had his nose broken in a few games, and each time it happened he returned to the bench and told Danny Whelan [the team trainer] to pop his nose back in. And then he went out again to play."[11]

The picture of a crippled Willis Reed hobbling onto the court to join his teammates scant minutes before the opening tip in Game 7 of the 1973 NBA Finals against the Lakers will forever be etched in my memory. Reed, matched up against Wilt Chamberlain, scored on his first two field-goal attempts—his only points of the game—to give his team the psychological boost it needed to close out the Lakers.

"There isn't a day in my life," Reid said more than two decades later, "that people don't remind me of that game."

Reggie Miller

A certain future Hall of Famer and star of the Indiana Pacers for 18 seasons, Reggie Miller said that his competitive juices really got stirred when playoff time rolled around: "I turn into a different person. I get cranky, moody. I get evil. I don't know how I turn it on or off, but it's Reggie Time."[12]

A perfect example of "Reggie Time" came in Game 1 of the 1995 NBA playoffs in New York when the Pacers trailed the Knicks by 6 points with 16.4 seconds to play. On the Pacers' possession, Reggie knocked down a 3-pointer, then stole the inbounds pass, dribbled back to the 3-point line, and hit another trey to tie the score. On the ensuing Knicks possession, John Starks was fouled and missed both free throws. Miller rebounded the second miss and was fouled. Reggie made both of his free throws for a 107–105 lead, and New York failed to score on its last attempt.

For New York Knicks fans of a certain age, those 16.4 seconds live on as an eternity in their nightmares.

Kareem & Wilt

Among great competitors, certain head-to-head encounters often drive the two heads involved to new competitive heights.

Kareem Abdul-Jabbar, the leading scorer in NBA history (38,387 points, which works out to 24.6 per game), faced such a challenge when playing against Wilt Chamberlain. The two had developed a special relationship when Kareem (then Lew Alcindor) was a young high school star in New York City and Chamberlain was a dominant player in the NBA. Chamberlain befriended the young man and brought him into his social circle in New York City. When the UCLA star entered the NBA with the Milwaukee Bucks as a 21-year-old in 1969—he wouldn't change his name until two years later—Wilt was still at the top of his game. The rookie feared that Chamberlain would dominate him, and the challenge stoked his competitive fires. Kareem remembered how it was when the two titans clashed:

[We] had a truly fierce competition. Later, after he retired, he said I played extra hard against him, as if I had something to prove. He is right. I did play extra hard against him. If I hadn't, he would have dominated me, embarrassed me in front of the league, and undermined my whole game and career. I'd seen him play too long to think I could just go out there and play and not be overwhelmed. Wilt demanded the best, and I gave it to him with a vengeance.[13]

Hakeem & The Admiral

Hakeem Olajuwon, one of the finest human beings I ever met in the NBA, was a fierce competitor whose game got a special boost when he was matched against San Antonio Spurs veteran David Robinson.

In 1995, Robinson was voted the NBA's most valuable player, and Olajuwon was not happy with the choice, feeling that he had played better than Robinson during the regular season. So Hakeem was especially motivated when the Rockets played the Spurs in the 1995 NBA Western Conference Finals. In a six-game series, which the Rockets won 4–2, Olajuwon averaged 35 points a game. He totally dominated Robinson. Olajuwon said that his great series was a direct result of what Robinson brought out in him:

*Because David is a great shot blocker and an excellent athlete, I had to play **beyond** my best to get by him. I used moves I never used before **because I had to**. Without them David would have stopped me. He made me work for every shot. If I made a mistake he was going to block it. He pushed me to a higher level.*[14]

Larry Bird

The great Celtics forward was a master innovator who made up ways to win games on the fly. Sometimes with a high-arching shot at the buzzer, sometimes with an offensive rebound and put-back score, sometimes with a steal of a pass, and occasionally with a spinning shot off the glass from the post position. You never knew how it would happen, just that it probably would. Why? Because of the competitive spirit that fired his on-court imagination.

Celtics great Bob Cousy, a television broadcaster during the years Bird played, has this to say about Bird's inborn competitive spirit: "He is always diving for loose balls, whether there are two minutes left in the game and he's up by 20 or the score is tied in the final 10 seconds. It's the only way he can play. It overshadows good sense, but it's effective. If that kind of competitive spirit is your bag, you really don't have control over it."[15]

Once, after a game in which Bird had knocked down a 3-pointer to beat my Portland team at the buzzer, I asked Celts 2-guard Dennis Johnson if Bird's winning shot came out of a play that Coach K. C. Jones had drawn up. "Nope," Dennis answered, "we just get the ball to Larry at times like that, and he works it out."

In another Blazers-Celtics game, a loose ball was rolling in my direction as I knelt on the sidelines in front of the Portland bench. I could see Bird hustling toward the ball and positioned myself to break his fall if the ball went out of bounds. Bird arrived under full throttle just as the ball crossed the sideline and into my hands. He knocked me through two rows of seats. I literally saw stars. Then I heard the Birdman say, "You all right, Coach?"

After the game Jim Lynam, my assistant, asked me if I was really all right. I assured him I was. Lynam said, "He gave you some hit, and I think he did it on purpose. He had his eyes right on you all the way." When I declined to believe Bird's personal intent, Lynam said, "Hey, you're part of the opposition. You're the enemy to someone like Bird."

Larry traces his fierce competitiveness back to growing up in a family in which older brothers pushed him athletically and helped stimulate his competitive juices:

I loved to compete. I was always trying to keep up with my older brothers, Mark and Mike. When I was little, they were always bigger and stronger, and they were constantly chal-

lenging me. I wanted so much to keep up with them. I hated to lose, and it seemed like I always lost to my brothers. It was a lousy feeling that I never forgot.[16]

Bird never took anything for granted. As great a shooter as he was, he always warmed up for a game the same way, starting with a regimen that began two hours before game time. It was just the Birdman and a ball boy on the court with a rack of balls. Bird started around the basket, shooting three six-footers. He then moved out to 15 feet, straight on, then to each side. Next he moved to midrange, then to 3-point distance.

The ball boy stood under the basket, catching Bird's shots as they swished through the net. As soon as the shot left Bird's hand, the ball boy fired a pass to Bird, who had moved to another position and readied himself to shoot again. There were typically two sounds: the swish of the ball as it went through the net and the slap of the ball in Bird's hands as he received the pass from the ball boy.

As an opposing coach, I watched that routine many times and seldom did I see Bird miss more than a couple of shots in the 45 minutes he was on the court. But those off-the-mark efforts clearly irked him. Bird was getting himself ready to compete in a basketball game, but it was more like he was preparing to go to war.

One year we trooped into the Garden early for a game accompanied by the "swish, slap" sounds coming from the dimly lit court. A rookie player on my team asked me what was going on. I told him to walk down to the court and watch Larry Bird in action: "He's getting ready for you."

Bill Walton, who played on Boston's great 1986 championship team, says this about his former teammate:

[Bird] was the antithesis of the player so prevalent in the NBA today. Most of the guys in the league these days think basketball is nothing more than running up and down the court and shooting jump shots. Not Bird. He was the ultimate competitor. No matter what it took, Bird would do it—or destroy himself trying. Despite the wear and tear on

his body, especially his back, he never avoided his respon-
sibility to the team or tired of his role as Celtics leader and
captain.[17]

Magic Johnson

Magic Johnson and Larry Bird first squared off in the 1979 NCAA Championship, when Magic's Michigan State Spartans beat Bird's Indiana State Sycamores. The rivalry continued in the NBA, where they led their teams to a combined eight championships (five for Magic's Lakers, three for Bird's Celtics). Head-to-head when their teams faced each other in three NBA Finals, Magic had a 2–1 edge over the Birdman. Throughout the 1980s, either the Lakers or Celtics were champions every year but two: 1983 (Philadelphia) and 1989 (Detroit). It seemed like Magic and Bird had taken up permanent residence on center stage.

When Magic came to the Lakers in 1980, my former assistant, Jack McKinney, was starting his first season in L.A. as head coach. McKinney told me during training camp that he was making the 6'9" Johnson his point guard. I questioned the decision, thinking Magic might have trouble handling the ball against quicker, smaller guards. McKinney responded that he had never coached anyone who could see the floor and make the scoring play like Magic.

As we all soon found out, Jack proved to be only 100 percent right.

But for a short while there, it looked like Magic was going to prove *me* right. In his rookie season, he did have problems with quick defensive guards, and he had a weak left-hand dribble. In a game in Portland, we forced Magic into nine turnovers by making him dribble to his left and then jamming him with a second defender. Our success was short-lived: by the following season, Magic could dribble equally well with his left and right hands.

Every season after that, Johnson added a dimension to his game to fix what he considered a weakness. He was an inconsistent perimeter shooter when he first came into the league, but he was excellent from 3-point range by the time he retired. He also developed an effective skyhook so that he could take smaller guards—which included just about everyone—into the low post when his team needed a clutch field goal. And right from the start, of course, he was the master of the open court.

I saw Magic one summer and asked him what he had been working on. He gave me his patented big smile and said, "I've got a surprise for you this year, Coach." I had to wait until the regular season, when he dropped in a sweeping hook shot from the paint, to see his new weapon. As he trotted into the backcourt, he looked over at me, gave me that big smile again, and nodded his head as if to say, "That's how I spent my summer vacation."

Pat Riley, Lakers coach from 1984 through 1990, developed a special relationship with Johnson, whom he called "Buck." Riley was amazed at Magic's competitiveness. "I never saw anything like it," he told me years later. "Practice is just like a game to Buck. *He will not lose.* He just will *not* lose."

On November 7, 1991, Johnson announced to a stunned world that he was HIV positive and would be retiring from basketball. Still a competitor to the core, Johnson didn't give up that battle either. At this writing, 19 years later, Magic is still competing, alive and well, running his business empire, and serving as vice president of the Lakers.

Michael Jordan

True story: Michael Jordan was cut from the Laney High School (Wilmington, North Carolina) varsity team as a sophomore (1978–79). You read right: *cut.*

MJ never forgot it. With that snub by the varsity coach constantly in his mind, Jordan played with fury on the jayvee team that season. Over the course of the next year, Michael grew four inches and became the star on the varsity for the next two seasons. He played well enough in his junior year to get an invitation to Dean Smith's basketball camp on the UNC campus. Jordan's athleticism and tremendous intensity were immediately apparent to Smith and his assistants, who decided then and there to offer Michael a scholarship to North Carolina after he finished high school in 1981.

But other people noticed Michael's performance at Smith's camp, and Jordan's name vaulted to near the top of the national list of rising high school seniors. Later that same summer, he was a last-minute invitee to Howard Garfinkel's prestigious 5-Star Basketball Camp, where he was a sensation.

The word was out. High-powered basketball colleges across the country pushed MJ to the top of their wish list. But playing for Dean Smith at UNC had been a dream of Jordan's for a while. That, along with Michael's fondness for Tar Heels assistant Roy Williams, shut out the other top colleges hoping to haul him in.

Certainly his physical growth and sheer talent had much to do with Michael's sudden emergence as a dominant player. But I think a bigger factor was his constant intensity stoked by that failure to make the varsity as a sophomore. He now played the total game at both ends of the floor, constantly harassing his man, stealing balls, blocking shots, rebounding the ball and jetting into the front court, then assisting teammates for scores, or finishing with thunder dunks at the hoop.

Much has been made of the 1984 NBA Draft in which Portland took Sam Bowie second (Houston had taken Hakeem Olajuwon with the top pick), leaving MJ available for Chicago at the third pick. Believe me, I still hear about it. Our reason for picking Bowie over Jordan was that we already had Jim Paxson and Clyde Drexler—very good players—at Michael's 2-guard position, but we badly needed a center.

A rational, well-considered decision?

Sure, and the biggest mistake in NBA history.

Michael has never passed up an opportunity to chide me about it. Later on, I was a staff member at the fantasy camps that MJ ran for 30-and-older basketball players. When Michael introduced me to the camp on the opening session, he always added, "and I want to thank Dr. Jack for not picking me at Portland, so I could have all of those great years with the Bulls."

You're welcome, Michael. You're very welcome.

The late David Halberstam noted that Michael never missed an opportunity to remind *someone* that they had erred in assessing his talent. When Jordan signed a shoe contract with Nike years later, he teased Sonny Vaccaro, the company's top basketball talent scout, for not inviting MJ to the Dapper Dan game, a prestige gathering at Pittsburgh of the top high school players in the country, the same year Michael had gone to the Dean Smith camp. [18]

Say this for MJ, he has a good memory.

"Michael had to be the first at everything," James Worthy, a teammate of Michael's at North Carolina, once told me. "Coach Smith always made us make a certain number of consecutive free throws before leaving practice. Michael would sprint to a basket to start shooting before anyone else. When he made the designated number before anyone else, it allowed him to be first in the shower room, first dressed, first out of the gym, first back at the dorm, first into the dining room, and first to look over the selection of steaks."

Worthy smiled and shook his head: "That routine was important to Michael. He took pride and delight in beating all of us on a daily basis."

At *everything*.

Jordan expected—make that *demanded*—his teammates to be as competitive as he was. He rode them hard if he thought they weren't competing up to his standards. Michael said, "I was always testing that aspect of my teammates' character, on and off the court. You pick on them and see if they will stand up. If they don't take it, you know you can trust them to come through when the pressure is on in the game."[19]

MJ was the catalyst for six NBA championship teams in Chicago. Except for a two-year hiatus when he tried his hand at baseball, MJ might well have led the Bulls to eight straight crowns, matching that of the Auerbach/Russell Celtics.

You probably won't be shocked to hear that I believe Michael Jordan was the greatest competitor ever to lace up a pair of sneakers.

Most great competitors are born with their competitiveness and then see it grow as they face greater challenges. But I also think that individuals can acquire a competitive personality by building their command of particular skills. Improvement gives them confidence, and confidence enables them to be successful in tough competition.

In other words, you can teach yourself to be a competitor.

I've watched this process take place with many players at all levels: high school, college, and professional. It applies to both offense and defense, and it begins on the practice floor with specific skill drills focusing on footwork, agility, hand-eye coordination, body position, and balance. Often this building comes in a one-on-one tutorial, just player and coach. When a good, motivated player senses that what he's learning will make him better, he'll work ceaselessly until he acquires the necessary level of performance.

Then the skill must be tested by competition on the practice floor. I preferred to isolate the "student" against one of his peers, setting up game situations, and then letting them go at it. Success is seldom immediate. Numerous repetitions are required. The player may need to have his confidence bolstered, but if he's had some success, he won't give up on his quest to fully develop his new skill.

The next step is to integrate the skill into the player's game on a team basis. Controlled scrimmaging provides an ideal setting for this to occur. Then comes the qualifying test, using the new skill capably in a game. Often it takes a while: a player might start slow and only bring it together over time, often beginning with summer workouts, then training camp, preseason games, and well into the NBA 82-game schedule.

That evolution takes physical skills, of course, but it also takes dedication and a passion to compete. The great ones, who already have an abundance of ability, never stop working to get better.

An example: after he had been banged around by more physical opponents in his first NBA seasons, Hall of Famer Bob Pettit, one of the game's greatest power forwards, found that concentrated weight work enabled him to become a much-improved player.

Another example: Larry Bird told me that his high school coach took him aside at one point and told him that if he really wanted to become a player, he had to learn to shoot better and to be aggressive going after his shot. Bird dedicated himself to improving his shooting technique to the point that, as he caught a pass, he automatically turned the ball in his hands so that his fingers were always placed across the seams of the ball before he shot it. I did that myself as a player, and always taught that to shooters, but Bird is the only player I know who did that every time he touched the ball.

People today mostly know Phil Jackson as the coach of 11 NBA championship teams rather than as the excellent off-the-bench defender for the great Knicks teams that I coached against in the late 1970s. Phil was the first big forward I ever saw who would leave his man to double team the opposing point guard in the backcourt and then recover to get back on his own man when the ball was in the front court. Very imaginative, very effective.

Coach Phil Jackson has brought the same creativity to his teams. As a radio and television analyst, I covered many Bulls and Lakers games that Jackson coached. I've been impressed by the way his teams played with intensity and a sense of purpose. Jackson seems to get his players to play with what he calls a "single-minded willfulness." He teaches them to compete, especially on defense.

Playing inspired defense, Jackson said, is a matter of will: "What are you *willing* to do as a group to help each other out? What are you *willing* to do as an individual to put the clamps on the opponent you're guarding?"

Jackson also believes that players must develop a "warrior mentality" if they are to compete effectively. Those who take on the warrior spirit play with a "sense of urgency" and with intensity:

> *Less talented teams with greater intensity defeat more talented teams all the time. Matching intensity does not mean initiating aggressive frenetic action. That often causes play-*

ers to go out of control, out of character. Matching intensity means competing with full alertness, with a commitment to sound principles of execution.[20]

Jackson will sometimes allow his teams to go through sluggish offensive segments without response. He's told me, "I wanted them to play through it," or "I wanted them to figure it out for themselves." But if there's the slightest lapse of defensive effort, Jackson leaps from the bench, signals for a timeout, and then blisters the culprits for their laxity. This is Phil Jackson's way of teaching his players how to compete. I think it's a good one.

Pat Riley, whether in Los Angeles, New York, or Miami, always demanded a full, all-out aggressiveness from his players, and he got it. His practices began with a routine that he learned from his high school coach, Walt Przbylo, called "backs to the bleachers." This was a meeting with the players, who sat in the bleachers or side court benches, while the coach critiqued recent team and player performances and stated the emphasis for practice that day.

I watched those meetings at Miami several times, and I was struck by the thoroughness of Riley's preparation, the rapt attention of the players, and the total response to the objectives of the practice as Riley had outlined them before floor work began. Players crisply carried out drills with focus and intensity. Nothing but maximum effort was permitted. Scrimmages were aggressive but controlled. Learning segments were well organized and taught effectively. Riley loved practice, and it showed. His players? Maybe not so much, but they understood it was the key to winning.

Doc Rivers, who played for Riley in New York, told me that the words players most dreaded to hear from Riles were, "There's been a little slippage." The players knew this meant that their next practice session would be particularly punishing.

Riley *taught* players how to compete.

At Portland, I met with every player at the beginning of the summer of 1977, the year I took over as coach. I started with Bill Walton. We met at his home, where I briefed him on the kind of game I wanted to play and his role in it. At the time, Bill had just had surgery on his right wrist and had his arm in a sling. He agreed with the offensive and defensive principles that I described, nodding his head frequently. I also talked to him about his own offensive skills. Coaching against the Blazers and Walton, I noticed that although he was a magnificent passer, a solid defender, a great rebounder, and a viscous shot-blocker, his shooting was mostly restricted to turn-around jump shots from 12 to 15 feet. I felt he could do much better by taking the ball into the paint and finishing with a jump hook, and I suggested that he work on those moves when his arm healed.

"One more thing, Coach," Bill said as I stood up to leave, "don't assume we know anything."

What he was saying—or at least what I heard—was that the Blazers *wanted* to be coached. Music to any coach's ears: I was walking on air as I left his house.

I stayed in Portland for another three weeks that summer while the Blazers participated in the NBA Draft, after which my assistant Jack McKinney and I conducted the team's rookie camp. Walton was a frequent observer at the workouts, and although I chatted with him often, I didn't see him on the court until the first day of training camp in the fall.

Bill didn't say anything, not "Hey, look at this," but began his prepractice warm-up with a series of jump hooks in the lane—using both left and right hands—and shooting with unerring accuracy. The demonstration wasn't lost on his teammates. Those who had played with him the previous two seasons looked at each other knowingly. Those new to the team gave "that's pretty nice stuff" expressions. I nodded in approval when I caught Bill's eye.

Walton was showing his teammates that he wanted to improve, that he wanted to compete at a higher level. In retrospect, that simple jump-hook warm-up drill that Bill performed on the first day of training camp was the first step toward what was to be the Blazers' championship season.

Becoming a winner at any level of athletic activity—amateur or professional—in any sport, requires that you know how to compete. You know how to give everything to reach your goal—winning.

Each of the players I've talked about here was, of course, immensely talented. But equally—perhaps more—important, each was an amazingly strong competitor. Each played with maximum energy in every game. None ever backed down from a challenge. All were "team" players. They all put winning first. They are role models for anyone who wants to know how to succeed, in sports and in life.

Sometimes it takes a pair of great competitors to make a championship team—like Shaquille O'Neal and Kobe Bryant with the Lakers and Shaq and Dwyane Wade with the Miami Heat.

Sometimes it takes a trio, like San Antonio has with Tim Duncan, Manu Ginobili and Tony Parker or Kevin Garnett, Paul Pierce, and Ray Allen with the 2008 NBA champion Celtics.

Sometimes, it takes all five and a couple off the bench who just won't be denied, like I had with my Portland Trailblazers championship team in 1977.

A coach must have at least one fiercely competitive player to have championship hopes for his team. Michael Jordan was that player in Chicago's six-title run. George Mikan was the compelling force behind the Minneapolis Lakers four-time-champion teams. Both had strong back-up support. Big George had Jim Pollard, Slater Martin, and Vern Mikkelsen. MJ had Scottie Pippen, John Paxson, and later, Dennis Rodman.

Although Bill Russell was *the* Celtic during Boston's magnificent run in the 1950s and 60s, Cousy, Sharman, Sam and K. C. Jones, Heinsohn, Havlicek, and Satch Sanders were tough-as-nails competitors. The later Celtic teams with Bird, Kevin McHale, and Robert Parish had the same level of competitiveness in the 1980s. The Los Angeles Lakers led by Earvin Johnson had Kareem Abdul-Jabbar, James Worthy, Byron Scott, and Michael Cooper to complement the spectacular "Show Time" game that Magic orchestrated.

It's conceded by most NBA basketball analysts that a team needs three highly skilled, competitive players to win it all. In today's NBA, that rule stands up when you break down the rosters of recent championship teams. The Spurs, winners of four titles from 1999 to 2007, had Tim Duncan, Tony Parker, and Manu Ginobili. The Lakers won three times with Kobe Bryant, Shaquille O'Neal, and Robert Horry; and twice more—and counting—with Bryant, Pau Gasol, and Derek Fisher.

And how long will it take upstart Oklahoma City to win a championship? The Thunder already have two pieces of the puzzle in place—Kevin Durant, a lithe 6'11" sharpshooter from anywhere on the court, who led the NBA in scoring in 2009–10; and Russell Westbrook, an explosive, strong, and quick point guard. Whether Jeff Green or James Harden can step up as a consistent third contributor remains to be seen. OKC won 50 games in 2009–10, is well-coached by Scott Brooks, and is definitely in the contending pack.

In the summer of 2010, Miami added LeBron James and Chris Bosh to its roster and re-signed its own free agent, Dwyane Wade. Highly talented players? For sure. Competitive? Of course. History will tell whether that trio of stars can blend together well enough to become champions.

Every team in the league will try to kick their butts!

7

TAKE CHARGE

Just before the 2009 NBA Finals began, I told Kobe Bryant the story about George Mikan coldcocking Red Holzman with an elbow in the 1951 Rochester Royals-Minneapolis Lakers playoffs because Red had the temerity to steal the ball from him.

Kobe threw back his head and laughed: "I love it!"

I told him that Mikan was the unquestioned leader of those great Lakers teams that won five NBA championships, and I asked Kobe about the leadership role he plays with the current Lakers.

Kobe Bryant at the Air Canada Centre in Toronto.

"Leadership is something that just happens," he said. "I've always been demanding of my teammates. I want to win ... and I want my teammates to have the same intensity and to work as hard as I do. We have the same goal. I'm going to push them to do that."

"And what happens," I asked, "if they don't respond?"

He gave me a big smile.

"I turn into George Mikan."

Championship teams *must* have a leader. Legendary UCLA coach John Wooden could have been describing himself when he said this about strong leadership:

> *Without organization and leadership toward a realistic goal there is no chance of realizing more than a small percentage of your full potential. Every effort should be made, in proper manner and keeping everything in proper perspective, toward maximum development of both the individual and group as a whole.*[1]

Wooden accomplished that level of organization and leadership with his scrupulous attention to the most fundamental details of practice. He taught his players on the practice floor how to perform in a game. He *prepared* his players to play and then allowed them to take over on the court. And take over they did: 10 NCAA championships in his last 12 seasons (1963–64 through 1974–75) at UCLA.

A pretty good measure of successful teaching, don't you think?

John Wooden was, in my view, the best pure teacher ever among basketball coaches at any level. Nobody was ever a greater stickler for detail. It began with basics: teaching players to lace their sneakers properly. Sure enough, I watched his former players when they got to the NBA, and their basketball shoes were all tied the same way—no loops and laced snugly to the top eyelet.

The Wooden-coached players I encountered were, to a man, fundamentally sound. They played on balance and with good agility. They caught the ball with two hands and with footwork that had them ready for the next play. They were patient in the team offense, making good passes and taking good shots. They had a sense for the basics of effective team defense and knew their responsibilities in it. These habits were products of Wooden's basic, fundamental practice drills and remained with the player wherever he played.

You could always tell a Wooden-coached player.

The team leader on the floor might be the point guard, the small forward, the big man who dominates the paint, or even a bench guy. It doesn't really matter. The team leader is the one who takes charge and sets the winning tone for his teammates to follow. The team leader is all about winning, always willing to subordinate his individual goals and do whatever's needed to drive his team to victory. To him, winning means more than individual glory.

The team leader is "The Man."

Some players are vocal and lead by being the coach on the floor. Others lead by example without saying a word. The latter do so by the force of their personalities as well as by how they play on the court.

The game revolves around the floor leader. He seems to be in the middle of the action all the time. He directs the offense without having to call a play. He's active on defense, challenging his matchup and helping out his teammates at the same time. He makes the big stop on defense, gets the critical steal or rebound, and is involved in game-winning plays on offense.

A team leader is unselfish. He supports his teammates enthusiastically and publicly, always directing the spotlight toward them when they've done something worthy. But he's also willing to challenge them, even at the risk of putting a strain on friendships, if that's needed to develop in them a winning attitude. If a guy needs his butt kicked to head him in the right direction, a true team leader is only too happy to provide that boot.

The late Dr. Bruce Ogilvie, the Portland psychologist when I took the job there, administered a battery of tests to the players each year and discussed his findings with me. I was fascinated by the insights into a player's psyche that he gained from those tests.

I always enjoyed talking with Dr. Bruce about the psychological aspects of coaching, especially leadership. He said that there are three principal traits of the most successful leaders: personality transparency, an insatiable desire for knowledge about their endeavor, and a fierce desire to succeed.

Bruce told me that a successful leader could be "Mr. Nice Guy" or an SOB. It doesn't really matter, so long as the leader maintains his personality traits *consistently*. It doesn't work for a leader to be one person under certain circumstances and somebody else under others. That's a prescription for failure. And if you think about it, that's true off the court as well—for all of us.

I found it fascinating to observe leadership traits among coaches and players in the NBA over my four decades (and counting) as a coach and radio and TV commentator.

Most players go through an adjustment period before taking over that special leadership role with their teams, but the coach must be the leader from the get-go. A coach-leader must demonstrate immediately that he knows the game, has an effective game plan, can teach his game, is able to fit his players into various roles, and can make game adjustments to handle the unique ebb and flow of the NBA game. He needs to do all of that in a firm, poised manner. He must show his players that he can help them win.

The coach-leader who can't do all these things soon acquires a new title: ex-coach.

Good players *want* organization and direction. They know instinctively when the game plan is sound and the style of play fits the personnel. They expect to work hard at practice and want that time to be productive. Players can sense when the coach makes the right adjustments during a game, and they expect his strategies to be on target. Although any player worth his salt wants to be in the starting lineup, he will accept decisions regarding playing time from a coach he respects.

Players expect their coach to be fair. They know that, for everyone's benefit, there must be certain rules of operation—being on time for all team functions is one of the most basic. Players want these rules to be applied equally throughout the roster. They don't like one set of rules for the stars and another set for the rest of the team. If the coach lives up to those player expectations, they will embrace him as their leader. In essence, players want a leader who is firm, fair, competent at his job, and can help them win.

Let's take a look at some of the NBA's great coach-leaders, starting with the greatest of them all, Arnold Jacob Auerbach (1917–2006).

Red Auerbach coached professional basketball for 20 years, beginning in 1946 with the Washington Capitals in the Basketball Association of America (BAA). He spent a season with Tri-Cities in the newly formed National Basketball Association (NBA) before taking over the Celtics in 1950. Red loved fast-break basketball. His Celtics were the first team to average 100 or more points a game for a season (1955), but they didn't start winning championships until Bill Russell came along.

I watched Russell's very first game as a Celtic on television. I was anxious to see how he adapted to the NBA game after winning back-to-back NCAA championships at the University of San Francisco (1955, 1956) and earning a gold medal as a member of the U.S. Olympic basketball team (1956).

Frankly, I was disappointed with what I saw. Russell didn't show an ability to score in the low post, and he wasn't dominant on defense in that game. But Auerbach was effusive in his praise of Russell in a postgame interview: "This guy will change the game with his defense."

Of course, Red was right on target. The Celtics not only maintained their ability to score 100 points a game, but they sharply reduced scoring by opponents because of Russell's shot-blocking, rebounding, and exuberant floor leadership. Russell averaged over 19 rebounds a game that season and blocked an unrecorded but significant number of shots. (The NBA didn't start keeping that stat until the 1973–74 season.)

Auerbach coached the Celtics to nine NBA championships, eight of them in a row. Russell was the defensive stopper on Celtics teams that won 11 NBA championships in the 13 years he played. In 1980, Auerbach was selected by the PBWA (Pro Basketball Writers Association) as the "Greatest Coach in the History of the NBA."

But he's also right up there among great general managers, if for no other reason than being shrewd enough to maneuver a trade with St. Louis to acquire the draft rights to Russell. He gave up two star players, "Easy Ed" McCauley and Cliff Hagan, to make the deal. He also had to include a Celtics preseason game at Rochester and schedule an appearance of the Ice Capades there to get the Royals to pass on Russell and select Sihugo Green.

Most of the smart guys who dissected every player move made every year argued that the Celtics had given up too much. But Auerbach still had Bob Cousy, Bill Sharman, Frank Ramsey, and Tom Heinsohn, all excellent at fast-break basketball. And Red saw that Russell would be the linchpin who could bring it all together.

Red had a game plan that was simplicity incarnate: a fast-break offense, with Cousy at the throttle, augmented by six half-court plays executed to perfection. The Celts' pressure defense was designed to funnel the ball to the intimidating, shot-blocking, rebounding Bill Russell.

That's how the Celtics played. Every team knew what was coming. No team could stop it.

I was in my second year of coaching at Saint Joseph's College in Philadelphia at that time, and I went to see Celtics-Warriors games whenever I could. I studied Auerbach very closely during those games, and I marveled at his apparent control of everything happening on the court.

The man had a brash, flamboyant, abrasive personality. Opponents hated him, and nothing made Red happier than to know he was driving them over the top. He verbally abused referees throughout the game, sometimes making sure to get himself ejected from a game in order to get extra effort from his players.

Red's players flat-out loved him, in no small measure because he had a rough and tough way of protecting their tender egos. I never saw him single out a player for a verbal reprimand in a game, not one time. Usually, a brief glare of scorn was all he needed to get his point across. Because he was on top of the game action 100 percent of the time, his game adjustments always seemed to work. Consequently, he was like E. F. Hutton: when Red talked, his players listened. On an immensely successful team packed with star players, Red Auerbach was clearly the team leader.

Years after his retirement as coach, I asked how he handled his players in order to establish such a high level of rapport. He stopped me midquestion: "You don't handle players, Jack," Red said. "You handle animals. I always treated my players with respect."

One time I was in the audience at a luncheon at which Auerbach and Russell were being honored. The two were sitting beside each other at the head table and talked animatedly throughout the meal, the conversation frequently punctuated by a Russell cackle. Someone later asked Russell what he and Red had talked about.

"Winning."

(Cackle.)

Shortly after I took over as coach of the Philadelphia 76ers in 1968, I received a phone call from Eddie Donovan, general manager of the Knicks. Eddie had coached at St. Bonaventure when I was at St. Joseph's College (now St. Joseph's University), my first coaching job above the high school level. Over the years, after we both went into the NBA, we became friends, often calling to chat about our teams and the league in general. Donovan had coached the Knicks without success before becoming their general manager.

The Sixers had traded Wilt Chamberlain to the Lakers earlier in the summer, so Eddie and I talked a lot about the trade and how it would affect the balance of power in the East. I told Eddie that I liked my team. I was confident that we'd be all right at the center position with Luke

Jackson, and that the other positions were solid. In support of that, I related to Donovan a comment by Alex Hannum, whom I was succeeding as Sixers coach, several months before the Chamberlain deal went down: "Don't ever let Luke Jackson go. You never know about Wilt, and Luke can be a good center in this league if Wilt ever decides to jump ship."

To close the chat, I asked Eddie if he had any advice about coaching in the NBA "Be the boss, Jack," he said. "Just be the boss and you'll be fine."

I discovered the wisdom of Donovan's advice in training camp that fall. I'd been the GM in Philly for the previous two years, so the players and I knew each other. But they didn't know me as a coach, and I was succeeding Hannum, regarded by NBA insiders as among the best in the league and for whom my players had great respect. I could sense at the first practice session that I was being compared and tested. But I had organized the practice well, and the session was crisp and productive. From the comments made by players after that practice, I knew that I had passed my first test.

Needless to say, more tests were to come.

At our first preseason game that year (against Donovan's Knicks), the pace was fast and furious, with a lot of scoring and not a whole lot of defense. It was the first game that I'd coached since I left St. Joe's two years earlier. In college basketball, of course, the games are played in two 20-minute halves, whereas in the NBA games are divided into four 12-minute quarters. For reasons that I still cannot begin to explain, I was in a college game time mode, and as the second period was drawing to a close, I took it to be the end of the game. That's right, the end of the second *half*, and thus the game, not the end of the second quarter.

We held a slight lead over the Knicks in the waning minutes of the ga…, sorry, *second quarter*, and when the horn sounded to end the period, I jumped off the bench with both fists clenched above my head. *We won!* Before my feet landed on the floor, I realized my mistake. I looked back at my players, hoping they hadn't noticed, but they were looking at me with bemused expressions on their faces. They'd noticed, all right.

I tried to recover, saying to them, "Good half … *good half!*" But as we trooped back to the dressing room, Billy Cunningham caught up with me, a huge grin splitting his face, and said, "Hey, Coach. You thought the game was over, didn't you?"

What could I say? I just rolled my eyes and nodded in the affirmative. Fortunately, he and his teammates shrugged it off as a rookie mistake.

For a coach, being a team leader is simply part of the job description. There are no special accolades for leading your team; that's what you were hired to do. But I always was vigilant about detecting signs that indicated I might not be fulfilling that vital part of my job.

In general, a coach knows if it's "his team" by the way players respond to his demands at practice, by how they listen at timeouts, and by their overall body language. In addition, comments made to the media and overheard bits of conversation will often tell a coach what he needs to know.

In that first season in Philadelphia, I overheard Cunningham talking to Archie Clark on the team bus after a close loss in Seattle. They were talking about me. "He never gives up, Arch," Billy C. said. "He's always figuring out a way for us to win." "I know, I know," Clark responded. "Jack's good. We're going to be all right."

I slept well that night.

In Buffalo, Jim McMillian told reporters, "When we don't play well, it's like the OK Corral. The door swings open and Coach storms into the locker room and really lets us have it. He jumps on everybody, then says, 'Anybody that has a problem with what I just said, come and see me, and we'll settle it any way you like.'"

McMillian added, "We have some big guys on this team. Nobody moved a muscle."

I felt good about my leadership status with the players in my first year at Indiana (1986–87). The Pacers had been 26–56 the previous season but improved to 41–41 and a playoff berth that year. Dick Harter, my assistant, and I felt a great sense of accomplishment even though we didn't get past Atlanta in the playoffs.

But the Pacers struggled through most of the second season, a result in part of the way I handled a confrontation with Chuck Person, a young player in his second NBA season. The Rookie of the Year in 1987, Chuck was a very good long-range shooter, but he was way too points conscious ("I've got to get my 20") by my standards, plus he was never in top physical condition and had problems defending. Late in the season, I got on Chuck pretty hard for his lack of defense in a practice scrimmage, and he barked back. We exchanged expletive remarks, and I sent him home. But Chuck didn't leave. He watched the rest of practice sitting high up in the stands. After practice I went to him and told him that his practice performance was unacceptable and that I didn't like the fact that he didn't follow my direction to leave the gym.

Chuck apologized profusely and offered to also apologize to the team. I told him that wouldn't be necessary so long as we understood each other. Chuck assured me that we were on the same page. I took no further disciplinary action.

I put the incident behind me. The other players didn't. They saw it as my backing down to a player. From that point, I sensed that my leadership of the team was being questioned. We finished that season by losing a playoff spot to New York in the last game of the year.

During the offseason, I recommended some roster changes before the next season—among them trading Person—but General Manager Donnie Walsh made none. We also lost the services of Steve Stepanovich, the team's most physical big man, due to a knee injury.

So going into the 1988–89 season, I wasn't pleased with my player personnel. At training camp, I didn't like the team attitude I encountered. Nor did I sense a commitment to winning as that season began. When the Pacers got off to an 0–7 start in 1988, I resigned as coach. It was no longer my team.

Pat Riley once told me about an encounter he had with Anthony Mason when both were with the Knicks. Mason was disrupting defensive practice by his lack of attention to detail one day. Riley stopped practice and said, "Mace, you can keep screwing things up here, and I'll just sit you out of the workout. If you want to do that, it's up to you. And whatever you decide is okay with me. But, I want you to know that I'm going to keep demanding that you do things the right way."

It worked. Riles sent a clear, strong message to Mason, and he did it in front of Mason's teammates to drive home his point. Riley said that his relationship with Mason improved after that.

(As Riley related that experience with Mason, I thought back to my confrontation with Chuck Person and how it might have ended differently if I had employed Riley's approach.)

There were many great coach-leaders during my time in the NBA. My list includes Red Auerbach, of course, plus (in alphabetical order) Cotton Fitzsimmons, Alex Hannum, Red Holzman, John Kundla, Dick Motta, and Bill Sharman.

In today's NBA, I rate San Antonio's Gregg Popovich as tops among coach-leaders. Pop coaches a game that fits his personnel. Tim Duncan, the Spurs multitalented big man, is the focus of the offense and defense. The Spurs attack plan, working through Duncan, is flexible enough to allow penetrating opportunities to the lightning-quick Tony Parker and expansive enough to give Manu Ginobili one-on-one creativity. The team's defense typically is one of the top three in field-goal percentage allowed.

Popovich has great rapport with his players, even though he blisters them from time to time—collectively or individually—when he feels they need it. Pop's also a sound tactician and usually finds ways to win close games down the stretch.

Pop is not only the leader as the team's coach, but he's also the leader of the Spurs franchise. The San Antonio team owner, Peter Holt, allows Pop to run the basketball operation. Along with right-hand man R. C. Buford, Pops has made some excellent personnel decisions, drafting Parker (France) and Ginobili (Argentina) among them.

The Spurs' four championships since he took over the coaching reins in 1996 are a pretty good indicator of what Pops brings to the party in San Antonio.

The Lakers were a veteran team headed up Abdul-Jabbar, Norm Nixon, and Jamaal Wilkes when they took Magic Johnson as the first pick overall in the 1979 NBA Draft.

Now, veteran stars typically take a "show me" attitude toward highly ballyhooed rookies. Conversely, many rookies, no matter how high their stack of press clippings coming in, are often shy about asserting themselves. But my good friend Jack McKinney, in his first year as head coach in Los Angeles, saw the point-guard potential in Magic and decided to move him into that position, which had been manned the previous season by Nixon.

Not surprisingly, Magic was initially reluctant to take charge of the team. His play in preseason scrimmages was tentative. After a week or so of training camp, McKinney called Magic over and said, "Kareem wants to know when you're going to take over the team." Magic was shocked: "Did Kareem say that?" "Yeah," McKinney answered, "and he also said he expects a lot more from you than you've shown."

Fact is, Kareem hadn't actually said anything of the sort to McKinney, but Jack used that little white lie to get Magic out of his deferential attitude toward his veteran teammates. It worked. Magic immediately became a more aggressive player, took over the team leader role Jack had envisioned him playing, and the Lakers were off and running.

Unfortunately, Jack was in a serious bike accident in November of that year—the Lakers were 10–4 at the time—and missed the rest of the season. McKinney's assistant, Paul Westhead, took over and coached the Lakers to the NBA championship, their first since 1954, when they were still in Minneapolis. And the team's undisputed floor leader? You guessed it: Magic Johnson, who capped a brilliant rookie season by winning MVP honors in the Finals.

Jack was still rehabbing from his near-fatal bike accident when the Lakers beat the Sixers in six games for the title, but his players didn't forget the role he'd played in getting the ball bouncing in the right direction the previous fall. At the championship celebration in Los Angeles, Abdul-Jabbar told the cheering throng, "Let's remember that it was Jack McKinney who got us started."

The most amazing demonstration of take-charge leadership that I witnessed in my two decades as an NBA coach took place in the NBA's predraft camp in 1984 in Chicago. There John Stockton, a little-known guard from tiny Gonzaga College, took a group of headstrong stars from different colleges and immediately welded them into an explosive, cohesive unit. The group had never played together, but after two practices Stockton had them looking like an outfit that had played together for years. That performance led me to make John my choice for Portland's second first-round pick in that year's draft.

You don't need to remind me that the 1984 draft was also the year we passed over Michael Jordan and took Sam Bowie with our first pick. Blazers fans are still crying over that spilt milk.

We were pretty confident that Stockton would still be available by the time our second first-round pick (18th overall) came around, and he almost was. Unfortunately for us, Frank Layden, Utah's coach/general manager at the time, had seen the same thing I saw in Stockton, and the Jazz made him their No. 1 pick (16th overall)—a choice, by the way, that was loudly booed at the time by Utah fans.

I was crushed. I believed that I'd lost the opportunity to nurture the development of a potentially great player, and I followed Stockton's subsequent NBA career with special interest. In his first three seasons in Utah, John started only 45 games, unable to beat out six-year veteran Rickey Green, a former first-rounder himself. I began to wonder if I'd been mistaken in my initial estimation of John's leadership and game skills. But in Stockton's fourth NBA season (1987–88), he took over as Utah's team leader, a role he retained until his retirement in 2003. Inducted into the Hall of Fame in 2009, John is the NBA career leader in assists and steals.

And he came *this* close to being a Blazer.

Avery Johnson's mother told him at age 13 that he was born to be a basketball coach. She saw something in her son that others didn't; mothers are good at that. Avery went undrafted and bounced around the NBA, playing for four teams over five seasons before finally earning a starting job in the 1992–93 season as point guard of the San Antonio Spurs, where he grew into the role of floor general and led the Spurs to their NBA championship in 1999.

San Antonio coach Gregg Popovich told me a classic AJ story about a game the Spurs were losing at halftime in Minnesota, playing poorly against a definitely inferior team. Superstar David Robinson's mind, Pop told me, was definitely somewhere other than the central time zone. As the team walked off the court, Pop sidled up to AJ and asked, "Do you want to get him or shall I?"

"I'll get him, Pop," Johnson answered. "I'll get him."

In the locker room, Pop settled the team down and then started his critique of the half. Avery interrupted him: "Excuse me, Pop, but I'd like to say something." Pop gave him the floor. AJ said, "Five-O, [Robinson wore No. 50 on his back] are you going to start playing, or are you just going to pussyfoot around like you did that first half?"

Robinson kept his head down. No response. Johnson approached Robinson, bent over, and looked directly into his eyes: "Tell me, Five-O, are you going to play like you know how, or did we waste all that hard work we did in training camp? *Tell me now, Five-O!*"

Robinson answered by playing an inspired second half, and the Spurs came back to win the game. That's player support and leadership at its best.

Late in the 2001–02 season—and even later in AJ's career: the 36-year-old was in his 13th NBA campaign—Dallas picked up Johnson from Denver to play a reserve role. The Mavs had a good team, one that included Steve Nash, Dirk Nowitzki, and Michael Finley. The following season, Johnson's first full one with the Mavericks, they won 60 games and advanced to the Western Conference Finals (where they lost to Johnson's old team, the Spurs). I remember posing this question to Steve Nash: "Who's your team leader?" Steve thought for a moment and then surprised me by offering up the name of a player who'd played in only 40 of the Mavericks' 82 games, starting not a single one: Avery Johnson.

Avery Johnson?

"That's right," Nash said. "Look, AJ played on a championship team. He has good, smart things to say. And the players listen to him."

Johnson became head coach at Dallas in 2005 and led the Mavs to a 60–22 record and the 2006 NBA Finals, where they lost to Miami after going up 2–0. The next two seasons the Mavs went 67–15 and 51–31 but were eliminated from the playoffs in the first round. Owner Mark Cuban fired Johnson after the 2008 season. AJ then became an NBA game analyst on television for two seasons.

Because of his love of the game and his great leadership skills, I assumed Avery Johnson would soon be coaching in the NBA again. I am pleased to see that the New Jersey Nets hired him as their head coach prior to the 2010–11 season.

Steve Nash served an apprenticeship under an established team leader (Jason Kidd) when he first came into the NBA with Phoenix in 1996. He expanded his game soon after he was traded to Dallas but returned to Phoenix as a free agent in 2004.

A seasoned NBA veteran, Nash, now in his midthirties, keeps a rigid (and very precise) conditioning regimen in the offseason. He has a personal trainer who stresses a lot of stretching exercises, and he mixes in a carefully selected group of weight drills. Steve also plays on two amateur soccer teams in the summer to maintain cardiovascular fitness. He positively adores soccer, despite the fact that his hands don't come in as, well, handy as they do in the NBA, where he's one of the game's elite floor leaders.

Michael Jordan joined a Chicago team with a core of veterans (Orlando Woolridge, Steve Johnson, David Greenwood, Quentin Dailey, Dave Corzine) in 1984. (Wasn't that the year my Portland Trail Blazers passed over that Jordan guy to take Sam Bowie?)

Hard as it to imagine now, Jordan hung back from asserting himself with the Bulls at first. I can only imagine it was out of respect for the veterans. But toward the end of that first season, Bulls coach Kevin Loughery anointed Jordan as his floor leader, a role MJ never relinquished.

Early in the 1984–85 season, I ran into Loughery, who had played for me in Philadelphia, and I asked him about his prize rookie. "Coach, this guy Jordan is something else," he said to me. "I coached Dr. J in the ABA, and he was great. But Michael's in a class by himself."

Loughery's coaching style was built around taking maximum advantage of mismatches, and Kevin quickly found that no one in the league could defend Jordan. No one. So Loughery set up MJ for one-on-one clear-outs with just about every half-court possession, and Michael had a picnic. He led the league in scoring that year with 28.2 ppg.

When Phil Jackson took over as coach of the Bulls in 1989, Jordan was commencing his sixth NBA season. He had led the league in scoring every year except his second, when he was limited to 18 games because of a foot injury. But while Jordan was tearing up the league with his individual play, the Bulls had no championship rings to show for it. Detroit's physical application of "The Jordan Rules," which forced MJ to his left, and then harassed him with a second defender, was the key factor in stopping the Bulls from advancing to the NBA Finals in 1989 and 1990.

After his first season, Jackson wanted to install the triangle offense designed by his assistant, Tex Winter, but knew he needed to get Jordan to sign off on it. (In the triangle, Jordan would have far fewer one-on-one opportunities to blow away his defender.) Jackson sat Michael down before the 1990–91 training camps opened and carefully explained the new offense, driving home his conviction that the triangle would give the Bulls a better shot at an NBA title, that there would be less physical wear and tear on Michael, and that MJ would still be able to score freely. Michael agreed to give the triangle a try.

As we all know, the experiment worked out pretty well: six NBA championships for the Bulls and six more scoring titles for Michael Jordan over the next eight seasons.

It was interesting to watch Michael adapt to the new system. In the 1990–91 season, he quickly mastered his role and everyone else's in the intricate scheme. He guided his team through its execution. And when he needed to score, he did. Michael was the Bulls coach on the floor: dominating when necessary, playmaking when called for, and always there to deliver the game-winning clutch plays that won big games.

The main reason the triangle worked so well, of course, is that Michael was Michael. I remember once asking him about his role in Phil's signature offense. "I can get my shot any time," he said. "The triangle is for the guys who can't get their own shots. We run it for them, not for me."

Some physically talented players attempt to exert leadership on a team before they're ready to do so. They've got the skills, but they lack the requisite maturity. Kobe Bryant, as a young player with the Lakers before Phil Jackson became his coach, was one such "preemie" leader.

Kobe had just turned 18 when he played his first NBA game in 1996. He joined a veteran team that included Shaquille O'Neal, Nick Van Exel, Eddie Jones, Elden Campbell, and Cedric Ceballos. Kobe averaged about 15 minutes of playing time and scored 7.6 points a game for Coach Del Harris. He was feeling his way into the NBA.

Jackson says that Kobe craved to be a leader right out of the box. But in his first few years as a Laker, Kobe's teammates didn't want to follow him. As Kobe told me years later, "Those guys weren't going to listen to some kid just out of high school."

Phil Jackson had a problem:

It was a kind of stalemate, and my idea was to convince Kobe to go along with the program until he matured into a leadership role. ... It was his mental attitude that bothered me. He simply had to find a way to involve himself with his teammates, trust them and give them credit where credit was due.[2]

There was friction early on between Bryant and Jackson, as Kobe rebelled against the slow-down, get-the-ball-to-Shaq offense. Kobe wanted to run more, and he wanted to play a stronger leadership role. It wasn't until the Lakers traded O'Neal to Miami in 2004 that Bryant became the team's unquestioned leader on the floor. Kobe and Phil are both all about winning, and as they learned to respect that fact in each other, they turned to the same page regarding the team's needs. Kobe told me how that often works during the course of a game. "There'll be times when I'll look over at Derek [Fisher], or Pao [Gasol], or Lamar [Odom], and I'll call out a sequence of options. Then we'll hear Phil's unbelievably loud, piercing whistle. We all look at him, and he just calls out the exact same thing I just called without knowing I'd done it. That's just how we are now. Me and Phil, we're in total synch."

Kobe likes to bide his time in the early going of a game, just feeling out his opponent, because he knows he can get his shot off whenever he wants it. (Who does that remind you of? Hint: his initials are MJ.) "I want to see what I can get from my teammates first," he says. "The sooner I can get them involved in the game, the easier it will be for all of us."

And Kobe knows that if that approach doesn't work, there's always Plan B—he takes over the game.

That's *leadership*.

The fifth pick in the first round of the 2003 NBA Draft, Dwyane Wade became the Miami Heat's team leader right out of the box, sparking a mediocre team to a strong finish, a playoff berth, and an upset win over New Orleans in the first round of the 2004 playoffs in his rookie season. In his third season (2005–06), he led the Heat to the NBA championship by sparking a crucial come-from-behind victory over the Dallas Mavericks in the NBA Finals.

Dallas won the first two games of that series and were up by 11 points in Game 3 midway through the fourth period. Time out, Miami. At the station break, my partner in the ESPN broadcast, Jim Durham, turned to me and said, "Sweep." It certainly had all the earmarks of one. Dallas had utterly dominated Miami to that point.

But those who were ready to stick a fork in the Heat because they were done had failed to reckon with the competitive leadership of DWade. After a stream of Coach Pat Riley's typically impassioned words, the Miami huddle broke to resume play, and DWade gathered his teammates about him.

"I ain't going out like this," he told them. *"I ain't going out like this."*

Wade then went on a rampage, scoring 10 points in the final minutes and deflecting a last-second Dallas lob pass toward the basket to preserve a 98–96 Miami victory. The Heat went on to win the next three games and became the 2006 NBA champions.

A separated shoulder limited DWade's playing time for the next two seasons, so we can only speculate whether he might have matched Michael Jordan with back-to-back-to-back championship rings. What we do know is that, like MJ, DWade is a defensive force who can cripple another team's offense, a generous passer to teammates who get open, and, in the final ticks of close games, a fearless gunner who knocks down winners.

Imagine where the Cleveland Cavaliers would be if LeBron James never showed up. It's pretty easy, really. Just look where they were at the end of the 2002–03 season: 17 Ws, 65 Ls.

Fortunately for the Cavs and their fans, that .207 W-L percentage gave Cleveland the first pick in the 2003 NBA Draft, which they used to turn their franchise around by selecting an 18-year-old graduate from St.

Vincent/St. Mary High School in Akron, Ohio, named LeBron James. Since then, the Cavaliers have had five winning seasons and five straight playoff appearances, including a trip to the 2007 NBA Finals.

A rare physical specimen (6'8" and 260 pounds of muscle), James has amazing speed and power and a relentless competitive drive. He was to the Cavs what Kobe has been to Lakers—or would have been if he ever got a supporting cast close in quality to the one that Bryant enjoys.

Coach Mike Brown wisely gave his superstar the green light to pretty much go on his own offensively. Also wisely, James kept his teammates involved and alert. He knows that talent wins games, but that leadership holds the key to championships.

The Cavs seemed to play their best when point guard Mo Williams initiated the offense and LeBron played off him. The offense bogged down when James was the primary handler, because that allowed defenses to overshift in his direction.

I talked with Coach Brown about that tactic early in the 2009–10 season. "We've talked about letting Williams be the primary ball handler, and I've talked to LeBron about it. He's okay with whatever we decide. He just wants to win." But the Cavs didn't win in 2010, and James opted out to join Miami, and Dwyane Wade and Chris Bosh. Cleveland struggled in the season after James' departure, losing 10 straight games early in the 2010–2011 season.

On the San Antonio Spurs, Tony Parker and Manu Ginobili handle the ball more frequently, but Tim Duncan is the acknowledged team leader. Spurs players know that Coach Pop's basic game plan in the half-court offense is to turn matters over to their 6'11" forward-center at the post and let him decide what the next moves should be.

Duncan understands that the ball goes to him to initiate the *team* game, and he's patient in reading opposing defenses and making plays that involve teammates.

Duncan also directs the Spurs defense. I've watched him, as his team leaves a timeout huddle, drape his arm around a teammate and speak very forcibly to him as the Spurs prepare to go for a critical end-of-the-game stop. More often a quiet, lead-by-example guy, Duncan can turn into a direct, in-your-face kind of leader if the situation calls for it.

Coach Popovich runs the game from the bench.

Duncan is the floor leader.

Each has four championship rings.

The division of labor works.

In his dozen seasons with the Minnesota Timberwolves, Kevin Garnett always inspired teammates and was the coach on the floor. I often watched him in practice, and I can assure you he prepared meticulously for every game. After a loss, he would make a point of getting together with his teammates to build their spirits for the next game. Like many other leaders, Kevin's not a great talker. But the aura about him says plenty.

The impact of his presence in Minnesota can be pretty easily summed up. In the Wolves' first 21 seasons in the NBA their W-L record topped .500 or better only eight times, all of them KG seasons. But it wasn't until after he joined the Celtics following the 2006–07 season that Garnett found himself supported by enough talent to win an NBA championship (2008). In his first two seasons with the Celtics, KG not only got the job done on the floor—that was never a problem—but he also strengthened Doc Rivers' authority with his players by going out of his way to shake his coach's hand as he left the floor near the end of another winning effort.

You just have to wonder how many championship rings KG would be sporting on that right hand—and maybe on his left—if he'd spent his entire illustrious career in the Boston Garden.

Abundant natural talent? To be sure. But Garnett's learned leadership skills are what have made him such a powerful force wherever he's played.

Karl Malone was a leader by example for the Utah Jazz throughout his career. A marvelously conditioned 6'9", 256-pound bull who could run like a deer, Malone teamed with John Stockton to form a tremendous scoring threat for opponents. Karl averaged 25 points a game and 10 rebounds for his career. He missed a total of 8 games during his 18 years with the Jazz.

Coach Jerry Sloan once said to me, "How can another player on this team take a game off when they see Karl lace 'em up every night?"

Technically, Larry Bird at 6'9" fit the definition of big forward. But on a Celtics team with two post-up teammates, Kevin McHale (6'10") and Robert Parish (7'0"), the Birdman just went out and played.

All over the court, wherever he thought he was needed.

I've racked my brain on this one, but I cannot think of a more competitive player in the history of the game. *As* competitive? Sure: MJ, Kobe, a handful of others come to mind. But *more* competitive than the Hick from French Lick?

Nobody.

Bird did whatever it took to give his team a W. Sometimes that would be a dazzling display of shooting and passing that left the bad guys on the ropes. Sometimes—make that many times—it would be a game-winning shot in the final seconds. But sometimes his contribution to a crucial Celtics victory wouldn't even make it into a box score. Dedicated Bird-watchers will all have their favorites in that category. Mine came in a game against Detroit in the 1987 Eastern Conference Finals when he intercepted an inbounds pass from Isiah Thomas to Bill Laimbeer and in the same motion flipped an on-target pass to Dennis Johnson for the game winner.

Although a lead-by-example player, Bird sometimes helped his coaches by serving as a "reinforcer." If the coach got on a player or prodded him to work harder on some aspect of his game, Bird followed up with the same message. In a different voice, for sure, with slightly different emphases, maybe, but always the same message.

Bill Fitch, Celtics coach from 1979 through 1983, and Bird teamed up on Robert Parish shortly after the Celtics acquired the big man from Golden State before the 1980–81 season.

"Right from the beginning," Bill told me, "I rode Robert just like Gene Autry rode Champion. Robert must have wanted to kill me on some of those days. Then Larry would get on him to do the same things I wanted from him, only Larry did it in a different way. And Robert seemed to take it better from him."

The Birdman was the sort of team leader who played injured when most guys with the same (or lesser) ailment took the night off. He told me of one home game after a road trip when his back was aching so bad that he had to be transported to the Boston Garden by ambulance, lying flat on his back. Needless to say, he played in the game.

A better team leader ever than Larry Bird?

Not in my book.

George Mikan's Minneapolis Lakers won a championship in the old National Basketball League, which merged in 1949 with the Basketball Association of America to form the National Basketball Association, and then went on to rack up four NBA titles. Over the years I spoke on several occasions with John Kundla, Mikan's coach during the Lakers' five championship runs. A Hall of Fame coach, Kundla remembers his team leader fondly: "George just loved to win. And he wouldn't let anyone or anything stand in his way."

I only saw Mikan play twice, once for the Chicago Gears (1946) and again in the NBA Finals against the Knicks (1952). In both instances, Mikan dominated the game. He was like a man playing with boys. He owned the paint at both ends of the floor.

On offense, he set up deep along the lane, received the ball, and then turned into the lane with a power hook that seldom failed to hit the target. Mikan hooked with either hand and always finished at the rim so that, on the rare occasions when he did miss, he was right there with the put-back.

On defense, he patrolled the defensive lane, just daring opponents to challenge him. The few that tried carried away scars for their effrontery.

Elsewhere in these pages I write a lot about Bill Russell's impact on the game of basketball and his part in Boston's mind-boggling string of 11 NBA championships—including eight straight!—in the 13 seasons he was a Celtic. That astonishing period of dominance has never been matched by any team in any sport—sorry, Yankees fans: the best your pinstripers have done was five straight world championships (1949–53).

And the No. 1 reason for that astonishing record?

William Felton Russell.

Where to start? How about with Jerry West, who played against Russell in six NBA Finals games: "He made all his teammates better by helping them to realize their potential. His record speaks for itself. He not only was the most valuable player I've ever known in basketball, but probably the most valuable in any sport.[3]

Next let's hear from teammate, K. C. Jones, who played with Russell both in college and with the Celtics: "[Russ] taught us to believe that we were not just one person—each one of us had the strength and skill of the group. We were never alone on the court." K. C. says Russell was sensitive to players who were struggling, and he often spent quality time with them: "Many times I saw Russ sense that a player was down in the dumps—it might be a guy that he wasn't really tight with—and there they'd be, out to dinner with each other. With Russ picking up the tab."[4]

It's one thing to be the designated leader when your team wins; it's quite another when you have to explain why you lost.

The Sixers beat the Celtics in the 1967 Eastern Division Finals, ending Boston's eight-year run of NBA championships, and Player-Coach Russell was on the floor until the final horn. He kept on battling even though Philadelphia won the game in a rout, 140–116—and even though, for the first time I ever witnessed, Wilt Chamberlain outplayed him. After the game, I got to the Celtics locker room in time to listen to Russell being interviewed.

There were tough questions from the Philly writers about Russell's coaching, the aging of his players, and the end of the Celtics' championship run. Russ answered every question calmly and directly before leaving the room to shower. He had played in his typical all-out manner. This time it wasn't enough.

End of run, end of story.

Postscript: the following season in the Eastern Division Finals, again versus Philadelphia, the Celtics overcame a 3–1 game deficit to win three straight and go on to the NBA Finals, where they beat the Lakers to earn Russ his 10th ring.

No one in Madison Square Garden was prepared for what they witnessed in Game 7 of the 1970 NBA Finals between the Knicks and the Lakers.

Knicks center Willis Reed, the team's leading scorer and rebounder during the regular season, had been badly injured in Game 5. He was unable to play in Game 6. And Reed did not accompany his teammates onto the court for warm-ups before Game 7. Then, shortly before tipoff, Willis hobbled out on the court, his thigh heavily bandaged.

Madison Square Garden erupted in a thunderstorm of noise that could be heard from the Bronx to Battery Park. Reed's teammates, who hadn't known for sure whether he would try to join them on the floor that night, were visibly pumped up by his mere presence. The Lakers, at the other end of the floor, looked on in stunned amazement.

In the first couple of minutes, Reed hit two jump shots over Wilt Chamberlain, and the Knicks were off and running. They were the only two field goals that Reed made in the game, but the Knicks rode an emotional high to win the game and the NBA championship.

Years after that memorable performance, I talked about it with Red Holzman, in just his third season (of 14) as Knicks coach that night. "Willis had gotten treatment all through the afternoon, then got more when he came to the Garden that night," Red told me. "He could hardly stand on that leg, couldn't bend it. I didn't think there was any way he could play. But Willis told me, '*I'm goin' to play, Red.*'"

At about 7 o'clock that evening, Red said, trainer Danny Whelan wrapped Reed's leg as tightly as he dared. The big man got down off the training table, took a couple of tiptoe jumps, and said, "Let's go."

"I still get goose bumps," Red told me, "remembering Willis coming out of the tunnel and onto the court that night."

So do I.

Reed was the acknowledged leader of the Knicks throughout his 10-year career with the team, even during the last three seasons when wear and tear took its toll on his powerful body and his game went into decline.

Teammate Bill Bradley describes how Reed took the reins:

The role seemed natural to him, and everyone accepted him. He was always the one to speak up when Holzman asked if anyone had something to add.... If Holzman was "the boss," Willis was "the players' boss." His dominance came in part with his position: A team is only as strong as its big man. A center has to fight for his teammates, or more specifically, he has to make the opponents believe he will fight. Willis never had trouble convincing anyone.[5]

Coaching against Willis was a special challenge for me because he was such a great team player. He had a strong low-post game, but he could also step out to 17 feet and knock down soft jumpers. Plus he was left-handed, and lefties somehow always seem to have an advantage in any sport. (No, I don't have any hard data to support that, but it's my gut feeling, and I'm sticking with it.)

Willis, at 6'10" and 240 pounds, was a wide body with good coordination and quickness. He was also the kind of leader who allowed his teammates to play their games. But when the Knicks needed a crucial hoop or stop, Willis was The Man.

The NBA has had many great centers over the last six decades, from George Mikan to Bill Russell to Shaquille O'Neal, but my personal favorite—key word *personal*—is Bill Walton.

Of course, I'm a little prejudiced. Bill was the main reason I have an NBA championship on my coaching résumé and a plaque in the Basketball Hall of Fame. And he's also been a cherished friend for the past three decades (and counting).

But speaking objectively, I rate Bill as the most versatile, most skilled, most team-first leader ever to play the center position. Unfortunately, multiple foot injuries severely limited Bill's career. His best play was at Portland in our 1976–77 championship season and the following year, when he was the NBA's MVP. He was also an integral part of the Boston Celtics in 1985–86, when the Celts won the NBA title and Bill won the NBA's Sixth Man of the Year Award, despite playing only about 20 minutes a game because of injuries.

Walton did everything well. He scored. He was a great passer. (The best passing center of all time, per me.) He rebounded, triggered fast breaks with pinpoint outlet passes, and blocked shots with the best of them—when he was healthy. Plus he was in constant communication with teammates at both ends of the floor.

Bill was also vocally supportive of me. After I gave my pregame talk in the locker room, he would stand and say, "All right, now let's go and get those bleepers." And then the Blazers would burst out of the locker room and onto the court. That always made Jack McKinney and me look at each other and smile. We knew our team was ready for a strong performance.

During timeouts, Bill sat at the edge of the scorer's table. I would see him out of the corner of my eye nodding in agreement with what I was saying. Then, when the timeout ended, he'd shout, "Let's go do it, goddamnit!"

He always, *always* showed us the way.

What about leadership over on the bench—you know, from the guys *not* wearing short pants?

In today's NBA, every team has a head coach and a staff of four or five assistants. A vital aspect of the head coach's leadership responsibility is to clearly define roles for his assistants. The head coach and his staff *must* be on the same page.

Typically, one assistant is in charge of the team offense while another runs the defense. These are the head coach's two main men. Another assistant prepares the scouting report on the upcoming opponent, another organizes the drill work at practice, and yet another might go on the road to act as an advance scout of opposing teams or to see prospective talent.

(As I write this, I'm thinking that today's NBA head coach has a pretty cushy job! But on second thought, I know better.)

See, in 1968, when I began coaching in the NBA, I had *no* assistant coaches. That's right, not a single one. No line item in the team budget for one; back then, the head coach did everything. That was what the job entailed, so I adapted to that condition. That was pretty much SOP in the NBA back in the "good" old days.

Hard to believe, isn't it?

My first NBA assistant was Bob McKinnon, who joined me in 1972, my first season at Buffalo. And that only happened because Braves GM Eddie Donovan asked me to take on Bob, an old friend of his, as a personal favor. Donovan had found out that McKinnon was about to be fired as head coach at Canisius College, and he wanted to hire Bob before that could happen to spare McKinnon the embarrassment. I knew McKinnon from my college coaching days, and regarded him as a good basketball man, so I agreed. But Bob had no NBA experience, and I didn't utilize him much.

When I left Buffalo in 1976 to take the top job in Portland, I brought Jack McKinney with me. Jack had played for me at St. James High School (Chester, Pennsylvania) and Saint Joseph's College (Philadelphia), and later he became my assistant at St. Joe's. (McKinney had assisted Larry Costello at Milwaukee the previous year (1975–76). The strong relationship we had established previously at St. Joe's helped us get off the ground quickly in installing the pressure defense, fast-break style that I wanted at Portland. McKinney knew instinctively what I wanted, and I had confidence in the ideas he presented. We were a good team.

At games, I wanted McKinney to feed me any observations he had. I told him to just say whatever he saw and not wait for me to acknowledge him, much less worry if he said something I didn't respond to. I would process what he told me on the fly and make a judgment about whether to act on it. That arrangement worked out very well for both of us and the Blazers.

When Phil Jackson took over as head coach of the Bulls he gave the team offense over to his assistant, Tex Winter. Jackson always acknowledged Winter as the author of that part of the team game in Chicago and later in Los Angeles with the Lakers. Like all strong, effective leaders, Phil is perfectly comfortable in delegating responsibility—and both taking the heat when things go bad and sharing the spotlight when things go well.

Coach Mike Brown had a unique system of using his assistants at Cleveland. In the 2009 season, Mike assigned an assistant to offense (current Pistons head coach John Kuester) and another (Michael Malone) to defense. Nothing unusual there. But during timeouts, each of them addressed the team, while Brown listened at the edge of the huddle, only sometimes adding a comment at the end. He's the only NBA coach that followed that practice during timeouts.

I was broadcasting the 2009 NBA Finals with Hubie Brown, a Hall of Fame coach, and I asked him what he thought of Mike Brown's procedure. Hubie's response: "That's okay if the assistants know more than you do." I took that to mean that Hubie didn't think much of Mike Brown's approach—and neither did the Cavs.

The team fired Brown in May 2010 and replaced him with former Nets and Hornets coach Byron Scott.

Team leaders like the ones I've talked about in this chapter have certain traits in common. They help establish a strong core of discipline and rapport among team members. They're extremely self-disciplined, highly reliable, and fiercely determined warriors. They need only to be pointed in the right direction, and they'll do the rest.

Personal styles vary, of course, but there is one thing that is common to all.

The passion to win.

Men with a passion to win: Dr. Jack Ramsay with Bill Walton and NBA Hall of Fame coach Hubie Brown at a 1993 clinic in Israel.

8

LEARNING FROM LOSING

Winning is joy, exultation, happiness.

Losing is frustration, depression, gloom.

Absolutes. Polar extremes. Irreconcilable.

Yet in his great poem "If," Rudyard Kipling was on the money when he wrote that "If you can meet with triumph and disaster / And treat those two imposters just the same," then you're on the road to your ultimate destination: "Yours is the Earth and everything that's in it / And—which is more—you'll be a Man, my son!"

But it takes a mature, sensible person to handle the yo-yo, back-and-forth swing of the emotional extremes, the triumph and disaster that characterize all sports.

And for much of my coaching career, I was not such a person.

I was okay with winning.

I still remember the giddy feeling that I felt after I played well for Harrisburg when we upset Lancaster on its court in a decisive Game 3 to get to the Eastern League Finals in my rookie season six decades ago.

I loved it when players and fans hoisted me on their shoulders and carried me off the floor after St. Joe's beat Temple for the Big Five championship in my first season of college coaching in 1956.

Ramsay leaving the court in 1965 after a St. Joseph's victory, his 200th as a college coach.

Ramsay addressing Brazilian coaches at a clinic by the Saint Joseph's team in Rio de Janeiro during the summer of 1965.

1955–1956 Saint Joseph's team (23–6, Big 5 champions, third place NIT), Ramsay's first year as a college coach.

I smile at the memory of running off the floor to the locker room at the Palestra in Philly after St. Joe's upset Nate Thurmond's Bowling Green team (ranked No. 1 at the time) in the Quaker City Tournament in 1962, as I jumped in the air to kick the door open and landed on my backside because the door was firmly locked. My Hawks players howled with laughter and joy. I joined their chorus, sore butt and all.

I sometimes celebrated victories wildly, once throwing my sports coat up in the air and into the stands in pure ecstasy after St. Joe's won a big game at Wake Forest. (Fortunately, I got the coat back from an honest fan, the envelope in the inside pocket containing our travel money still sealed.)

I still like telling the story about a time early in my NBA career with Philadelphia when I was walking back to the hotel after dinner on an off night in Detroit. I was with the two Philadelphia beat writers who covered the Sixers, Jack Kiser of the *Daily News* (now part of the *Inquirer*) and George Kiseda of the *Evening Bulletin* (now defunct), and Andy Musser, the team's radio announcer (WCAU). The Sixers were off to a slow start that year (1979), and both writers had zinged me in their columns about the way the team was playing. I had gotten back at them in a good-natured way during dinner by questioning their qualifications to question me. There were some good shots taken all around—better ones than I was getting for my players, somebody suggested—and we all enjoyed the interplay. After dinner, Musser and I walked ahead, as Kiser and Kiseda lagged behind, involved in conversation. As they rounded a corner near the hotel, they saw me flat on my back on the sidewalk at a bus stop, with Musser bending over me. The writers thought I must have had a heart attack and rushed up. Musser played the role of the frantic friend, asking if either knew CPR. When I sensed their anxiety was at a high-enough level, I opened my eyes and pointed to a sign above me with an arrow pointing down that read: "Board Coach Here." It was the perfect capper on a good evening on the road.

The most exhilarating shower I ever took in my 85 years (and counting) on this planet came under an endless spray of champagne administered by my players in the Blazers' locker room after we won the NBA championship in 1977. Later that day, I hung the sports shirt and slacks that I was wearing at that moment in my closet at home, where I left them untouched for years. Every time I entered that closet, the sweet scent coming from the champagne-soaked garments evoked happy memories of that triumphant moment.

I also recall the mixed feelings of joy and humility that came over me in 1992 when I learned that I had been elected to the Naismith Basketball Hall of Fame.

I had played in college against teams coached by some of the legends of the game, men such as Nat Holman (CCNY), Hank Iba (Oklahoma A&M), Joe Lapchick (St. John's), and Frank Keaney (Rhode Island State). All were in the Hall for their monumental contributions to the game of basketball.

I coached against some of the game's greatest college and NBA coaches, men like Jack Gardner, Ben Carnevale, Red Holzman, and Harry Litwack who were already in the "Hallowed Hall." I didn't keep tabs, and I'm not about to go to the record books and check, so all I can say is that my teams won some and lost some against those great coaches.

On enshrinement day in May 1992, I was extremely honored to be in the company of those and other great basketball figures, but I also felt like something of an intruder. I felt the others were much more qualified than I was. But over the years, I've been able to squelch those feelings of being a party crasher and have enjoyed belonging to that elite club.

Those were special times, long-ago times, times that still evoke happy reveries (and occasional goose bumps) many years later.

And losing?

That was something else. I treated it as a personal failure, and I walled myself off from others. I brooded and acted immaturely. I was a poor loser. Still am.

I haven't forgotten the Harrisburg team that lost to Williamsport in the 1950 Eastern League Finals in a decisive Game 3 mostly because their point guard, a fellow named Jack Ramsay, allowed the game tempo to escalate rather than keeping it at the ball-control pace of our game plan. After the game, the coach, Billy Binder, said to me, "So much for controlling the tempo, huh Jack?" I drove the four hours back home with several of my teammates without saying a word.

Back when I was coaching at St. Joe's, I remember storming out of the Palestra in Philadelphia after a loss to La Salle and driving home at a reckless speed, forgetting that I was supposed to join my wife, Jean, and another couple after the game for a late dinner. Only when I opened the door and my daughter, Susan, asked, "Where's Mom?" did I realize how my inability to handle losing could warp my behavior.

I was so ashamed of my team's performance after St. Joe's lost to Navy in a consolation game in the 1965 NCAA Eastern Regional tournament that I wouldn't allow the players to go on the court to receive their fourth-place medals. Even now, over four decades later, I shake my head in disbelief and remorse for my behavior.

I recall after a close loss to the Bulls in my first season as coach of the Sixers that I walked deserted Chicago streets alone in the wee small hours of the morning, hoping that someone would try to mug me so that I could unleash my anger on him. Later, an assistant started hanging around with me after road losses—mostly, I now understand, to keep me out of harm's way. We'd go on long, sometimes bitter-cold walks in silence, while I got rid of my postgame wrath.

After a close loss to Seattle in my first year with the Sixers, I banged on the door of the officials' dressing room, demanding an explanation for a noncall as Billy Cunningham drove to the hoop at the end of the game. No response. More banging on the door by me. Finally Richie Powers, the lead official, said through the still-closed door, "Forget it, Jack. Go get your team ready for the next game."

Good advice.

Assistants like Jack McKinney, Jim Lynam, Dick Harter, and Rick Adelman and coaching friends like the late Cotton Fitzsimmons helped me over the years to become more sensible about accepting defeat.

Fitzsimmons and I were kindred spirits. We both came from college coaching backgrounds—he'd been at Kansas State before taking over the Phoenix Suns in 1970—and we both loved the challenge of the NBA. Cotton was an excellent coach and was twice named NBA Coach of the Year (1979 and 1989). Cotton knew me well and often chided me for my paranoia about losing. "Now listen, Doc," he said to me on one occasion before a Suns-Blazers game, "we *are* going to go out and have a nice meal together after the game, no matter who wins. Okay?"

Phoenix won the game, and we did go out to dinner that night.

Cotton succumbed to lung cancer in 2004, the same year that melanoma got rooted in my foot. I talked to him by telephone shortly before he passed away. As we finished our conversation, he said, "I love you, Doc." I replied, "I love you too, Cotton." Those were the last words we spoke to each other.

Over time, the 82-game NBA schedule helps make even an irrational person (read: me) realize that you can't withdraw from society just because your team lost a basketball game. I never became what anybody would call a "good loser," but I got better at accepting defeat and moving on.

I found that physical workouts helped me deal with postgame frustrations so I started putting a good, hard workout at the top of my agenda for the day following a game. (Sure, I skipped a day now and then, but never after a loss.) I also made it a point to talk to each of my players the day after a loss. If the team was on the road, I was first on the team bus taking us to the airport, and I'd look each player in the eye and greet him with a "Good morning." Doesn't sound like much, but at least it broke the silence and opened the lines of communication.

A loss, once recorded, can't be changed. Funny how hard it is emotionally to accept that basic truth. A coach can't do anything about a loss except to use it as a tool to gain the next victory. For an NBA coach, there's a very simple process for doing just that:

1. Break down the game video to show the players the

reasons for the loss. In most cases, turnovers, a failure to block out and rebound, a slow transition defense, and quick or shoddy execution of offense are the culprits.

2. Use drill work on the practice floor to correct those errors.

3. Examine your coaching performance regarding game plan, substitutions, and strategy to see if you could have done better from the bench.

Players are almost universally receptive to this sort of approach. They acknowledge their mistakes when they see them on video. "The video don't lie" is a comment I heard over and over.

Specific practice work on the areas of deficiency helped forge confidence, and improved performance almost always followed. To improve ball-handling and reduce turnovers, I used a two-on-two, half-court drill in which the defenders were encouraged to be very aggressive and had the freedom to double-team the player with the ball, forcing him to make good passing decisions. Block-out drills for rebounding are tough, physical work, but they always paid dividends by reducing second-chance points by opponents. Transition defense drills—sprinting to the backcourt while keeping the ball within your vision—renewed the importance of that fundamental.

Improving a team's offense takes more time, patience, and focus to bring about. Ball handling, defense, and rebounding are functions, for the most, of greater effort and attention to fundamentals. Turning poor shooters into good shooters is a taller hill to climb.

My parting words to my players after a bad loss were variations of this basic theme: "We've got work to do." They knew that meant we'd be going back to fundamentals in the next practice session.

"You'll have a lot of time off when we win," Red Holzman used to tell his Knicks just before the season opener, "but if we lose, you're mine." Translation: at least three hours of work the next time they all got together on things he knew they knew they should know how to do.

I don't remember ever saying to my team that we *had* to win a particular game. I didn't need to—my players knew as well as I did when we were heading into a "must win" game. Prior to a game, after reviewing all the tactics we had gone over on the practice floor, my concluding words to my team were simply, "Now, let's go do it."

Sharing the experience of winning with team members forms a bond that lasts forever. In December 2009 I visited Maurice Lucas, the Blazers' power forward on the 1977 NBA champions, in a hospital just outside of Portland. Luke, battling bladder cancer, was propped up in a chair, taking both drip chemo and nourishment intravenously. He was drifting between sleep and consciousness. He opened his eyes, saw me, smiled, and said, "The Doctor … the Doctor is here."

We talked for about an hour, as Luke recalled the joy and love he and his teammates on that championship team felt for each other. We talked about how special that team was to both of us: "We had it all, Doc. Too bad it couldn't have lasted."

Luke told me that many of his teammates visited him. "I woke up the other day and Lloyd [Neal] was just sitting there," Luke said. "I don't know how long he had been there. He just wanted me to know he was there for me. [Memphis Grizzlies coaches] JD [Johnny Davis] and Train [Lionel Hollins] drop by when they're in town. Bobby (Gross) stops by quite a bit."

We talked about our families, the NBA, mutual friends, and even some politics. But the conversation always came back to the championship team, recalling incidents with vivid clarity from games played over 30 years ago. We had some good laughs and shared some great memories.

I also told Luke about my own cancer experience and how I was free of the disease at that time. I wanted him to know that cancer cures take place every day and that he shouldn't give up.

No fear of that. He was still the Blazers tough guy.

Luke gave me a hug when I was ready to leave. I kissed his forehead and whispered, "God bless you, Luke."

Tears were in my eyes as I left the room.

Luke and I kept in touch by phone and e-mail after that. I was working the 2010 NBA Finals in Los Angeles on June 5th, when I got a voice mail from him. "Thirty-three years ago today, Doctor—a special day for all of us Blazers." He was referring to the day in 1977 when we beat Philadelphia to win the NBA title.

I didn't see Luke again until October 2010. I knew that he'd had a period of remission but that the cancer had returned to his bladder. He'd just returned home after a lengthy stay in the hospital. I made arrangements to visit him.

Luke was sitting up in bed when I walked into the room. He looked thinner than the last time I'd seen him, but he was smiling and his eyes were bright as we exchanged hugs. He said, "It's good to see you, Man."

This time we talked mostly about life and family values. He told me how special it was to have his loving wife, Pamela, and his adult children with him. He said he was off chemo treatment for the time, while his doctors deliberated on the next steps in his recovery. "I hope the docs come up with something. I'm not giving up, but I'm ready for whatever will be. I had a good visit with my minister. My family is here. I'm in God's hands now."

Luke passed away about three weeks after my last visit. He was 58 years old.

May The Big Man forever smile upon you, Maurice Lucas.

Phil Jackson, who's had a little experience with the concept of winning—one championship as a player, 11 (and still counting) as a coach—is as good an authority on the subject as anybody I know:

> *The greatest part about winning is how you feel as a group. You're happy for one another. You look at small plays that happen in a game, the people who come off the bench and provide something the group needs.... It is not just the best player. It's from one to twelve, the coaches included, and your appreciation for each is very high.*[1]

Immediately after his Lakers won the NBA title in 2009, I watched Jackson, standing apart from his players, beam like a proud parent as they hugged each other and shouted with happiness. Afterward he told me that while he was still driven to win as a competitor, what he most enjoys at this point in his career is watching the response of his players to winning. "It's nice to sit back and see how much joy they get out of winning," he said. "I still remember that first championship with the Bulls [1992] as being something very special. It was a new experience for all of us. Very, very special."

Red Auerbach said the same thing when I asked him, many years after he retired, which of his nine championships meant the most to him: "The first one, 1957. We had just gotten Russell. Tommy Heinsohn was young, but Frank Ramsey, Cousy, and Sharman had been around long enough to wonder if they would ever win one. It was a great feeling—and I never got tired of it."

I was associated with two championship teams in the NBA, the 1967 Philadelphia 76ers as general manager and the 1977 Trail Blazers as coach. I had a great sense of satisfaction as GM when the Sixers won, but I didn't have the same connection with the team that Alex Hannum had as its coach. General managers oversee the whole program, but the coach is in the trenches with his players. He's there every day with them, charting the course, guiding them over the bumps, urging them on, driving them when fatigue saps their energy. The coach is an active part of the team.

Rookies just entering the NBA are concerned, first and foremost, with staying there. (Rightly so. Some mighty big college names have had one-year-and-out NBA careers.) Once they get over that anxiety hump, the next goal is to hear the compliment "He can play" from his peers. That may not sound like much to the layman, but to an NBA player it's a huge source of pride. And next?

The toughest accomplishment of all: getting fitted for a championship ring. Some fine players complete long, outstanding careers and retire ringless. They may not say it out loud, but failing to win a championship leaves true competitors feeling unfilled when they leave the game. And the ones who do win one? They want another and another and another …

Winning can take on different meanings. At Boston during the Bill Russell era, making the playoffs was a given—a mere formality that the Celtics endured before getting down to the real business, squaring off against another team in the championship series. In my first year coaching Philadelphia, we played the Celtics four times in the preseason. We won the first three games handily. Before the fourth game, Hal Greer, the Sixers' future Hall of Fame 2-guard, said to me, "This game will be different. The Celts will want to win this one. You'll see a different Bill Russell tonight." Hal was right. The C's came out with a purpose, as if to say, "Enough of this. We've got to get ready to win another championship."

And they did.

Russell appeared to place winning and losing in what I would call a balanced light. But for Red Auerbach, the only coach that Bill ever played for in the NBA (except for the three seasons that Russ was player-coach), this was most assuredly not the case. Here's Russ on Red:

> He thought about winning more than I thought about eat-ing when I was little. He ached when we didn't win; his whole body would be thrown out of whack when we lost. He didn't care about any player's statistics or reputation in the newspapers; all he thought about was the final score and who had helped put it on the board. He was our gyro-scope, programmed solely for winning.[2]

But Russell discovered when he took over the Seattle and Sacra-mento teams as a bench coach that a team without himself as a player was very different from the Celtic teams on which he was the key performer.

Jerry Reynolds, who served as Russell's assistant when he came back to the NBA in 1987–88 after a 10-year hiatus to coach the Sacra-mento Kings, told me that he could see the pain in Russell's eyes after a loss. Finally the pain became too much to bear: Russ stepped aside as coach with 24 games left in the season. The Kings' record at the time of his departure: 17–41.

I talked to Bill many years later about his five seasons (make that *almost* five seasons) as a nonplaying coach. By the time he took over in Sacramento in 1973–74 after being away from the NBA for three seasons, he had established something of a don't-give-a-damn attitude toward the media, and he was known to shortcut team practices. Pretty clearly, coming back into the game after being away from the NBA for so long hadn't been such a good idea.

"I guess I could have put more into it," he said softly. "I could have put more into it."

But again Reynolds came to his defense: "What the team missed most was a player *like* Bill. When he worked out at practice at the age of 45, he was still the best player on the court. He worked hard with the big men we had [LaSalle Thompson and Otis Thorpe], but they just weren't good enough."

Red Holzman had one goal, *only* one goal: "You can win all the games you want during the regular season, but if you don't win the championship, all the work and effort of training camp and eighty-two games means nothing."[3]

Of course, Red could say that when he had players like Willis Reed, Dave DeBusschere, Bill Bradley, and Walt Frazier. But I also remember hearing Red say he was "doing the best he can with the players I have." That was when the Knicks brought him out of retirement to replace Willis Reed as coach 14 games into the 1978 season; he finished the year with a 25–43 mark. Red was as good a coach then as when the Knicks won championships, but his players were no longer good enough to compete for the title. A coach's perspective has to be realistic.

For my first Buffalo team, which won only 21 games, "winning" was expressed in seeing modest skills improvement in the players who were going to be members of my teams of the future.

Winning was in getting center Elmore Smith to make a fundamental back-door pass from the post. A fellow teammate, John Hummer, a cerebral player from Princeton, said to me after watching me work with Smith on some passing drills at training camp, "Coach, you'll never get 'E' to make that pass." But we did.

Winning was getting Randy Smith to drive to the basket with a left-hand dribble and getting Bob McAdoo to recognize the difference between a good shot and a bad one. And it was getting Bob Kauffman to accept the role of rebounder and defender coming off the bench. By the end of that first season, all four had achieved those goals and were ready to play on teams that made the playoffs.

Philadelphia had already won two NBA championships before I took over as coach there in 1968, so making the playoffs was a minimum expectation. My Sixers teams met that standard three of the four seasons I was there. No big deal.

But for the other three teams I coached in the NBA, "winning" was defined as just squeezing into the playoffs. Buffalo and Portland had never been there before; Indiana had been to one NBA playoffs and was eliminated in the first round after three straight losses. Of course, a team doesn't get to the playoffs without winning consistently during the regular season. But for teams in the middle of the pack in talent, that playoff goal is the everyday focus of the coach and players.

When the Blazers clinched a playoff spot in my first season in Portland, the scoreboard flashed "PLAYOFFS ... PLAYOFFS ... PLAYOFFS" as jubilant fans celebrated in the arena for about an hour after the game ended. The season was already a success. Imagine the euphoria when that team went on to win the championship! That was over 30 years ago, but it's still the biggest thing to happen in Oregon sports history.

When Buffalo made it to the playoffs in 1974, the third year of the franchise's existence, the fans were ecstatic. But unfortunately for those fans, the franchise left Buffalo after the 1978 season, and the city hasn't had an NBA team since.

Winning typically occurs only when a team plays its game well. No, that's not exactly an earth-shattering observation, but I make it because teams can also win when they don't play especially well. The name for that, of course, is "winning ugly."

I recall a game my Braves won in 1976—it happened to be our 11th straight win—when we'd played poorly, at least by my standards. We were just lucky that on that night our opponents had played a whole lot worse. I was none too pleased with our performance, and I told my guys that in no uncertain terms back in the locker room after the game. They all knew how we'd played, and many nodded in assent at my critique. I noticed Jack Marin looking at me with a knowing smile on his face. I said, "Do you have something to add, Jack?"

"I agree with your assessment about the game," Jack said, "but let's not forget how tough it is to win 11 in a row in this league and not get too bent out of shape about how we played. We did win the game after all."

"I'll take the win, of course," I responded. "But we're not going to win many games playing like that. I want us to play better. If we do, the winning will take care of itself."

The bottom line? Don't count on winning ugly. Sooner or later, ugly becomes the team's norm and losing sets in.

My Blazers won a game in Chicago as we wheeled into the last quarter of the season following our 1977 championship. We had given up a go-ahead field goal off a turnover on a poorly executed play in the closing seconds. Then, with the game clock winding down to zero, Lionel Hollins banked in a running one-hander from near midcourt to win the game for us.

Lionel's teammates leaped in the air and high-fived him as they ran to the locker room. But Coach Killjoy didn't like the way the Blazers played the whole game, and especially down the stretch. I walked slowly off the court. When I got to the locker room, I wrote on the chalk board the time the bus was leaving for the airport, said not a word, and walked out of the room. I waited until the next day to tell the team that we'd been damned lucky to win, and then I ran down a list of specific screw-ups and examples of general sloppiness. Just making the playoffs wasn't an issue. Falling into bad habits, taking things for granted, getting sloppy—those were the things we needed to worry about.

"Let's play at our best level," I told them, "and then we won't have to be lucky to win."

The flip side to winning, of course, is losing, and how miserable it makes everyone associated with it feel. When a team has a losing season, everyone associated with the franchise feels it and wants to change the situation. I recounted in a previous chapter how team rosters were turned over in my early years at Buffalo and Portland to transform losing teams into winners. That's not always going to happen. I wanted to do the same thing at Indiana, but Donny Walsh was unable to make the trades to do it. Sometimes a coach just has to gut it out.

"Losing causes more than a number in the loss column," says Rudy Tomjanovich, referring to the 2001–02 season, when his Rockets went 28–54 on the heels of a 45–37 record the year before. "It tests your constitution. It tests your faith. It clouds the true issues. Everyone starts searching for reasons why this could be happening to us."[4]

Tomjanovich's first head coaching job came two-thirds of the way through the 1991–92 season, when Don Chaney was fired for not living up to ownership expectations. The season before, the Rockets won the Midwest Division with a 52–30 record. At the time Chaney got the axe, the Rockets were spinning their wheels at 26–26.

Rudy's first game was at home against the Sixers, and I was there to help televise it back to Philadelphia. I interviewed Rudy before the game, and let me tell you, the man was a nervous wreck. He even expressed some doubt on air that night that he could do the job—not exactly the sort of thing you want to hear from a brand-new coach. (Or any kind of coach, for that matter.) He was so uptight and lacking in self-confidence that I wasn't sure he'd last the season. But Rudy gained some measure of confidence (or at least mitigated his panic) as the Rockets finished 16–14. The following season, they went 55–27 to finish first in the Midwest Division. And the season after that (1993–94), Rudy's Rockets won the first of back-to-back NBA championships. By then, Rudolph Tomjanovich from Hamtramck, Michigan, had gotten over his crisis of confidence. That didn't mean the 28–54 nightmare in 2001–02 was easy to take. But Rudy had proven he was a winner, and that made it at least marginally easier.

Losing is no fun wherever or whenever it takes place.

When I coached Saint Joseph's College in Philadelphia, there were alumni of all the other Big Five colleges (Villanova, La Salle, Temple, and Penn) in my Andorra neighborhood. If one of their teams beat the Hawks, they waited for me to appear on the street the next day. As soon as I showed my face, my neighbors from the other four schools would start shouting "The Hawk is dead" and keep shouting it until I either got in my car and drove off or went back into the house. The rivalries were that intense. Mind you, I liked all the people. We socialized frequently throughout the year and had great times together. This only happened during the basketball season, and only if one of their teams beat St. Joe's, and—fortunately—that didn't happen very often. But, given my near psychotic aversion to losing, I didn't look forward one bit to their playful taunting after an L.

Losing is even worse, Bill Bradley says, if you lose in New York: "Daily encounters with the public become painful. Walking down the street as a winner invites hellos and congratulations. Walking down the same street after losing produces criticism and derision."[5]

Bradley goes on, "Learning to cope with defeat was not easy. From the time I was in high school, I used to turn a basketball loss over and over in my mind. Asking myself what I could have done differently. Often I replayed the game so relentlessly that it would interfere with my sleep. The loss hung for days, like a fog."[6]

(Sounds a lot like somebody I know. Somebody I see every morning in the bathroom mirror.)

Senator Bill says it took him several years before he came to handle losing in a more balanced manner. In his second year in the NBA he had just made the Knicks team as the starting forward when his team lost a close game to Philadelphia. I was coaching the Sixers then, and I remember the game. The Knicks had a late lead, and we started pressing them. The game turned when Bradley made a bad pass in the closing seconds. I subsequently learned that Bill was utterly disconsolate after the game, the essence of an abject dejection so intense so that a trusted teammate had to give him a little talking to:

Back at the hotel Dave DeBusschere, an experienced pro who had joined the team two months earlier, and was my new roommate, put me straight: "You can't go through a season like this. There are too many games. Sure, you blew it tonight, but when it's over, it's over. Let it go. Otherwise you won't be ready to play tomorrow night."

That piece of advice changed my whole attitude.... I realized that the more you carry the bad past around with you in the present, the less likely it is that the future will improve.[7]

As readers of a certain age will recall, the future improved *dramatically* for Bradley and the Knicks. Bradley became the team's most reliable passer and shooter. Not spectacular like Frazier with his eyes-defying sleight of hand, nor as great a scorer as DeBusschere, but steady as a luxury liner of the sort that used to dock at Hudson River piers in New York. I don't ever remember seeing Bradley commit a key turnover again.

Not ever. Not once. That's saying something.

"When you win," wrote Red Holzman, Bradley's coach in New York, "everything is better. You sleep better, you look forward to the day, your coffee is just right in the morning, the sun is usually shining, and everyone looks at you with a smile on his face."

Red loved coaching in the NBA. "What's better than this, Jack?" he asked me once. "We travel first class to the best cities in the country, we stay in the best hotels, our rooms are paid for, we eat at the best restaurants, and we practice on the best basketball floors." Then he added with a twinkle in his eye: "If only we didn't have to play the games."

Phil Jackson, who hasn't experienced as much losing as most of us mere mortals, always has a game plan in hand that he believes will, eventually, be effective regardless of what opponents might do to counter it. Consequently, Phil typically doesn't make many adjustments during games. An opposing team can run off 15 straight points, and Phil will sit on the bench with his arms folded. He often won't even call for a timeout.

After one such game in which his Bulls went through a bad stretch before racking up a W in the 1992 NBA Finals against the Lakers, I asked Phil why he hadn't called for time so that his team could regroup.

"I wanted my guys to play through it," Phil answered. "I wanted them to find a way to win."

(P.S.: they did.)

Jackson had a great team in Chicago and he knew it. I felt he was willing to sacrifice a victory if need be so that his players could learn a lesson for the future. Phil still uses the same philosophy in Los Angeles. I asked Kobe Bryant about that approach in crises, and his answer was quick and unequivocal: "I like it. Phil puts it on us, and on me in particular—to figure things out. It shows he has confidence in us."

Some coaches privately question Jackson's reluctance to involve himself more in game situations like that, but it's hard to argue with those 11 NBA championships on his résumé.

John Wooden once said to me that his job was to prepare his team to play the game but that it was up to them to go out and win it. Like Jackson, Wooden didn't make many adjustments during a game. But Wooden's record for winning is unmatched in NCAA competition.

That's a luxury that may apply only to coaches with abundant talent. If you coach a team with lesser talent, one that must scratch and claw on every possession, a competitive coach must step in and try to help his team find a way to win. When I coached, if what I planned didn't work the way I thought it would, I made changes, sometimes several changes, looking for something that would work.

For those of us coaches not named Wooden or Jackson, that's part of the job description.

At times—too many times—during my coaching career I wouldn't speak to anyone after a loss: not my players, not my assistants, not my friends, not even my family. Losing cost me years of sleep. I'd toss and turn and sometimes not sleep at all. One of my college players, Bob McNeill, said many years later that for me "losing was like having a death in the family."

"Ramsay may be a good coach," Red Auerbach once said, "but he won't talk to anybody after a loss. He's got to get over that."

I finally reached a compromise with myself: I would meet with my assistant after a loss to talk about the way we played. Together we would analyze what we could do to correct our shortcomings. Then the next morning, I'd get up early and have a vigorous physical workout before meeting with the team at practice. I made a point of speaking personally with each player. At a team meeting, I outlined the plan my coaches and I had developed for eliminating the previous game's mistakes and for improving various team situations. Then we'd head out to the practice court to prepare for the next game.

Rick Adelman, one of my assistants at Portland (and now coach of the Rockets), later told me that he felt my change in comportment and conduct following losses turned out to be one of my greatest strengths as a coach, and something he tried to emulate. Now with two decades of head coaching under his belt, Rick passed my career win total (864 wins early in the 2009–10 campaign). When asked if he had gained anything from his time as my assistant that helped him achieve coaching success in the NBA, Rick referred back to that trait: "One thing I learned from Jack was how to bounce back after losses. He was always upbeat and optimistic the next day after a loss and transmitted that enthusiasm to the players."

(Good thing Rick wasn't around me during the early years.)

Players, I discovered, are generally able to shed the sting of defeat much quicker than their coaches. From my observations, most players put a game out of their minds by the time they leave the locker room after a defeat. By the next game, they're ready to go all out to win. When you're playing an 82-game schedule, there's merit in that approach. (See the advice Dave DeBusschere gave Bill Bradley.)

I'm not the only one who struggled to find a way to handle defeat. The unflappable Phil Jackson, the coach who likes to let his players "play through" the bad times, says that in high school and college, winning was a matter of life and death:

As a kid, I often threw temper tantrums when I lost, especially if I was competing against my older brothers. Losing made me feel humiliated and worthless, as if I didn't exist.... My obsession with winning was often my undoing. I would push so hard to succeed when things weren't going my way that it would hurt my performance.[8]

Mr. Clutch, Jerry West, was also inconsolable after critical losses in the NBA playoffs, games in which he felt he and his team had played well enough to win:

I don't think people understand the real trauma associated with losing. ... I don't think they realize how miserable you can be.... It got to the point with me that I wanted to quit basketball. I really did. I didn't think it was fair that you could give so much and play until there was nothing left in your body to give and you couldn't win.... The closer you come to the magic circle, the more enticing it becomes. I imagine in some ways, it's like a drug. It's seductive because it's always there, and the desire is always there to win one more game.[9]

West struggled as a coach in great measure because he couldn't accept less than the very maximum effort from his players. I once had a chat with him before a game in Portland when he coached the Lakers. He was unhappy with the way his team was playing and said, "And I don't know when that big stiff is going to start playing." I looked out at the floor where the players were warming up, not knowing which "big stiff" he was referring to, when I saw that he meant Kareem Abdul-Jabbar!

When West was president of the Memphis Grizzlies team that Hubie Brown coached, he sometimes came into the locker room after a loss and tore into the players for their shoddy performance. That sort of visitation by management is considered a no-no in the NBA.

Like West, Michael Jordan had zero tolerance for anything less than the maximum effort from his teammates, 100 percent of the time:

A lot of other guys ... might think, "It's only a game and you are supposed to have fun, so you shouldn't make a game larger than life." I don't agree with that. If I'm going to play, then when I walk in between those white lines, I'm going to play to win. I'm not out there just to be playing. That's just not me. That's not my attitude.[10]

Michael led the league in scoring 11 times—every season he was with Chicago, except when he was injured and played in only 18 games (1986) and when he came back from baseball near the end of the season (1995). But the only accomplishment that meant anything to him was winning championships.

"It's all about the rings, Doc," he said to me more than once. "It's all about the rings."

Given how much we all love Ws and hate Ls, it's sort of ironic that there are more lessons to be learned from losing than from winning.

After a loss, a coach can dissect the game and find out what didn't work. Whatever the reasons for a loss, you can pinpoint them and develop a game plan to prevent their recurrence, then test that plan on the practice court.

When you win, on the other hand, it's easy to gloss over a lot of things. You don't analyze the game as carefully because, hey, you won, didn't you? Sometimes, when you go over a video of a win, you wonder how your guys managed to pull it off. You may discover that your team actually didn't play that well and just got plain lucky. Losing is a better teacher, even when the lessons it teaches are painful.

After Utah blew out San Antonio 109–83 in a game in the 2007 playoffs, I asked Spurs coach Gregg Popovich what he planned to do to get his guys ready for the next game. Pop just shook his head: "They all know that we played like bleep. My message to them was pretty simple: we were terrible, they were good, and we don't want to be terrible."

Smart call, Pop

What else can you say to a good team after it gets blown out? They don't need to have their performance sliced and diced and gone over in detail. *Close* games against inferior teams that end up in the loss column, they're different. They do bear close examination. Maybe the L came about as a result of some small thing that can be identified and fixed. At least you make sure the next day that you bust your butt trying to fix what went wrong.

(P.S.: the Spurs won the series with Utah and went on to sweep Cleveland in the NBA Finals.)

Popovich has a great sense of what the Spurs need from him. When they need to get ripped after a loss, he minces no words, either with an individual player or the team as a group. The players all accept it and respond positively.

Pat Riley saw benefits in losing, particularly if a loss comes after a good team has played poorly and loses to a team it should have beaten:

> *Sometimes losing is more constructive than winning.... When you play lousy and you win, you lose perspective. You start believing that lack of effort doesn't matter. Other teams are intimidated by your record. Momentum is on your side. Then playing lousy becomes part of your style and your psyche. You set yourself up to get beat and demoralized somewhere down the road.* [11]

I can still hear Riley saying to his Heat players after a sluggish performance, "I see some slippage." At that single word, they'd cringe, knowing how hard Riles would drill them on the practice floor the next day.

John Wooden said that losing provided the feedback needed to become a winner: "Long before any championships were won at UCLA, I came to understand that losing is only temporary and not all-encompassing. You must study it, learn from it, and try hard not to lose the same way again. Then you must have the self-control to forget about it." [12]

I was privileged to participate in several coaching clinics with Coach Wooden. His sessions were always packed, and the audience, mostly high school and small-college coaches, sat mesmerized at the feet of a master clinician. Wooden would speak for an hour or more, using no notes, but without hesitation. He seemed to speak to each individual in the room. There was rich meaning in everything he said or wrote.

Winning and losing.

Some of both will turn up in everyone's life.

The trick is in how you handle those two imposters.

Dave Cowens   George Karl

Dick Motta   Jack Ramsay

1992 staff for an NBA clinic in Mexico: Dr. Jack with Hall of Fame Celtics player Dave Cowens, Denver Nuggets coach George Karl (who recorded 1,000 wins during the 2010–2011 season) and legendary NBA coach Dick Motta, who won an NBA championship in 1979 with Washington.

9

THE FUN
IN WINNING

The Big Three of American sports—football, baseball, and basketball—are all team games. My favorite, it will come as no surprise to hear, is basketball. One big reason, maybe the biggest, is what sets basketball apart from the other two team games—namely, that you don't need to be part of a team to enjoy it.

You've read here about the likes of Jerry West and Pete Maravich and Magic Johnson, all of whom spent hours and hours every day when they were kids, all alone, shooting buckets on outdoor courts in the neighborhoods where they grew up.

You've read about Ernie DiGregorio, a marvelous ball handler whom I coached in Buffalo in the mid-1970s, who once told me that he didn't remember a time as a kid when he didn't have a basketball in his hands. Ernie dribbled his ball on the way to school, while doing errands for his mother, and—of course—on his way to and from the playground. I didn't ask him, but I wouldn't be surprised if Ernie slept at nights with his basketball next to him in bed.

I was like them.

Not as good mind you, but every bit as much in love with basketball.

When I was about 12 years old, my father hung a basket on the barn in back of our house in Milford, Connecticut. Every day during the school year, in all but the worst weather, I'd make a beeline for the barn the minute after I got home from school. That was my haven—and my heaven. I spent hours there shooting and dribbling, rebounding missed shots, and playing in imaginary games until dinnertime. Then, since there was an outside light on the barn, I'd go again after I finished my meal.

I remember many dark, cold winter nights, first shoveling the snow from the driveway and then going to work on parts of my game that needed special attention. I worked on improving my left-hand dribble and layup, shooting off the dribble, and learning how to spin the ball off the backboard—in this case the side of the barn—and into the hoop. I'd stay out there, my hands nearly frozen, until my mother called me to the house to do homework. It was great.

I played shortstop on a local baseball team in the summers, but I still found time to visit the barn to shoot hoops after the sun went down in the early evenings.

From that beginning, I became good enough to play on my grade school and high school teams and eventually received an athletic scholarship to St. Joseph's College in Philadelphia. I played there four years. After graduation from St. Joe's, I got a job coaching basketball at St. James High School in Chester, Pennsylvania, and then at Mount Pleasant High School in Wilmington, Delaware. I combined teaching and coaching at the two schools with playing six years in the Eastern Pro League. I also played for an independent team, the Norristown Blocks, a couple of times a week, sometimes in a prelim before the old Philadelphia Warriors' NBA games in the Philadelphia Arena. The $15 a week plus gas money I got helped pay the bills at home and kept me in good shape for the Eastern League games on the weekends.

In all of that time, the lure of the court never diminished for me. I still feel the same way about all of my associations with basketball, whether playing, coaching, conducting clinics, doing radio and television broadcasts of games, or writing about it.

Love of the game? You'd better believe it!

Although the beautiful solitude of "you, a ball, and a basket" is often a life-altering experience, the joy of competing in the great game of basketball is ratcheted up to even higher levels with participation on a talented team. The Portland Trail Blazers that I coached were that kind of team. That team "came

Ramsay with Harry Litwack, his presenter at Ramsay's 1992 induction into the Naismith Basketball Hall of Fame in Springfield, Mass.

together" at training camp to win the NBA championship in 1977. It was a wondrous season in which we exceeded expectations time and again. The pure joy of the way that team played together was reward enough, but winning the title was icing on the cake.

The "journey" and "destination" that Coach John Wooden talked about were equally gratifying. The year after we won the championship, the Blazers were even better, running on high octane right out of the chute and beating everybody in the league, at home or away. But after reaching a 50–10 record, we were decimated by injuries, to Bill Walton and others, and our season crumbled. We went 8–14 the rest of the way and got knocked out of the playoffs in the second round by Seattle. But during that first 60-game period, our team was close to invincible.

That run provided the most enjoyment I've ever had in basketball, and it gave me more satisfaction than *any* activity in my life, except for being with my family. Not only were we dominating the league; we were also having a great time doing it. I got daily pleasure from just being with that group.

We had fun at practice. We were all involved, players and coaches alike. I loved competing against the players in free throw shooting contests at the end of practices. As a player, my best effort from the line in a game was 15 for 15 in the Eastern League, and 75 straight on the practice floor. So I usually held my own. My wins were occasions for much good-natured needling.

Guard Dave Twardzik and I also got into one-on-one action that was great fun. Twardzik was my height (6' 1") and had played the post on an undersized but very good high school team in Middletown, Pennsylvania, before going on to star at Old Dominion College. A six-year veteran, Dave had some very clever moves in the paint and beat me consistently, but we had a lot of fun banging each other around.

I was often seated next to players on plane trips, which gave me a chance to get to know them more personally. Each of us had come from a different background, but fate, and a good selection process, had brought us together. I discovered some interesting facets of their lives.

For instance, I learned that Walton was an avid student of U.S. history and geography. He often commented on locations and events as we looked down on the country from on high. Mo Lucas told me about growing up in Pittsburgh and how an older brother was adjusting following his recent release from prison. John Davis talked about the difficulty of living in a segregated, tough section of Detroit. Lionel Hollins, now coach of the Memphis Grizzlies, thought like a coach even then, and we would often X-and-O through entire flights.

I learned a lot about my players that helped me relate to them on the basketball court. It was a special time.

My players still talk about it today.

And, as you've just seen, so do I.

Players often wax eloquent and enthusiastic about how much fun the game of basketball has been for them over the course of their lives. No surprise there. Even jaded veterans were little boys once. The exhilaration they experienced while learning to play drove them to improve their game so that it could become a profession. Basketball became a job, but it started as pure, unadulterated fun.

For Spud Webb, who logged 11 years (and part of a 12th) in the NBA, the fun never ended. As an opposing coach, I could tell that the diminutive Spud (5'6") flat-out loved to play just by the way he warmed up for a game. There was always joy on his face, a bounce to his step, and a visible affection for his teammates as he went through pregame layup drills. After he'd loosened up, Spud would drive to the hoop, rise above the rim, throw down slam dunks, and then beam as his teammates saluted him with high fives.

Spud expressed his attachment to basketball quite eloquently:

I love basketball so much you can't believe it. It is the greatest game in the world.... I'd play for free. I'm gonna play as long as I can and, who knows maybe they'll even have basketball in heaven.... For me, pursuing a basketball career with all my heart and soul was just that easy—the game is that much fun.[1]

Bill Walton also loved everything about playing basketball, especially contributing to a championship team, and later stayed with the game as a prominent game analyst for ESPN. Bill honed his skills early on by playing more than 100 games of AAU competition in the spring and summer months in the late 1960s, in addition to playing at Helix High School in La Mesa, California. Walton had great across-the-board skills as a center and loved playing in a style where teamwork was a high priority. I do believe he enjoyed making an assist more than scoring himself.

After the foot injury that felled him (and the Blazers!) late in the 1977–78 season, Bill managed to play only 14 games over the next three years. Several painful reconstructive surgeries to correct foot and ankle problems allowed him to come back, and he won a championship ring with the Celtics in 1986, but he was never the same Bill Walton who'd led us to the NBA Championship in 1977. I talk to Bill several times a year. He never fails to reminisce about how much fun it was being part of that great Blazers team.

Walton's chief adversary at that time, Kareem Abdul-Jabbar, saluted Bill's passion for the game: "Walton played with true playground enthusiasm; he would have played basketball even if there was no prestige or pay involved … he was out there having fun for a living."[2]

Bill derived a different kind of enjoyment from basketball when he joined the Celtics in 1985–86, his last full season in the NBA. He had recovered sufficiently from injuries to play again, but only on a on a part-time basis; he was no longer his team's kingpin the way he'd been for us at Portland. But the chance to play with Larry Bird, and on a team with great chemistry, made playing for the Celtics a lot of fun: "The Celtics were everything I thought basketball should be. I've always wanted to have fun playing basketball.… I was happiest playing basketball, and playing for a championship team. I always played for the joy of the game."[3]

Coaching allowed a few former NBA players to continue their love affair with the game. Pat Riley was an outstanding college player at Kentucky and mostly an off-the-bench guy for the San Diego Rockets, Lakers, and Phoenix Suns. He was a valued sixth man on the Lakers team that won 33 games in a row and the NBA championship in 1972. Riles then went on to become "consumed with coaching" after he took over the top job in L.A. in 1981.

Winning an NBA championship as a rookie coach might have had something to do with the emergence of his newfound passion. And the other four rings Riles won over his illustrious 23-year coaching career kept that love affair aflame. Riley was elected to the Naismith Basketball Hall of Fame in 2008.

Riley resigned two times when coaching Miami, once after a disappointing 25–47 season in 2002–03 and again in 2007–08 following a disastrous (15–67) year. He came back to coach after his first resignation in 2005–06, replacing Stan Van Gundy, when the Heat were struggling (11–10) in the early season. Miami went on to finish 52–30, then defeated Chicago, New

Jersey, and Detroit in the early playoff rounds, and concluded the season by winning the NBA title against Dallas (4–2). It appears that Riles didn't like losing any more than I did.

Riley once told me that the time he played in college (Kentucky) and the NBA (San Diego, Phoenix, and the Lakers) was "the best time to be involved in basketball. There simply was a greater sincerity and purity on the part of all individuals involved. The goal then was to be a part of a team and want to accomplish things as a team. That's the kind of experience that you remember as long as you live."

He added, "Much more of *me* has crept into the game. It's more about the money (today)."

As an executive, Riley has made more positive adjustments than anyone in the NBA since Red Auerbach. As president/coach, he took over a Miami team that was 32–50 the year before (1994–95) and made two blockbuster trades to acquire Alonzo Mourning and Tim Hardaway. The Heat made the playoffs (42–40) that season and improved to 61–21 the following year.

He later orchestrated deals that brought top-level players like Shaquille O'Neal, Lamar Odom, Dan Majerle, Eddie Jones, Brian Grant, Terry Porter, Bruce Bowen, Gary Payton, and P.J.

LeBron James splits the Piston defenders.

Magic Johnson

Brown to the Heat; and added a couple of good draft picks (Caron Butler and Udonis Haslem) and one especially astute selection, Dwyane Wade, in the 2003 NBA Draft.

In the summer of 2010, Riley pulled off the greatest NBA heist of all time. He maneuvered his roster to clear salary cap space for superstars LeBron James, Chris Bosh, and Wade, his team's own free agent. Riley signed them all! Going into the 2010–11 season, the Heat can put that dynamic trio on the floor with a combination of free agents (Mike Miller, Zydrunas Ilgauskas) or holdovers Haslem, Carlos Arroyo, Joel Anthony, and Mario Chalmers. Eric Spoelstra, Riley's hand-picked successor in 2008, coaches the team.

"There's a lot of luck involved in something like that," Riley said to me. I say that it also takes a lot of negotiating skill to bring it about.

There was a part of the negotiations that must have warmed Riley's heart. All three of the superstars—James, Wade, and Bosh—agreed to contracts for less money than the maximum amounts they could have received under the rules of the NBA salary cap. That was noteworthy. But then Wade went a huge step further. Because Udonis Haslem was renounced by the Heat to allow for the signing of the "Big Three," he was tendered contracts as a free agent from Denver and Dallas for more money than the Heat could pay him. When Wade heard that Haslem was going to take the more lucrative offer, he went to his new teammates, James and Bosh, and said, "We need to put together some money so that the team can keep Udonis."

How much, he was asked?

"I need $15 million from each of you; I'll kick in $17 mil," Wade told them. Both James and Bosh agreed immediately. The total amount ($47 million dollars) allowed the Heat to re-sign Haslem and also bring Mike Miller onto the roster. Both Haslem and Miller agreed to contracts for less money than they would have received from other teams. They did this because they all wanted to play together on a team with the chance to win a ring!

Just like in the old days, huh, Riles?

LeBron James was skewered by the Cleveland fans and media for leaving the Cavs. I have no quarrel with his decision. James had a great stay in Cleveland. He was a two-time MVP and twice led his team to the league's best record. Despite efforts to surround him with complementary players good enough to win a championship, it didn't happen.

James wanted a (championship) ring. He used his free agency status to join with two other great players to be better able to get one. He used legal means to accomplish that goal. The only criticism I have is that he should have used better judgment in making known his decision to join Miami. The hour-long television presentation only antagonized the Cleveland fans who adored him as a Cavs player.

Phil Jackson made the jump into coaching somewhat like Riley. Phil played high school basketball at Williston, North Dakota, where an away game often meant a bus trip of 150 miles (or more). Phil told me that those long hauls gave him a lot of time to think about himself and his game, and he became determined to play at the college level. At North Dakota State College, he averaged 27 points and 14 rebounds as a senior, good enough for the Knicks to select him in the second round of the 1967 NBA Draft.

Phil played 807 games over 12 seasons in the NBA (10 with the Knicks, the last two with the Nets) without starting a single one. But for a patch he was the most valuable sixth man in the game and a fan favorite in Madison Square Garden, where his entrance into a game always triggered a roar. With his maniacal defense, Phil was a major contributor to Red Holzman's 1973 championship Knicks team. After his retirement from basketball in 1980, he decided he wanted back in, and so he became head coach of the Albany Patroons in the Continental Basketball Association. There he won the league championship in 1984, capping his first full season at the reins.

But "just" coaching wasn't enough. During the five seasons Jackson was with Albany, he and some former college and Eastern League players formed a team that played benefit games in the region after the CBA season was over. They played anybody, local amateur and All-Star teams, even prison teams. They did it because they loved to play and were still juiced by the game. "It was far from NBA level," Phil told me once, "but that didn't matter. We just loved getting together to play."

I've always wondered if Phil's flailing arms and elbows played as big a part in his Albany game as they did in the NBA. I'm guessing they did.

Magic Johnson will tell you that he enjoyed every second he spent on the basketball floor. And in 906 games over his NBA career, all with the Lakers, that added up to a lot of seconds. Magic beamed his signature smile, one that lit up an entire arena, as he orchestrated the Lakers' "Show Time" game to five NBA championships during the 1980s. Magic's constant refrain was "I just love winning," as if that weren't patently obvious, and that joy inspired his teammates to reach for the same euphoria.

Kareem Abdul-Jabbar, as taciturn a player as I've ever seen, says Johnson's enthusiasm for the game even rubbed off on him:

In a game, at practice, at pickup scrimmages, wherever he happened to be, Magic was very thrilled to be playing basketball. He was a boy living a dream and his enthusiasm was infectious. He was also a showman who was totally capable of playing the kind of intense winning basketball that I responded to and at the same time make the crowd feel like they were participating. And in some sense they were, because the more the place roared, the more he would make it roar.[4]

I can personally attest to the positive effect that Magic's joyful approach to the game had on Kareem, who became more outgoing and relaxed from the moment the two became teammates in 1979. Prior to an early season game between the Lakers and my Blazers that season, Kareem joked with me about the similarity between my coaching style and that of his new coach, Jack McKinney, whom he clearly respected.

This was the very first time Kareem had ever initiated a pleasant conversation with me. The most Kareem had said to me before Magic joined the Lakers was a challenging, "You want some, too?" after he had put a chokehold on Dave Twardzik in a skirmish, and I ran on the floor to intervene. My response: "Yeah, if you think you're big enough."

That encounter probably didn't do much to encourage a lot of future repartee. Magic's presence, on the other hand, did. And on the court, Kareem seemed more confident, more demonstrative, with Magic running the show. I got the feeling that Kareem was beginning to love the game that had been drudgery to him before. Chalk it all up to Johnson's "Magic."

To Reggie Miller, the greatest pleasure in basketball came from making a game-winning shot in the last seconds of play:

The big shots are what get me going more than anything else....
Big shots are the absolute greatest. There's no better feeling
than coming off the break in a playoff game, with the crowd
going crazy, and hitting the game winning three. There's no
feeling like it. People can't understand the fan noise. It's inde-
scribable, the way the applause lifts you up. That's why I feel
so lucky to be a part of this game. I get to experience what
other people dream about.[5]

Reggie's heroics were no accident. He prepared himself thoroughly on the practice court for those moments and reveled in his ability to meet the challenge. I coached Miller for just one season, but I knew from his confident attitude as a rookie that he was going to be a player who would take and make big shots.

Bill Bradley, who was to achieve great success off the basketball court in both business and politics, remembers to this day the pure joy and delight he felt in the Knicks locker room after New York won the NBA title in 1973:

The high of a championship is unequaled in my experience.
On days when I ask myself why I play, I remember those few
moments after victory, in the locker room with the team, when
there was a total oneness with the world and smiles grew broad
enough to ache. The chance it could happen again is suffi-
cient lure to continue. The money is important, but the chance
to relive the moment outweighs dollars.[6]

Funny how winning and fun so often go hand in hand.

Isiah Thomas exuded joy as a player. He had a perpetual little smile on his face even in the most stressful game situations. He smiled a lot on the basketball court for the simple reason that he was enjoying himself: "I was playing a game I loved. I was happy when they handed me the ball. I was happy when I got to shoot and even happier when the damn thing went in. I was jubilant when we won, but even when we were losing, I loved being wrapped up in the game that was my refuge, my outlet, and in many ways my salvation."[7]

Unfortunately, Thomas couldn't carry over the love for the game that he experienced while playing to the job of coaching it. As a player, he was on two championship teams. As a coach, he led Indiana to the playoffs three straight years, but in two seasons in New York, his Knicks finished next-to-last and dead last in the Atlantic Division. The dismal 23–59 record in his second season (2007–08) with the Knicks tied for second-worst W-L record in the NBA. Thomas was fired at the end it, never having found in coaching anything close to the joy (and success) he experienced as a player.

I coached against Thomas when he played for the Pistons and then broadcast his games when he coached Indiana and New York. I didn't see the same joyous attitude when Thomas coached. Reports circulated that he was sometimes late for practice at Indiana and that practices were loosely organized. At games, Isiah was impeccably dressed, but the smile was gone and he sat impassively, giving the impression that it was up to his players to find a way to win. And if they couldn't do it … so be it.

Rick Pitino was known as a great motivator as a college coach and when he coached the Knicks in 1987 and 1988. I learned from my son-in-law, Jim O'Brien, who was Rick's assistant at the time, that Rick sometimes told his team to go out and play for the fun of it rather than to focus on winning. The Knicks' final game of the 1987–88 season against my Indiana Pacers at Market Square Arena in Indianapolis was one of those occasions. This was a game that would decide which team went to the playoffs. I remember the game very well but was unaware that Pitino had said this to his team before-hand:

You have had a great season, whether you win or lose. You have won thirteen more games than you did last year. You have brought the crowds back to the Garden. You have changed the writers' attitudes. You have brought the excitement back. You have had a great season, and nothing that happens tonight can take that away. That's the thing to remember. So go out and have fun tonight, because these are the moments to cherish, ones you will remember when your careers are over.[8]

As it turned out, Pitino sent his team exactly the right message. The Knicks played with poise and toughness and won the pressure game by two points, 88–86. We had a chance to tie the game with four seconds left but failed to score.

Great players cherish the chance to compete against other players of their caliber. These players seek intense, competitive situations because of the thrills they'll find there. John Wooden understood what competition was all about and why it produces great pleasure to those who thrive on it: "There is great joy and satisfaction in competing against an opponent who forces you to dig deep and produce your best. That is the only way to get real joy out of competition itself. The worthy opponent brings out the very best in you. This is thrilling."[9]

I can't say it any better than that—as usual, Coach Wooden was right on target.

For those who really love the game, the opportunity to compete is more important than the rewards attached to it. These players seem driven to seek out competitive opportunities for their own sake. Michael Jordan, the game's greatest competitor ever, says simply, "I just love the competition. I like the challenge. I could play for a dollar."[10]

The great players of today love the game every bit as much as did Bill Bradley, Magic Johnson, Reggie Miller, Bill Walton, and Michael Jordan.

"Basketball is a wonderful, wonderful sport," says Dwyane Wade, Miami's do-everything player. "Sure, basketball is a job to us. We have to earn a living, like anyone working 9–5. It's just that if we weren't playing basketball for a living, we'd be playing after our 9–5 job, just for the love of it."

In my two decades in the NBA, I either coached or coached against every player mentioned in this chapter—except, of course, for the currently active players, and those I've interviewed countless times for television and radio broadcasts.

We all had—still have—one thing in common: a deep, abiding love for the game. When I made the decision to make coaching basketball my career, money didn't matter. I fully expected to coach high school basketball forever. But once I got involved in the game, I wanted to move up to the next competitive level. But it still wasn't about the money. In fact, I took a sizeable pay cut from high school coaching at Mt. Pleasant High School in Delaware to coach at St. Joseph's College. But I just couldn't pass up the chance to coach at a more competitive level.

In basketball, much of the affection comes from a single, basic interrelationship—you, the ball, and the basket—that makes the game accessible at some level to just about anyone.

Some of the joy comes from competing against those who feel just as passionate as you do about the game.

Some comes from feeling the response from fans, who are far closer to the action than in the other two Big Three sports.

And some comes from instinctive, emotional love for the totality of the game itself.

Basketball is a simple game. It's creative. It allows for self-expression. It's physically demanding. It fires the competitive juices of its participants. It's easily accessible at a basic level to bother genders and all ages. It's just plain exciting, to watch or to play. And sometimes, as in my personal experience over the past few years, just thinking about it can be such an enormous source of solace and inspiration.

What's not to love?

CONSULTATIONS WITH PLAYERS AND COACHES

Interviews

Bryant, Kobe – Guard (Lakers)

Chamberlain, Wilt – Center (Sixers, Lakers)

Drexler, Clyde – Guard/Forward (Trail Blazers, Rockets)

Duncan, Tim – Forward/Center (Spurs)

Erving, Julius – Forward (Sixers)

Fitch, Bill – Coach (Celtics and four other teams)

Fitzsimmons, Cotton – Coach (Suns, Hawks, Spurs)

Garnet, Kevin – Forward (Timberwolves, Celtics)

Ginobili, Manu – Guard (Spurs)

Holzman, Red – Guard (Royals), Coach (Knicks)

James, LeBron – Forward (Cavaliers, Heat)

Johnson, Avery – Guard (Spurs and five other teams), Coach (Mavericks, Nets)

Johnson, Dennis – Guard (Celtics, SuperSonics, Suns)

Johnson, Earvin "Magic" – Guard (Lakers)

Kundla, John – Coach (Minneapolis Lakers)

Lucas, Maurice – Forward (Trail Blazers and five other teams)

Lynam, Jim – Coach (Clippers, Sixers, Bullets)

McKinney, Jack – Coach (Pacers, Lakers, Kings)

Nash, Steve – Guard (Suns)

O'Brien, Jim – Coach (Pacers, Sixers, Celtics)

Paul, Chris – Guard (Hornets)

Paxson, Jim – Guard (Trail Blazers, Celtics)

Pollard, Jim – Forward (Minneapolis Lakers)

Popovich, Gregg – Coach (Spurs)

Riley, Pat – Guard (Rockets, Lakers, Suns), Coach (Lakers, Knicks, Heat)

Silas, Paul – Forward (Celtics, SuperSonics, and three other teams), Coach (Cavs, Clippers, Hornets)

Skiles, Scott – Guard (Magic and four other teams), Coach (Suns, Bulls, Bucks)

Wade, Dwyane – Guard (Heat)

Walton, Bill – Center (Trail Blazers, Clippers, Celtics)

Webb, Anthony "Spud" – Guard (Hawks, Kings, and two other teams)

Worthy, James – Forward (Lakers)

Writings

Abdul-Jabbar, Kareem – Center (Lakers)

Auerbach, Arnold "Red" – Coach (Celtics)

Barkley, Charles – Forward (Sixers, Suns, Rockets)

Barry, Rick – Forward (Warriors and five other teams)

Bird, Larry – Forward (Celtics), Coach (Pacers)

Bogues, Tyrone "Muggsy" – Guard (Hornets and three other teams)

Bradley, Bill – Forward (Knicks)

Cooper, Michael – Forward (Lakers)

Cousy, Bob – Guard (Celtics), Coach (Royals)

Drexler, Clyde – Guard/Forward (Trail Blazers, Rockets)

Dumars, Joe – Guard (Pistons)

Frazier, Walt "Clyde" – Guard (Knicks, Cavaliers)

Holzman, Red – Guard (Royals), Coach (Knicks)

Jackson, Phil – Forward, (Knicks), Coach (Bulls, Lakers)

Johnson, Earvin, "Magic" – Guard (Lakers)

Jones, K. C. – Guard (Celtics), Coach (Bullets, Celtics, Supersonics)

Jordan, Michael – Guard (Bulls, Wizards)

Mahorn, Rick – Forward (Bullets, Pistons, and four other teams)

Maravich, Pete – Guard (Hawks, Jazz, Celtics)

Mikan, George – Center (Minneapolis Lakers)

Miller, Reggie – Guard (Pacers)

Olajuwon, Hakeem – Center (Rockets, Raptors)

O'Neal, Shaquille – Center (Magic, Lakers, Suns, Cavs, Celtics)

Riley, Pat – Guard (Rockets, Lakers, Suns), Coach (Lakers, Knicks, Heat)

Robertson, Oscar – Guard (Royals, Bucks)

Russell, Bill – Center (Celtics), Coach (Celtics, Supersonics, Kings)

Smith, Dean – Coach (University of North Carolina)

Starks, John – Guard (Warriors, Knicks, and two other teams)

Thomas, Isiah – Guard (Pistons), Coach (Pacers, Knicks)

Tomjanovich, Rudy – Forward (Rockets), Coach (Rockets)

Walton, Bill – Center (Trail Blazers, Clippers, Celtics)

Webb, Anthony "Spud" – Guard (Hawks, Kings, and two other teams)

West, Jerry – Guard (Lakers), Coach (Lakers)

Wilkens, Lenny – Guard (Hawks and three other teams), Coach (Supersonics and five other teams)

Wooden, John – Coach (UCLA)

NOTES

Chapter 1: Play Smart

1. West, Jerry with Libby, Bill. *Basketball My Way.* Englewood Cliffs, NJ: Prentice-Hall, 1973, p.162.

2. Abdul-Jabbar, Kareem and Knobler, Peter. *Giant Steps: The Autobiography of Kareem Abdul-Jabbar.* New York: Bantam Books, 1983, p. 212.

3. Miller, Reggie. *I Love Being the Enemy.* New York: Simon and Schuster, 1995, p. 66.

4. Bogues, Tyrone "Muggsy" and Levine, David. *In the Land of Giants: My Life in Basketball.* New York: Little Brown & Company, 1994, p. 132.

5. Russell, Bill and Falkner, David. *Russell Rules: 11 Lessons on Leadership from the Twentieth Century's Greatest Winner.* New York: Penguin Putnam, 2001.

6. Riley, Pat. *The Winner Within: A Life Plan for Team Players.* New York: Penguin Putnam, 1993, p. 33.

7. Auerbach, Arnold "Red" and Feinstein, John. *Let Me Tell You a Story: A Life in the Game.* New York: Little, Brown & Co, 2004, p. 149.

8. Walton, Bill. *Nothing But Net: Just Give Me the Ball and*

Get Out of the Way. New York: Hyperion, 1994, p. 221.

9. Russell, Bill and Branch, Taylor. *Second Wind: The Memoirs of an Opinionated Man.* New York: Random House, 1979, p. 166.

10. Frazier, Walt "Clyde" and Sachare, Alex. *The Complete Idoit's Guide to Basketball.* New York: Simon & Schuster, 1998, p. 235.

11. Ibid.

12. Johnson, Earvin "Magic" with Novak, William. *My Life.* New York: Random House, 1992, pp. 117–118.

13. Ibid.

14. Ibid.

15. Wooden, John with Jamison, Steve. *Wooden: A Lifetime of Observations and Reflections On and Off the Court.* Chicago: NTC/Contemporary, 1997, p. 56.

16. Johnson, Earvin "Magic" and Roy S. Johnson. *Magic's Touch.* New York: Addison-Wesley, 1989, p. 142.

17. Russell, *Second Wind*, p. 154.

18. Ibid.

19. West, Jerry with Libby, Bill. *Mr. Clutch: The Jerry West Story.* Englewood Cliffs, NJ: Prentice-Hall, 1969, p. 165.

20. Walton, *Nothing But Net*, p. 217.

21. Jordan, Michael. *For the Love of the Game: My Story.* New York: Crown Publishers, 1998, p 60.

22. Bird, Larry with MacMullan, Jackie. *Bird Watching: On Playing and Coaching the Game I Love.* New York: Warner Books, 2000, p. 273.

23. Starks, John with Karkowitz, Dan. *John Starks: My Life* Champaign, IL: Sports Publishing, 2004, p. 44.

24. Johnson and Johnson, *Magic's Touch*, 1989, p. 5.

25. Bird, *Bird Watching*, p. 125.

26. Bradley, Bill. *Life on the Run*. New York: Vintage Books, 1995, pp. 34–35.

27. Abdul-Jabbar, Kareem with Singular, Stephen. *A Season on the Reservation: My Sojourn with the White Mountain Apache*. New York: William Morrow, 2000, p. 59.

28. Walton, *Nothing But Net*, p. 20.

29. Jabbar, *Giant Steps*, p. 37.

30. Auerbach, Arnold "Red." *Basketball for the Player, the Fan and the Coach*. New York: Simon and Schuster, 1975, p. 50.

31. Bradley, *Life on the Run*, p. 197.

Chapter 2: Live in the Here and Now

1. Jackson, Phil and Rosen, Charley. *More Than a Game*. New York: Simon & Schuster, 2002, p. 123.

2. Riley, Pat *The Winner Within: A Life Plan for Team Players*. New York: Penguin Putnam, 1993, p. 51.

3. Robertson, Oscar. *The Big O: My Life, Times, My Game*. Rodale, 2003, p. 258.

4. Wooden, John with Tobin, Jack. *They Call Me Coach*. New York: McGraw Hill, 2004, p. 57.

5. Walton, Bill. *Nothing But Net: Just Give Me the Ball and Get Out of the Way*. New York: Hyperion, 1994, pp. 63–64.

6. Russell, Bill and Branch, Taylor. *Second Wind: The Memoirs of an Opinionated Man*. New York: Random House, 1979, p. 148.

7. Hundley, Rod with McEachin, Tom. *Hot Rod Hundley: You Gotta Love It, Baby*. Champaign, IL: Sports Publishing, 1998, p. 235.

8. Bird, Larry with Bischoff, John. *Bird on Basketball: How-to Strategies from the Great Celtics Champion*. Menlo Park,

CA: Addison-Wesley, 1985, p. 114.

Chapter 3: See It, Feel It, Do It

1. Bird, Larry with MacMullan, Jackie. *Bird Watching: On Playing and Coaching the Game I Love.* New York: Warner Books, 2000, p. 273.

2. Johnson, Earvin "Magic" with Novak, William. *My Life.* New York: Random House, 1992, p. 206.

3. Jackson, Phil and Rosen, Charles. *Maverick: More Than a Game.* New York: Playboy Press, 1975, p. 242.

4. Tomjanovich, Rudy with Falkoff, Robert. *Rocket at Heart: My Life and My Team.* New York: Simon & Schuster, 1997, p. 89.

5. Ibid., p.256.

6. Jackson, Phil with Arkush, Michael. *The Last Season: A Team in Search of its Soul.* New York: Penguin Press, 2004, p. 136.

7. Jordan, Michael. *For the Love of the Game: My Story.* New York: Crown Publishers, 1998, p. 153.

Chapter 4: Practice, Practice, Practice

1. Olajuwon, Hakeem and Knobler, Peter. *Living the Dream: My Life and Basketball.* New York: Little Brown & Company, 1996, p. 280.

2. Ibid., p. 289.

3. Bird, Larry with Bischoff, John. *Bird on Basketball: How-to Strategies from the Great Celtics Champion.* Menlo Park, CA: Addison-Wesley, 1985, p. 114.

4. Frazier, Walt "Clyde" and Sachare, Alex. *The Complete Idiot's Guide to Basketball.* New York: Simon & Schuster, 1998, p. 90.

5. Jordan, Michael. *For the Love of the Game: My Story.* New York: Crown, 1998, p. 17.

6. Jordan, *For the Love of the Game*, pp. 64–65.

7. Ibid.

8. Russell, Bill and Falkner, David. *Russell Rules: 11 Lessons on Leadership from the Twentieth Century's Greatest Winner*. New York: Penguin Putnam, 2001, p. 185.

9. Starks, John with Karkowitz, Dan. *John Starks: My Life*. Champaign, IL: Sports Publishing, 2004, p. 164.

10. Ibid., p. xii.

11. Jackson, Phil and Delehanty, Hugh. *Sacred Hoops: Spiritual Lessons of a Hardcourt Warrior*. New York: Hyperion, 1995, p. 38.

12. Cooper, Michael J. with Lynn, Theodore J. Jr. *No Slack*. Albuquerque, NM: CompuPress, 1987, p. 18.

13. Ibid., p. 18.

14. Ibid., p. 44.

15. Maravich, Pete and Campbell, Darrel. *Pistol Pete: Heir to a Dream*. Nashville, TN: Thomas Nelson, 1987, p. 70.

16. Johnson, Earvin "Magic" and Johnson, Roy S. *Magic's Touch*. New York: Addison-Wesley, 1989, p. 26.

17. Tomjanovich, Rudy with Falkoff, Robert. *Rocket at Heart: My Life and My Team*. New York: Simon & Schuster, 1997, p. 113.

Chapter 5: Believe in Yourself

1. Jackson, Phil with Arkush, Michael. *The Last Season: A Team in Search of its Soul*. New York: The Penguin Press, 2004, p.190.

2. Bradley, Bill. *Values of the Game*. New York: Workman, 1998, p. 34.

3. Ibid.

4. Bird, Larry with Bischoff, John. *Bird on Basketball: How-to*

Strategies from the Great Celtics Champion. Menlo Park, CA: Addison-Wesley, 1985, p.111.

5. Ibid.

6. West, Jerry with Libby, Bill. *Mr. Clutch: The Jerry West Story.* Englewood Cliffs, NJ: Prentice-Hall, 1969, p. 21.

7. Barkley, Charles. *I May Be Wrong but I Doubt It.* New York: Random House, 2002, p. 175.

8. Ibid.

9. Olajuwon, Hakeem and Knobler, Peter. *Living the Dream: My Life and Basketball.* New York: Little Brown & Company, 1996, p. 102.

10. Webb, Spud with Slaughter, Reid. *Flying High.* New York: Harper & Row, 1988, p. 179.

11. Jordan, Michael and Ioose, Walter Jr. *Rare Air: Michael on Michael.* San Francisco: Collins, 1993, p. 36.

12. Ibid.

13. Lazenby, Roland. *Mindgames: Phil Jackson's Long Strange Journey.* New York: McGraw Hill, 2002, p. 178.

14. Drexler, Clyde with Eggers, Kenny. *Clyde the Glide.* Champaign, IL: Sports Publishing, 2004, p. 219.

15. Barry, Rick with Libby, Bill *Confessions of a Basketball Gypsy: The Rick Barry Story.* New York: Dell, 1972, p. 105.

16. Ibid.

17. Frazier, Walt "Clyde" and Sachare, Alex. *The Complete Idiot's Guide to Basketball.* New York: Simon & Schuster, 1998, p. 240.

18. Bird, *Bird on Basketball*, p. 114.

19. Bradley, *Values of the Game*, p. 134.

20. Williams, Pat. *Quotable Michael Jordan.* Henderson, TN: TowleHouse, 2004, p. 70.

21. Ibid.

22. Miller, Reggie. *I Love Being the Enemy.* New York: Simon & Schuster, 1995, p. 53.

23. West, *Mr. Clutch: The Jerry West Story*, dust jacket.

Chapter 6: Kick Some Butt

1. Barkley, Charles and Williams, Roy S. *Outrageous: The Fine Life and Flagrant Good Times of Basketball's Irresistible Force.* New York: Simon & Schuster, 1992, p. 197.

2. Wooden, John with Jamison, Steve. *Wooden: A Lifetime of Observations and Reflections on and off the Court.* Chicago: NTC/Contemporary, 1997, p. 86.

3. Robertson, Oscar. *The Big O: My Life, Times, My Game.* Emmaus, PA: Rodale, 2003, p. 87.

4. Holzman, Red with Lewin, Leonard. *A View From the Bench.* New York: W. W. Norton, 1980, p. 88.

5. Barry, Rick with Libby, Bill. *Confessions of a Basketball Gypsy: The Rick Barry Story.* New York: Dell, 1972, p. 200.

6. Bradley, Bill. *Values of the Game.* New York: Workman, 1998, p. 31.

7. Holzman, *A View From the Bench*, p. 76.

8. Bradley, *Values of the Game,* p. 31.

9. Webb, Spud with Slaughter, Reid. *Flying High.* New York: Harper & Row, 1988, pp. 161, 181.

10. Tomjanovich, Rudy with Falkoff, Robert. *Rocket at Heart: My Life and My Team.* New York: Simon & Schuster, 1997, p. 86.

11. Holzman, *A View From the Bench,* p. 68.

12. Miller, Reggie. *I Love Being the Enemy.* New York: Simon & Schuster, 1995, p. 219.

13. Abdul-Jabbar, Kareem and Knobler, Peter. *Giant Steps: The Autobiography of Kareem Abdul-Jabbar.* New York: Bantam Books, 1983, p. 217.

14. Olajuwon, Hakeem and Knobler. Peter. *Living the Dream: My Life and Basketball.* New York: Little Brown, 1996, p. 290.

15. Cousy, Bob and Ryan, Rob. *Cousy on the Celtic Mystique.* New York: McGraw-Hill, 1988, p. 183.

16. Bird, Larry with MacMullan, Jackie. *Bird Watching: On Playing and Coaching the Game I Love.* New York: Warner Books, 2000, p. 149.

17. Walton, Bill. *Nothing But Net: Just Give Me the Ball and Get Out of the Way.* New York: Hyperion, 1994, p. 107.

18. Halberstam, David. *Playing for Keeps.* New York: Random House, 1999, p. 62.

19. Williams, Pat. *Quotable Michael Jordan.* Henderson, Tennessee: TowleHouse, 2004, p. 93.

20. Jackson, Phil, with Arkush, Michael. *The Last Season: A Team in Search of Its Soul.* New York: Penguin Press, 2004, p. 48.

Chapter 7: Take Charge

1. Wooden, John with Tobin, Jack. *They Call Me Coach.* New York: McGraw Hill, 2004, p. 84.

2. Jackson, Phil and Rosen, Charley. *More Than a Game.* New York: Simon & Schuster, 2002, p. 41.

3. West, Jerry with Libby, Bill. *Basketball My Way.* Englewood Cliffs, NJ: Prentice-Hall, 1973, p. 141.

4. Jones, K. C. with Warner, Jack. *Rebound.* Boston: Quinlan Press, 1986, p. 85.

5. Bradley, Bill. *Life on the Run.* New York: Vintage Books, 1995, p. 75.

Chapter 8: Learning from Losing

1. Lazenby, Roland. *Mindgames: Phil Jackson's Long Strange Journey.* New York: McGraw Hill, 2002, p. 179.

2. Russell, Bill and Branch, Taylor. *Second Wind: The Memoirs of an Opinionated Man.* New York: Random House, 1979, p.125.

3. Holzman, Red with Lewin, Leonard. *A View From the Bench.* New York: W.W. Norton & Company, 1980, p. 65.

4. Tomjanovich, Rudy with Falkoff, Robert. *Rocket at Heart: My Life and My Team.* New York: Simon & Schuster, 1997, p. 179.

5. Bradley, Bill. *Life on the Run.* New York: Vintage Books, 1995, p. 103.

6. Bradley, Bill. *Values of the Game.* New York: Workman, 1998, p. 131.

7. Ibid., pp. 131–132.

8. Jackson, Phil and Delehanty, Hugh. *Sacred Hoops: Spiritual Lessons of a Hardcourt Warrior.* New York: Hyperion, 1995, p. 31.

9. West, Jerry with Libby, Bill. *Mr. Clutch: The Jerry West Story.* Englewood Cliffs, NJ: Prentice-Hall, 1969, p. 198.

10. Jordan, Michael and Ioose, Walter Jr. *Rare Air: Michael on Michael.* San Francisco: Collins, 1993, p. 28.

11. Riley, Pat. *Show Time: Inside the Lakers Breakthrough Season.* New York: Warner Books, 1988, p. 13.

12. Wooden, John with Jamison, Steve. *Wooden: A Lifetime of Observations and Reflections On and Off the Court.* Chicago: NTC/Contemporary, 1997, p. 80.

Chapter 9: The Fun in Winning

1. Webb, Spud with Slaughter, Reid. *Flying High.* New York: Harper & Row, 1988, pp. 2–3.

2. Abdul-Jabbar, and Knobler, Peter. *Giant Steps: The Autobiography of Kareem Abdul-Jabbar.* New York: Bantam Books, 1983, pp. 274–275.

3. Walton, Bill. *Nothing But Net: Just Give Me the Ball and Get Out of the Way.* New York: Hyperion, 1994, p. 82.

4. Abdul-Jabbar and Knobler, *Giant Steps,* p. 313.

5. Miller, Reggie. *I Love Being the Enemy.* New York: Simon and Schuster, 1995, p. 54.

6. Bradley, Bill. *Life on the Run.* New York: Vintage Books, 1995, p. 210.

7. Thomas, Isiah. *The Fundamentals*: *8 Plays for Winning the Games of Business and Life.* New York: HarperCollins, 2001, p. 85.

8. Pitino, Rick and Reynolds, Bill. *Born to Coach: A Season with the New York Knicks.* New York: Penguin Books, 1988, p. 255.

9. Wooden, John with Jamison, Steve. *Wooden: A Lifetime of Observations and Reflections On and Off the Court.* Chicago: NTC/Contemporary, 1997, p. 65.

10. Jordan, Michael and Ioose, Walter Jr. *Rare Air: Michael on Michael.* San Francisco: Collins, 1993, p.76.

About the Authors

Jack Ramsay coached basketball for six years at the high school level and 11 years at St. Joseph's University in Philadelphia before moving to the NBA. Over the course of 20 seasons, he coached four NBA teams, including the 1977 Portland Trail Blazers team that won the NBA championship. In 1978 he was Basketball *magazine NBA Coach of the Year and was elected in 1992 to the Naismith Basketball Hall of Fame. He has two decades of broadcasting experience, serving as a TV game analyst for the '76ers and the Heat and, since the early 1990s, as an analyst for NBA TV, ESPN, and ESPN Radio. He is the author of* Pressure Basketball, The Coach's Art, *and* Dr. Jack's Leadership Lessons Learned from a Lifetime in Basketball. *Ramsay holds a doctorate in education from the University of Pennsylvania.*

Neal Vahle is the author of seven books, including, with Buddy Bell, Smart Baseball: How Professionals Play the Mental Game *and, with Dick Donaldson,* Scrapper/Panther Athletics, 1900–2000: Sports in a Minnesota Small Town. *He has served as a journal and magazine editor and as publishing director of Heldref Publications in Washington, D.C. Vahle holds a doctorate in American history from Georgetown University.*

Acknowledgments

A work like this would not be possible without the contributions of many people. Four people from ESPN deserve special thanks. John Walsh, Executive Vice President and Executive Editor, and Steve Wulf, Executive Editor, *ESPN The Magazine*, provided support and encouragement and the conviction that this work makes an important contribution to our understanding of how the game of basketball is played. Glen Waggoner, founding editor of *ESPN The Magazine* and author of the *New York Times* best-selling *My Life In and Out of the Rough* (with John Daly), spent long hours providing expert counsel and advice, as well as editorial input, on each of the book's chapters. My son Chris Ramsay, Senior Deputy Editor, ESPN.com, read the manuscript as it was being written and provided valuable suggestions that improved its overall quality.